WITHDRAWN

ADULT LITERACY

Contexts & Challenges

Anabel Powell Newman
Caroline Beverstock
Indiana University

WITHDRAWN

International Reading Association, Inc.
800 Barksdale Road, Newark, Delaware 19714

ERIC Clearinghouse on Reading and Communication Skills
Indiana University
Bloomington, Indiana 47405

ERIC/RCS
Director Carl B. Smith

The ERIC Clearinghouse on Reading and Communication Skills (RCS) is sponsored by the Office of Educational Research and Improvement, U.S. Department of Education. ERIC/RCS gathers and disseminates information in areas related to language arts and mass communication under DE contract No. RI 88062001. Contractors undertaking such projects under government sponsorship are encouraged to express freely their judgment in professional and technical matters. Points of view or opinions, however, do not necessarily represent the official view or opinions of the Office of Educational Research and Improvement.

Copyright 1990 by the
International Reading Association, Inc.

Library of Congress Cataloging in Publication Data

Newman, Anabel Powell.
    Adult literacy : contexts and challenges / Anabel Powell Newman, Caroline Beverstock.
        p.   cm.
Includes bibliographical references.
    1. Literacy—United States 2. Literacy—United States—History.
I. Beverstock, Caroline. II. Title.
LC151.N49 1990   90-38481
374'.012—dc20   CIP
ISBN 0-87207-356-4

Contents

Foreword

T oday is yesterday's tomorrow. The present status of adult literacy as a pervasive value in American society is rooted in the work of literacy pioneers such as Cora Stewart, William S. Gray, Frank Laubach, and Welthy Honsinger Fisher. More recently, Sarah Gudschinsky, Don Brown, Anabel Newman, H.S. Bhola, and Paulo Freire have expanded our understanding of the unique literacy needs of adults and of our pedagogical, psychological, and sociological resources for meeting them. Even so, we still have limited knowledge of illiterate adults and how to assist them. However, as the 1990s begin, so begin some promising breakthroughs in adult literacy.

One of the most significant developments in adult literacy during the 1980s was the recognition that the research base for decision making and the affirmation of progress was extremely limited. The response of dedicated individuals, institutions, organizations, and corporations to this need has been vigorous and already has begun to produce valid, quantified knowledge to replace assumptions. Clarification of the relationships among learning theory, cultural/social factors, and workplace demands as they apply to the literacy needs of today's adults is leading to instructional change. Most important, new questions are being raised and new programs developed; concurrently, our perspectives are broadening. Two recent trends are: (1) intergenerational/family literacy, designed to break the cycle of adult/child "undereducation," and (2) workplace literacy, which focuses attention on individuals in relation to the societal and economic concerns of the nation.

A second major development over the past decade has been the creation in 1981 of the National Coalition for Literacy, which has provided a means for better communication, cooperation, and collaboration among groups from the public, private, corporate, and professional sectors that are committed to the literacy effort. In 1985, with the assistance of the American Advertising Council, nationwide advertising campaigns were begun. Today, as never before, Americans are "sensitized" to the nation's literacy needs. Enrollment in literacy programs and the number of volunteer teachers have increased. Funding for literacy programs has increased as well, and innovative initiatives are appearing in virtually every state.

But challenges remain. What are our national literacy goals? Who will provide the leadership for meeting them? Who will fund new programs? How can the public and private sectors become more productively collaborative? What is the role of industry? Who will plan, fund, and execute research? What are the more promising practices—programatically and instructionally?

Today will soon be tomorrow's yesterday. To make every tomorrow one in which new advancements are made toward literacy for people everywhere, the International Reading Association dedicates its resources and its will. This volume, offered during International Literacy Year, affirms this commitment and honors all who have contributed, are contributing, and will contribute to the realization of a more literate tomorrow for every child and adult who seeks the freedom and fulfillment of learning to read and write. Through a past-to-present view, these pages define the status of literacy education today and point to tomorrow's challenges.

Betty H. Yarborough
Old Dominion University

Introduction

A merica changed its mind for the better about adult literacy during the 1980s. We have been brought by the adult literacy movement from a slight (but growing) awareness of the problem of illiteracy in the previous generation to national recognition of the literacy needs of adults. Now we are ready as a nation to affirm full literacy as a value that we cannot do without.

For some, awareness of the problem came as a result of the media blitz sponsored by the National Coalition for Literacy. For others, awareness came through hearing about disturbing test results in U.S. classrooms, or by meeting people at work—nice and otherwise competent people—who could not hack it because they could not read and write well enough to do their job. Some of us became aware of the problem because we were part of the problem. Our personal experience with spiraling technological developments and economic demands forced us to acknowledge our own specific illiteracies. Some of us became aware of the literacy problem in America before World War II, and this awareness was nurtured through years of federally funded and state-managed literacy programs.

Literacy workers are a heterogeneous and dispersed group, and they face unique challenges in their work. The results of their advocacy, research, and fieldwork often are published—when they *do* get published—in forums other than traditional research journals. Both the funding and the status of literacy programs vary, from slickly presented training in industry to informal classes held in church basements.

The adult literacy movement now confronts the standard problems of all progressive movements: how to direct its energy into organized productivity and how to organize these beginnings into ongoing, successful programs. We are convinced that the growing pains of adult literacy in America are more an opportunity than a problem. Therefore, commissioned by the International Reading Association, we have written this volume with the purpose of reporting recent and significant studies across the spectrum of the literacy movement in order to help plan America's literacy future, and to contribute to the effort for worldwide literacy.

We call for concerted action on the part of adult educators, researchers, trainers in industry, policy makers, funding agencies, volunteer organizations, members of IRA and other professional groups, state and federal officials, and all concerned citizens. We submit that collaboration for literacy at all levels can proceed informed by the data presented here. With this knowledge of the history, definitions, research, and practices of the adult literacy movement, we can avoid misspending our efforts.

The time. We present this publication in 1990, designated as International Literacy Year by the United Nations. The potential for international communication is greater now than ever before. And yet, even with satellites circling the globe and high quality communications systems available in every media type, we see the gap growing wider between the technologically adept and the technologically deprived. This does not mean that we are entering a terminal crisis of literacy. We offer this study partly to link the discussion of adult literacy to cultural, social, political, and economic realities, and partly to make suggestions about how to achieve worldwide literacy at a level never before enjoyed.

Perspectives. We are researcher-teachers. Each of us has had direct experience with adult illiterates. We have directed literacy research, developed literacy materials (films, videos, and print matter), and conducted literacy programs. We care about the adult new reader. We have seen progress, and we know the challenges.

Weiss and Bucuvalas (1980) examined the processes decision makers employ in assessing the usefulness of social science research. Their analysis revealed five frames of reference: relevance, quality, conformity of results with expectations, orientation to action, and challenge to existing policy. Interactions among these

vii

frames suggested that decision makers apply both a truth test and a utility test in screening social science research. We have endeavored to apply these tests of truth and utility to the studies we have reviewed. As Weiss and Bucuvalas suggest, we have judged the truth of the work reported on two bases: research quality and conformity with prior knowledge and expectations. We have looked at utility from the standpoint of feasibility for real-world implementation with new readers. We address current policy, both political and pedagogical, in terms of what best serves the newly literate. In this report, we examine primarily the United States, but we have included international perspectives as space and knowledge allow.

The challenge. We are aware of contradictions implicit in writing about literacy. Your interest in this book suggests that you are concerned about advancing literacy. Your knowledge of literacy will permeate your understanding of these pages, but what you see as literacy may be quite different from our images of literacy.

We all have had years of contact with people who possess varying degrees of literacy. We enjoy the richness of multiple literacies—the literacy of our specialized field of endeavor, the jargon of our favorite sport or hobby, the dialect of our hometown or ethnic heritage. Presumably, each one of us has felt that sinking feeling of having to pass as literate when faced with insurance policies, legal documents, IRS forms, or instructions for assembling a VCR. We had to admit to ourselves that in some sense we were inadequately literate. Both the positive and the negative experiences give us hints about people who are less literate than they prefer to be and than society demands they be.

Writers and workers in the field of literacy come to the task with a variety of human experiences that color their perception of the needs for, responses to, and ways of literacy. There is no one right way to teach literacy to an adult new reader; no one approach or program is so superior that all other efforts should be abandoned. We invite multiple, reflective approaches to challenges, just as we celebrate our variety of human perspectives.

Literacy is intensely personal, and is therefore a human challenge. Literacy is personal because language, interaction with adult learners, and collaboration with fellow literacy workers are personal. Our sense is that most people who work in the adult literacy movement do so for personally satisfying reasons. We have seasoned these pages of academic reporting with narratives about new readers, samples of their writing, and personal accounts of the human effect of their new literacy. By maintaining the human variety and the personal touch in our programs and approaches, we will meet the challenges of literacy.

Through the coaching of the newly literate, we have become aware of their intense aversion to the term *illiterate*. "We are not illiterate or stupid," they say. "We just haven't learned to read." Substitute terms such as *underliterate* and *insufficiently literate* also have drawbacks, however. To our newly literate friends and to prospective literates we say that we see no one right way of referring to those who for any reason do not read and write as capably as they might wish, but we do have increased awareness of the feelings of people trying to become more literate.

In this volume, we discuss the history of the adult literacy movement, especially in America, and the emergent definitions of adult literacy. We report on the scholarship about, practice of, and challenges confronting the adult literacy movement. In addition, because we believe that communication, cooperation, and collaboration are essential if progress is to be achieved, we outline the current status of the National Coalition for Literacy and other initiatives.

Reference
Weiss, C.H., & Bucuvalas, M.J. (1980). Truth tests and utility tests: Decision-makers' frames of reference for social science research. *American Sociological Review, 45,* 302-313.

Acknowledgments

T he patience, friendship, and collaboration of many friends and colleagues have made this book possible. Our staff at the Reading Practicum Center—Elizabeth Metz, Tonya Venstra, Julie Stuffle, Ruth Whitbeck, and Sibel Cakmak—covered classes, did library research, and performed myriad other tasks. Kurt Messick helped with his word processing skills, William Bintz read and reacted at several crucial junctures, and Michael Ginsberg was editor-cum-writer.

The ERIC staff smoothed many a rough turn for us; we are grateful to Bruce Tone, Mary Morgan, Ellie MacFarlane, Carl Smith, and our major editor, Warren Lewis. We also wish to thank Joye Coy, Linda Farrell, and Mary Andis for their help and insight. Indiana University faculty members H.S. Bhola, Larry Mikulecky, Martha Nyikos, and Leo Fay were generous in their responses as the book progressed.

So many people helped us: the reviewers who steered us into more productive channels for the book, Ron Pugsley and others at the U.S. Department of Education, Nickie Askov at the Institute for the Study of Adult Literacy, Linda Church and Muriel Medina at Laubach Literacy Action, and Gisela Fitzgerald. Anne Jungeblut and Irwin Kirsch gave permission to reproduce tables from the Young Adult Literacy Study, and members of the National Coalition for Literacy provided information on their respective organizations. Jennifer Stevenson and the staff editors at IRA were wonderful as we worked through the numerous revisions.

Thanks to IRA for providing a forum for our thoughts and the research findings of literacy workers past and present.

Anabel says: To my husband, Philip Newman, my continuing gratitude and love for his forbearance and good deeds.

Caroline says: For a lifetime of support and encouragement I salute my father, Bev Beverstock.

APN

CB

1

Adult Literacy: A New American Value

T en years ago, a team of literacy instructors, working in a project with 80 mothers on welfare, made some important discoveries (Newman, 1980). As the team and the women worked together on reading, writing, and arithmetic, the preeminently social character of the literacy undertaking became increasingly clear. The mothers made solid progress only when group activities were initiated. Group review sessions, group participation in the production of a weekly letter, group exercise programs, and group rap sessions were the turning points of progress in learning.

The instructors learned a powerful lesson. The values the emerging literates placed on their new literacy were different from the values of longtime literates. Most of the women came from homes with few magazines, no newspapers, and no books. Communication was primarily oral—over the back fence or via television. Progress was slow until we took their cultural environment into consideration and adjusted our instruction accordingly.

The welfare mothers took to one aspect of their literacy learning with special enthusiasm. They participated wholeheartedly in producing the weekly newsletter started part way through the program. They had been keeping journals from the start of the program, but it was a major turning point when they saw in print their stories, poems, letters to the editor, and gripes. This informal, student-produced newsletter became a source of emotional support for these women. The women were willing to work harder and longer to prepare their copy for the newsletter than for any of the classes.

They were hungry for the recognition they generated for themselves by getting their words and names in print.

The importance these women placed on the newsletter highlights how much we depend on printed media. Our local papers provide most of us with a vital communication tool. When Tomilea Allison, the mayor of Bloomington, Indiana, wanted to inform people about major streets to be closed for repairs, she assumed the newspaper was the best means of distributing this information. She asked the local paper to publish the street names, hours of closing, and other details. The editor cooperated, and the information was printed on the front page. Allison commented:

> I assume that objective citizens will read the daily paper to keep track of crucial local items. I count on it as a means of communication for the most basic news—from street closings to handling the concerns of hazardous waste. I think we have to count on the good judgment and common sense of citizens, plus time to analyze the facts, to provide checks and balances when a community has to offset the one-paper, one-point-of-view idea (personal interview with Tomilea Allison, 7/25/89).

Allison valued literacy and, like most literate adults, took for granted that the citizenry of Bloomington (a university town) had the ability to read the daily papers. It has become clear, however, that mayors and other political leaders dare not assume that all voters can read printed information.

In our experience of working with the welfare mothers, we became acutely aware that they desperately wanted to "get off the dole." One middle-aged woman worked day and night, even at one point with a broken ankle, to keep up her basic skills and job-training classes. "My three sons have no hope of getting out of the ghetto," she told us, "unless I can get off welfare and get a decent-paying job." Literacy had become this woman's new value.

Literacy Is Rooted in Cultural Values

What we value determines the direction of our lives. Starving people value food more than they do reading material.

Newman and Beverstock

Businesspeople value return on investment. People teaching literacy value all three: food, reading material, and a return on the investment of their energy. They value the votes cast in Congress by their representatives who support the literacy effort.

Literacy learning for the new reader is as basic to that person's values as food is to the body. In literacy work, we have been slow to realize that the programs and practices we assign to illiterate learners often are at variance with the learners' cultural background and the values that govern their lives. This often has been the case in overcrowded, understaffed programs where simply assigning a text on the "right" reading level was deemed adequate to individualize instruction.

BIZARRO   By DAN PIRARO

**"'See Spot. See Spot run. See Spot run
and play...' What IS this garbage?"**

The "Bizarro" cartoon by Dan Piraro is reprinted by permission of Chronicle Features, San Francisco.

A generation of literacy instructors has been supplied with inappropriate teaching materials. New readers are bored with uninspiring workbooks filled with routine exercises that allow too little fun in learning, prompt no mental explorations, and fail to relate to the personal circumstances of the literacy learner. Commercial book publishers might have found a market in the millions of new readers by supplying the richly varied array of materials needed in a typical literacy class filled with people from many cultures and language backgrounds, working at different levels. But like everyone else, commercial publishers must watch the bottom line. Newly literate people tend to be poor, and programs funded for them—whether by government or by private agencies—tend to be underfunded. Only industry, working to educate its own workers, has had the wherewithal to pay for interesting materials. The market and the need are there, but the money is not.

In today's information-rich environment, the day of routinized literacy instruction is, we hope, coming to an end. Programs are still underfunded, and many materials are still uninspiring, but at least the means exist for correcting this unacceptable situation. Desktop publishing software makes it possible in principle for literacy instruction centers to publish their own specifically relevant literary materials to meet the needs of each group of new readers.

We are still so far from the actualization of this potential that computer-generated, individualized literacy instruction material sounds Utopian to the typical worker in the typically impoverished program. Nevertheless, this technological power could enable the literacy teacher to meet the demands placed on our profession by researchers and workers in the field. Research has shown that more than a learner's reading level must be taken into account if appropriate instruction is to be provided. The findings of five workers in the field who are especially responsive to cultural values speak eloquently to the need for more than merely generic literacy materials.

Paolo Freire. To Freire (1985a), literacy is active creation rather than passive transference. He sees literacy learning occurring when learners are encouraged and supported by other learners, when they analyze and reflect on problems in their personal experience, and when they work actively together to transform their social worlds. Freire's years of work in Brazil and other developing nations have led him to the belief that education is simultaneously an act of knowing, a political act, and an artistic event (Freire, 1985b). For Freire, the recognition of cultural integrity and economic necessity demands a far more basic grasp of people's values than is reflected by generic materials.

David Harman. Harman (1985) speaks forcefully in support of viewing literacy in its cultural context. He argues that the definition of literacy as simply the ability to read and write is absolutist, reductionistic, and value-neutral, and that it leaves out the sociocultural and context-dependent nature of literacy. He argues for multiple definitions of literacy based on specific cultural, social, and contextual factors.

Arlene Hanna Fingeret. Writing in support of the kind of ethnographic research for which she has become well known, Fingeret (1987) notes that few ethnographic research projects have been conducted in adult literacy. She urges that more work be done to illuminate how adults view themselves as learners, to understand student perspectives of instructional programs, to describe the relationship between students' cultural and classroom behavior, and to observe the functions of literacy in settings other than schools.

In evaluating statewide Adult Basic Education (ABE) programs—the federally funded, state-administered literacy instruction programs established in the mid-1960s—Fingeret (1985) found that programs and programmatic decisions were made by external forces rather than by active participants. Given Fingeret's findings that ABE personnel are dedicated people who emphasize nurturance and responsiveness, we can draw a simple and obvious conclusion: literacy professionals need to redirect their good intentions into more effective teaching that takes into account the cultural needs of the learner.

Francis Kazemek. Kazemek (1985, 1988a, 1988b) calls into question both the validity and the widespread acceptance of the definition of functional literacy as the most useful approach to adult literacy and adult literacy education. He urges recognition of the following:

1. Literacy is both a personal and a social process of coming to know that is political, cultural, and context-dependent.
2. Adult literacy instruction needs to be viewed as a process of mutual discussion.
3. Adult literacy instructors need an understanding of the adult learner.

Kazemek's viewpoint implies criticism of the generic approach to literacy materials.

Shirley Brice Heath. The functions and uses of literacy are based on the interpretive needs of a particular cultural community, according to Heath (1980, 1983, 1984). Functional literacy is a highly contextual and culturally dependent phenomenon. Thus, instead of providing learners with new skills, or replacing ones they already have with ones many teachers might regard as dysfunctional, we need to build on the literacy skills learners demonstrate across a variety of contexts, for a variety of purposes.

Fingeret especially has pointed out the importance of recognizing that some portions of society depend more on oral than on written communication. Without pencil and paper, Native Americans, for example, teach their children how to catch fish. Innercity "pocket cultures" depend little on written communication other than graffiti that graces neighborhood walls. One must conclude that literacy is culturally defined; it derives from the needs and values of the community.

Many of the newly literate do not depend on the nuances of argument or the discussions of the traditionally literate to reason through tough issues. A new adult reader, after sitting in on a state coalition meeting and listening to 5 hours of discussion surrounding the possibility of developing a foundation to receive and dispense monies for literacy purposes, commented, "You sure know how to take a simple idea and make it difficult." Ready to vote yea on the measure, this newly literate person summed up the situation this way: "We need money and this is a way to get money. What are we waiting for?"

Food for the mind and the gold of literacy in their pocket—these are rock-solid values for the newly literate, so long as their new literacy comes to them in culturally meaningful terms. This quintet of researchers speaks out unanimously in favor of more attention to the cultural aspects of learners. The narrow, one-dimensional approaches of the past no longer can be conceived to meet the new reader's needs. All literacy leaders and instructors, whether in official or volunteer programs, must answer the questions raised by these five thinkers: Do we continue to be content with talking about the glories of literacy in professional jargon while dispensing literacy to our learners through restricted, artificial, contextually vapid materials that leave the new reader unsatisfied? Or do we engage in dialogue with our learners, incorporate their interests into the program, and make their values the cultural norm of the reading and writing skills we are teaching?

Open Communication and Cultural Pluralism

For many years, literacy was narrowly defined according to one of its many dimensions. A person who could barely read and write was judged to be literate. As a nation, we are now coming to realize that literacy involves the many dimensions of our many cultures, and we are redefining literacy accordingly. To acknowledge the richness of American cultural pluralism is to reaffirm its Constitutional basis and the freedoms of communication that are guaranteed in the Bill of Rights: freedom of speech, freedom of assembly, freedom of the press, and freedom of religion. Political freedom needs to be paralleled by similar freedoms characterizing our social transactions. Frightened people are not free, but people do not remain frightened when they can hear and talk to one another. As long as communication remains open to the free expression of our polycultural energies, we can be hopeful about the future.

In the past, we have refused to allow property and possessions to undermine the freedoms that guaranteed the rights of ownership and wealth. Now we must ensure that the complex information technology that serves our American value of openness so well does not define a new line of demarcation between the haves and the have-nots, thereby undermining the free exchange of information. Open access to the powerful tools of communication holds the promise of ever-expanding democracy and places greater literacy demands on all citizens. That power in the hands of a few would hack at the very root of our democracy. If we fail to achieve adult literacy, if we fail to provide open access to information for all the people, we are putting democracy at risk.

An American man, bound to China by marriage to a Chinese woman, wrote of the impact of technological openness on a group of his students in China.

> I gave a campuswide slide show of American life with an array of photographs of how we live, what we drive, where we shop. When a photograph of a pay telephone booth appeared on the screen, I explained to my students that the telecommunications technology made in the U.S. was advanced to the point that anyone could call any other phone in the country...from that pay phone, even using a credit card. This amazed everyone in the crowded auditorium. It [the phone] was a symbol that ties together scientific knowhow, material well-being, and intellectual freedom — a machine that was the epitome of a democratic state and its free flow of information (Kullander, 1989, p. 17).

In an open society — the kind of society that America continues to want to be — literacy has come to be an assumed value, as native to the soil of democracy as our liberties, and as taken for granted as any other human right. Because literacy is a value intrinsic to our society, it is a "demand" that our society places on individual citizens. Because literacy is a precondition for full participation in our economic life, it has become part of an urgent political agenda.

Literacy as a Social Event

The social sciences, attuned to taking a human measure of reality, characterize literacy as a profoundly social process. While we write, thoughts unfold, take shape, clarify, and are aimed at publication, even if only for one other reader. While we read, others'

ideas touch us, nourish us, and transform our thinking. As readers and writers, we are members of the interpretive communities standing invisibly at our elbow while we read and write, no matter how physically isolated we may seem. These interpretive communities shape both the meaning we construct from the words on the page and the words we choose to use as we write.

Consider the comment: "That is really **bad!**" Depending on the hearer's or reader's interpretive community, these words can be either a negative or a positive statement. The word *bad* can have vastly different meanings, and a familiarity with the speaker's or writer's neighborhood is required for the original intention to be understood within its proper context.

Membership in an interpretive community is often referred to as a specific literacy, as when we speak of *computer literacy*—that mixture of acronyms, jargon, and cyberspeak by which computer whizzes exclude the rest of us from their arcane discourse. Some words in these subdialects move from the highly specific uses within their unique communities to metaphoric use by wider, yet uninitiated, communities. For example, default settings, a technical term that once was used to refer only to computer hardware and what it would do if it were not given alternative instructions, now has been extended to the personal realm as a synonym for habits.

Special literacies function as avenues of human growth and understanding (of the self and the community); of reinforcement of present views; and of escape, confrontation, emotional highs, and psychic depths. As points of power within a literate society, reading and writing serve both as symbols of social status and as tools for economic, social, and personal changes. Literacy itself becomes the basis of our social transactions, a measure of our self-esteem, and the instrument of our confidence that we can make social progress (Sticht, 1988).

Learning to read goes hand-in-hand with life's changes. One example is the young worker who joined a literacy program when his promotion to shop steward became imminent, so he could learn to read the shop steward's manual. Another example is the woman who, as she was learning to read, decided that now she had enough self-respect to get a set of false teeth and start "getting out in the world."

To the adult learners who attended the First National Literacy Congress in Philadelphia in September 1987, their newly acquired literacy was a heady experience. We could sense their joy, their confidence, and the affection they held for others who had become literate. As they exuberantly and confidently exchanged anecdotes from their experience, we could not see the shy, diffident, inarticulate "shadow behavior" so often associated with the nonreading adult.

The Social Potential of Literacy

Another community of literacy is the subculture of people who are TV-induced aliterates—people who *can* read but choose not to (Harste & Mikulecky, 1984; Thimmesch, 1984). Some aliterate people watch the tube for hours every day. Researchers say the TV goes on in the morning when the family gets up and goes off at night when they go to bed. They never read a book or magazine (other than *TV Guide*), their literary allusions are chiefly to commercials, and their best friends are electronic images.

In the era of the couch potato, we are witnessing the transfer of communication activity from the print medium, which requires the reader's active construction of meaning, to the passive medium of visual receptivity. Anxiety over this sagging state is no mere paranoia when you consider that the ongoing consolidation of the major media is putting into the hands of a few the power to educate, influence, and control large segments of our population. One cause of this anxiety is that although we value literacy, we do not value it enough to make it available to all our citizens.

One result of this tendency might be a massive loss of literacy. According to philosopher Henry Sauerwein, "A profound challenge currently confronts our society." In a recent lecture at the University of New Mexico, he asked, "Can we rise anew to great art? Can we work hard enough to reexamine humanity, create something new...in order to realize in society the value of our better selves as generous, caring, and inventive human beings?"

Simple literacy is not to be equated with great art, and literacy itself is essential only to literary art. But whatever answer one gives to Sauerwein's questions, the same answer applies to literacy. In a sense, it applies to literacy before it applies to great art. If the values implicit in the production of art were extended to adult literacy environments—the workplace, the military, the correctional facility, the ghetto—they would bring about a literacy renaissance. This renaissance would be a work of great art in which humans are the medium, and would eventually lead to works of literary art arising from a broader base of literate humanity. Without a commitment to literacy as great as the dedication to art, the odds seem slender of achieving greatness in either.

Great art, like a great oak, begins small. At the Reading Practicum Center at Indiana University, we work with learners of all ages. One of our students wanted to work with adults and was placed at a small center where adults gathered for a hot lunch, social activities, and some classes. She started to work with four women who, prior to her arrival, had been working individually in standardized workbooks. As their work became group work and as they imagined together, the women wrote and shared stories and poems. Sometimes they illustrated their stories in watercolor. The results pleased the women immensely. A warm camaraderie developed; they delighted in one another's creativity.

At this same center, four other women and a different instructor decided to write a history of their town out of their own experiences and memories. The resulting booklet captured funny, otherwise unknown, personal glimpses, changing oral history into a form others could read and enjoy. Through sociable literacy, these women reveled in the pleasure of one another's company.

Another quartet of newly literate women composed a booklet on quilting, which reinforces the connections among literacy, the community, and art. They had started out working individually in generic workbooks—filling in the blanks of cookie-cutter literacy materials that filled an elementary purpose but failed to inspire aesthetic response. These women had long since graduated to the authorship of their own publication on quilting, and they asked, "Oh, do we have to go back to workbooks?" No longer illiterate, these women were ready for bigger and better things. Their newfound literacy had freed them to achieve a new level of social communion.

dot
plain and print
bright, gay, warm
a pretty dress I had
colorful

Helen Hastings

flower
color and design
merry, cheerful, action
the middle flower shows better
clover

Margaret Harris

pioneers
plain print
square and stripe, one on top
they are my great grandparents
red and blue

Bernice Gaskins

four leaf clover
circle for the moon
day and night
bright and summer
the beauty in it

Flora Fuka

From "Thoughts on Patterns," part of a booklet on quilting produced by four newly literate women.

Literacy's Contribution to Society

Many social welfare agencies have begun to make reading or English-language ability a condition for receiving services, welfare payments, and early paroles. The Armed Forces require improving literacy as a qualification for advancement in rank (Kelly, 1989), and they provide meaningful literacy materials for new recruits to improve inadequate reading and writing skills.

Some people object to making literacy a requirement for the attainment of rank, but the objection misses the point. Literacy is required not as a punitive measure or as a means of depriving someone of needed assistance, but because literacy is the sine qua non for functioning in a democratic society, necessary for enabling welfare recipients to become independent and for unlettered recruits to make something of themselves. Since the 1940s, the Armed Forces have been aware of the importance of literacy. Stephen Steurer, executive director of the Correctional Education Association, tells of drastic changes for the better that have taken place in prisoners' lives when hope entered through literacy.

In some situations, especially those connected with penal correction, society must value its own safety above the rehabilitation of those who have failed to find a socially acceptable niche. However, when citizens realize that it would be more cost-effective to rehabilitate people than to keep them in storage, and better still to take therapeutic and preventive steps prior to imprisonment, both the sense of threat and the high price of crime will come down. If one traces back the cause-effect link from crime to poverty to illiteracy, it takes little logic to realize that we put many people in prison merely because they cannot read and write. Literacy is not a cure for evil; but many inmates would have a better chance of getting jobs, becoming better citizens, escaping the criminalizing effects of poverty, and staying out of jail if they were literate. America's choice is an economic one: either spend a few thousand dollars teaching a potential perpetrator to read and write, or spend hundreds of thousand of dollars keeping him or her locked up.

The demand for adult literacy for the good of a democratic society is vital. And the potential is unlimited.

The Economic Value of Literacy

The American business community is becoming painfully aware of its need for greater literacy in the marketplace. U.S. companies are nervous about what is *not* going on in their industries — from workers who cannot read the danger signs around the plant to supervisors whose secretaries have to write their letters for them. When one CEO was asked if he had any literacy problems in his company, he said no; but when he was asked if any of his vice presidents needed help writing business letters, he said yes. Illiteracy comes in people of all shapes and sizes of bank accounts.

Used by permission of Don Wright, *The Palm Beach Post.*

Large segments of North American business and industry are economically threatened by foreign pressures and the decreasing competitiveness of U.S. businesses in world trade. This situation must be linked in part to a lack of literacy among American workers. U.S. industry has been driven to the competitive brink by Japan, West Germany, and other more literate, technologically oriented industrial nations. Fulfillment of the American dream is being redefined in the era of new technology as depending on upgrading the literacy of the American workforce by providing job-related, lifelong relearning for the adult worker.

Many companies also realize that their customers need to be literate. Clients need to be able to read advertisements, follow instructions for assembling a product, and comprehend warning labels which, if misunderstood, could lead to injury and expensive litigation. Corporations are becoming more involved with the community environment in which they are located or are about to locate. Are the schools good? Is there a trained, trainable, and literate labor force? Are other resources that depend on literacy (including communications and transportation) available and efficient?

In a commercial climate based on complex technology that requires a high degree of sophistication to use standard electronic equipment, employers and personnel managers must be concerned about selecting employees who are suited for high-tech tasks or can be brought up to speed quickly. Standardized tests used for sorting and qualifying candidates have been illegal since 1971, when the Supreme Court ruled in *Griggs v. Duke Power Co.* that all testing conducted for either recruitment or promotion must be drawn from job-specific materials rather than from general references. Determining minimum reading requirements for a given job poses problems: "There are few documented attempts to establish minimum reading requirements for various occupations" (Park et al., 1985).

The result of all these concerns is that American business is playing a larger and more overt role in making decisions about what literacy is and who will be literate. Mikulecky (1988) suggested that the business community has three options: (1) it can lower wages and simplify jobs, (2) it can send jobs "off the continent," or (3) it can improve the effectiveness of American employees by increasing their literacy. The third option seems to be the only desirable one: many jobs will become more complex, workers will demand higher pay, and the United States does not want to give its jobs away. U.S. businesspeople have no other choice than to become literacy activists. Mikulecky noted that people are expected to learn new tasks every 3 to 4 months; he contended that problem-solving must be taught and explicitly linked to the work that people are hired to do.

The teaching and learning of the critical, job-specific skills of problemsolving require increasing literacy.

Literacy for Employer and Employee

Literacy programs in industry are divided into two kinds: those designed by the employer to teach workers new job skills as quickly as possible and those that are more employee-centered, designed for personal empowerment and career advancement. Programs that empower workers have not always been perceived by management to be in the best interests of the company, but a shift is taking place in this perception. Through the common value of literacy, and its economic value for both labor and management, a new singleness of mind is emerging in U.S. industry.

Along with the spread of interest in conflict management and management by negotiation, and a decline in the adversarial relationships that characterized the management-vs.-labor stance of the past, a cooperative partnership in educating the workforce also is emerging. Most corporations once hesitated because of the cost of retraining programs; now many companies ask what it will cost *not* to retrain workers who want to improve their skills and work at a higher level. Some corporations provide in-house local training programs; others arrange for employee release time to go outside the plant for additional training.

Given the high cost of training, management's regard for the worker's literacy sometimes is defined narrowly. Businesses must decide who is worth additional training, since they are "investing in human capital" (Bedenbaugh, 1985). The issue then becomes human resource development and utilization as company policy, and the industrial educators must justify instruction in terms of payoff for the company (Mikulecky, class presentation, 1988). This narrow definition of skills and attainment tends to tie education directly to productivity, and sets up a preference for teaching the kind of literacy that is quantifiable and easily tested.

The new concern for literacy also challenges industry to entertain more aspects of employee literacy as indirectly related to a broader efficiency: job-related mental health, personal fulfillment, workplace morality, and other concerns often overlooked in the past are now being addressed. According to Sondra Stein (1989), deputy director of Massachusetts' Commonwealth Literacy Campaign, many of the employers she has worked with have found it more productive to offer a broad array of literacy classes, integrating basic skills with specific job literacies. The employers cite as gains higher morale, improved teamwork, increased communication, and decreased absenteeism.

The pressure for profit leads to complex ethical quandaries about workers displaced by new technologies and the need for intelligent recycling of human talent. In some cases, it may be cheaper to retrain than replace workers rendered obsolete in their old jobs but unable to move into a technologically more demanding job. In other cases—such as a 60-year-old laid off just short of retirement because the company can get younger workers trained more quickly—the worker may not be so fortunate. Companies and unions now must consider how to address the complexity of these practical, ethical, moral, and economic dilemmas.

Anticipating the need for a solution to these problems, the First National Adult Literacy Congress (1987) published the following mandate in their summary:

> Companies need to be informed about the problems of illiteracy. When students go to companies and commit themselves to work on their GEDs, their rights must be protected. It should be illegal for an employer to fire someone who does not read. When students make a commitment to overcoming their reading problems, they should ask their employers for their help and commitment. Companies should encourage employees to seek help.

Literacy has meant economic security for some. Studies show that income rises commensurately with education (Bowen, 1977; Schwartz, 1988). However, literacy training does not automatically provide economic guarantees, as Karier (1975, p. 2) observed:

> Just as one of the controlling myths of the nineteenth century was the belief that westward movement would result in

social mobility, so too, one of the central myths of the twentieth century is that schooling *will result* in social mobility.

At the same time, the underprivileged literate worker's chance at a job is immeasurably greater than is the chance of the underprivileged illiterate worker. Representative Major Owens (D-NY) said of the chances of young black males in America:

> Most of them have a choice between zero and the drug trade. They don't have a choice of a legitimate job that pays wages sufficient to climb out of poverty. Part of the problem is the changing nature of the American job. U.S. industry is phasing out many of the unskilled and semiskilled factory jobs which were the traditional bottom rungs on the economic ladder for poorly educated minority men. Between 1973 and 1987, black male dropouts saw their annual earnings, after adjustment for inflation, decline an average of 44 percent, says Andrew Sum, director of Northeastern University's Center for Labor Market Studies (Hey, 1989, p. 7).

The value of literacy in the American marketplace has become crucial for boss and worker alike. Can the United States, struggling to keep up in a rapidly expanding world economy, keep pace with other industrial nations whose workforce is better educated and more literate than ours? In the competitive climate of a global economy, can the United States afford to carry the added weight of an intolerably and unnecessarily high national illiteracy rate, a burden that takes its toll in the enormous reduction of America's workforce?

Goldberg (1951, p. 4) offered advice on the basis of his study of the Armed Forces that is still applicable to business and industry today:

> America cannot afford, at this critical juncture in her history, to discount the potential capacities, intellectual and productive, of her many millions of illiterate adults. The

source of this country's strength lies more in the vigor of its people than in its natural resources or industrial capacity. It is the job of education, properly supported by local, state, and federal funds, to ensure that all of the people are better prepared to assume the duties and responsibilities consonant with citizenship. Educators have the task of seeing that education gets its job done.

Business and industry may have difficult and expensive choices to make, but in view of the world economy and the global marketplace, the basic choice seems inevitable: employers must now regard themselves as educators. Beyond this choice, finer decisions must be made. Will managers invest in the whole worker or merely develop a narrow set of skills for the immediate future? Will they retrain or lay off? Will they use exclusionary testing techniques that may have a heavy impact on a cultural minority group? Should cost/benefit ratios be considered only for the present, or should they be considered in terms of our societal needs as a whole?

Business and industry should not have to answer these questions alone. As our national recognition of literacy becomes clearer, state and federal legislation will mandate some of the answers. One example of congressional action is the Senate's passage of the Illiteracy Elimination Act in February 1990. While this proposal has not completed the full congressional review, it is expected to be passed into law, thereby increasing the authorization of funds by $100 million a year during fiscal 1991-1995. However, businesspeople listen more readily to other businesspeople than they do to legislators or educators. As the challenge to U.S. commerce has come most strongly from other industrialized nations that are more literate than the United States, the U.S. business community is likely to learn the lesson of marketplace literacy from its most distinguished schoolmaster, Professor Competition. Similarly, the greatest single source of leadership toward a worldwide development of literacy, whether in industrialized or nonindustrialized nations, has come not from the United States but from abroad. The United States is learning a lesson on the global value of literacy from the United Nations.

UNESCO: The Global Leader in World Literacy

Literacy has become an American value partly because it has become an international value. The value of literacy for the global human community was succinctly stated by the United Nations Educational, Scientific, and Cultural Organization (UNESCO) in its 1975 International Symposium for Literacy. At the symposium, literacy was defined as being inseparable from "participation." Structures of government and society favorable to literacy were defined as those that would (1) foster the effective participation of every citizen in decision making at all levels of human life, (2) not make education a privilege of class, (3) provide local communities with control of learning technologies, and (4) favor concerted approaches and permanent cooperation. In short, the International Symposium for Literacy proposed a declaration of literacy for all the people of the world, and with it, the attending, inherently democratic, liberation of humanity.

This highly refined definition had been a long time coming. UNESCO had taken a worldwide leadership role in promoting literacy among its member states since 1946, and over the years its definition of literacy evolved substantially. Even in the early years of its founding, UNESCO's promotion of literacy was far in advance of any national initiative. The development of the worldwide literacy movement can be tracked through UNESCO's seven major conferences on adult education: Elsinore, 1949; Montreal, 1960; Teheran, 1965; Tokyo, 1972; Persepolis, 1975; Paris, 1985; and Bangkok, 1990. (The United States was one of the original signatories of the UNESCO charter; however, Cold War politics of the 1980s, compounded by the Arab-Israeli conflict, led to the withdrawal of the United States from UNESCO in 1984.)

At the Elsinore conference, literacy was regarded as a part of adult education. The delegates did not declare literacy to be indispensable; nonetheless, they affirmed that literacy enables people to broaden their knowledge through independent sharing of cultural improvements.

At the Montreal conference, UNESCO moved a step forward in its literacy concerns. Literacy was defined to be indispensable to human society, and the immediacy of the need for literacy in education and development was recognized. The conference called for the worldwide eradication of illiteracy as soon as possible. To achieve this goal, UNESCO invited affluent nations to provide a special fund for an international campaign. This proposal, however, was never put into effect.

The Teheran conference (the World Conference of Ministers of Education on the Eradication of Illiteracy) expanded the scope of literacy considerably with the adoption of the concept of *functional literacy*. This redefinition far surpassed the previous meaning of literacy; but the new concept, termed *work-oriented literacy*, with its exclusive focus on economic aspects and productivity, was essentially limited (Bhola, 1984). Implementation of the effort for functional literacy was conducted by the Experimental World Literacy Program (EWLP) between 1967 and 1973 in 11 Third World countries.

At the Tokyo conference, there was dissatisfaction with the narrowly conceived functional literacy concept. UNESCO responded by asking member states to make the elimination of illiteracy a priority by conducting large-scale literacy campaigns based on a revised definition of functional literacy to include personal fulfillment, social progress, and economic development. Consequently, a critical review of EWLP's work and the 1975 conference changed the meaning of functionality. The exclusive focus on economic skills was transformed into adopting the Freirian stance that literacy as a strategy of liberation teaches people to read not only the word but also the world. This message, stemming from Freire's early work with the economically disadvantaged, broadens horizons and implies an awareness and acceptance of a much larger perception of self in relation to one's own world and to the world of others.

The UNESCO conference in Paris reemphasized the intention to achieve functional literacy—according to the new definition—by global campaign, and it set a deadline for the eradication of functional illiteracy by the year 2000 (Bhola, 1989). In 1987, the United Nations General Assembly unanimously named 1990 a year of global summons to the task of the new decade. The yearlong celebration began with the Fourth World Assembly on Adult Education, held in Bangkok, Thailand, in January. The Bangkok meeting, entitled Literacy, Popular Education, and Democracy: Building the Movement, was designed with a people's emphasis in mind. A dialogue with donors on adult literacy kept centermost the ever-troublesome matter of funding. A consensus emerged to work toward education for all by the year 2000 and to allocate resources to that end. However, federal governments remain unwilling to pay for all of adult literacy; private angels must be found to fund the movement. Other major conferences during the year were the World Conference on Education for All in March, also held in Bangkok, and the International Education Conference, held in Geneva, Switzerland, in September.

As member states have responded to UNESCO's moral leadership, universalization of primary education generally has been accepted as standard policy. National adult literacy campaigns in many countries have contributed to a significant reduction in illiteracy. UNESCO has acknowledged the industrialized nations' fostering of functional literacy according to the expanded definition. According to UNESCO, between 1950 and 1985 illiteracy among the world's adult population decreased from an estimated 44.3 percent to 27.7 percent (Bhola, 1989). UNESCO's 1985 statistics showed that 1 billion adults — one in every four living on the globe — were still illiterate. This figure does not suggest the criteria by which anyone was determined to be illiterate, though; nor does it address the difficulties of cross-country comparisons.

The figures are devastating for the Third World, where 98 percent of the earth's adult illiterates live. In one sense, however, a 25 percent functional illiteracy rate is even more traumatic for the functionally illiterate people living in the industrialized countries. In Third World lands, traditional styles of existence do not necessarily require literacy for survival or for active participation in society. In the United States, functional illiteracy keeps one-fifth to one-fourth of our population from dealing independently with the demands of the economy, society, and politics.

UNESCO also took the lead in developing a comprehensive approach toward literacy in an effort to achieve universal primary education. One important consequence of adult literacy is the positive attitude toward schooling for children that develops in families and communities. UNESCO supports the coordination (frequently neglected) between literacy campaigns for adults and out-of-school youth and children. Based on the interrelationship between the education of parents (especially mothers) and children, UNESCO's Second Medium-Term Plan (1984-1989) proposed the simultaneous education of all children, youth, and adults.

Despite various efforts toward the eradication of illiteracy at all levels, counterarguments continued against the international education of adults. A literacy skeptic quoted by Bhola (1989, p. 23) argued that literacy is oversold, meaning that it is a myth to believe that literacy necessarily brings democratization and modernization. The skeptic continued, "[There is]...no use wasting resources on adults who did not take the opportunity when first offered, and who are not motivated even now to read and write. Available educational resources should be allocated to more urgent things"—especially the education of children.

Bhola countered that even developing nations have learned that "neither modernization nor democratization is possible without literacy" (Bhola, 1989, p. 66). Through their experiences, they have come to realize that neither technology (broadcast media) nor democracy can be a substitute for literacy. "Literacy is the only passport for independent learning, and for citizenship in the knowledge society" (Bhola, 1988a, p. 23). In terms of policy, Bhola and UNESCO urged that literacy be retained at the core of program planning for development in both underindustrialized and industrialized countries, and that appropriate modes of delivery and methods of teaching literacy be created to suit the different political and cultural contexts.

In 1990, International Literacy Year, U.N. member nations committed themselves to the promotion of discussions about literacy among policymakers concerned with the mutual effects of development and education, to the training of planners and practitioners for literacy work, and to the ongoing systematization of the literacy campaign. Simultaneously, field experience continued to refine the concept of literacy and the methods used to achieve it worldwide.

Literacy: One More American Right

People who cannot read and write are, to the degree of their illiteracy, not free; they are personally limited and politically restricted. Although they may be smart, wise, and witty, they are enslaved by ignorance and excluded from full participation in the social, political, and cultural processes of our society.

The most shameful American example of the slavery of illiteracy was the illiteracy of the slaves. Education and literacy were denied to black slaves in America. Anyone who did not count in the political arena had no need of reading and writing; furthermore, the black population was perceived as presenting both social and political threats. Education was an assumed value for enfranchised white males, but systematically denied to disenfranchised slaves and women.

In the laws of many states, slaves were forbidden to read, and it was illegal to teach them the skills of literacy.

> Every Southern state except Maryland and Kentucky had stringent laws forbidding anyone to teach slaves reading and writing, and in some states the penalties applied to the education of free Negroes and mulattoes as well....In North Carolina it was a crime to distribute among them any pamphlet or book, not excluding the Bible....In the slave system of the United States—so finely circumscribed and so cleanly self-contained—virtually all avenues of recourse for the slave, all lines of communication to society at large, originated and ended with the master (Elkins, 1968, pp. 59-63).

If a slave did learn to read or write, the consequences could be terrible. In some places, the punishment for learning to read and write was amputation. According to one former slave, "The first time you was caught trying to read or write, you was whipped with a cowhide, the next time with a cat-o'-nine-tails, and the third time they cut the first joint offen your forefinger." The testimony of another ex-slave makes even clearer the threat of literacy perceived by the ruling elite: "If they caught you trying to write they would cut your finger off and if they caught you again they would cut your head off" (Cornelius, 1983, pp. 171-178).

Despite these terrors, many slaves did learn to read and

write. Ex-slaves most often cited the adolescent children of their white owners as their teachers, although white teachers hired by slave owners, daring the reprisals of their neighbors, also taught the slaves. Often slaves were self-taught, and then brothers and sisters would teach one another (Cornelius, pp. 171-183).

Coy (1988, p. 13) analyzed adult literacy in terms of "the value and belief system that is operating in the legislative and policy making areas of society." She pointed out that during the time women were excluded from political equality in America, they also were excluded from equality of literacy. Before the Civil War, about 20 percent of the U.S. male population was literate, but "the new nation had not yet included women in its framework for literacy expectations." A few privileged, and some adventuresome, women enjoyed private schooling and perfected their skills on their own. But as a rule, girls were neither sent to school nor taught to read and write. They, like the black slaves, were not intended by the Founding Fathers to be included in the resounding affirmation that "all men are created equal." This was a political statement about free, white, property-owning males, not women and slaves. Not until 1920 — 133 years after the signing of the Constitution — would women win the right to vote. Unlike slaves, women were "allowed" schooling, but relatively few could take advantage of any formal education. White males had laid for themselves a democratic groundwork for "life, liberty, and the pursuit of happiness," but only in the building of democracy's superstructure would those rights and liberties gradually be extended to all the people.

Following the Civil War, the victorious North realized the need for free, public schools as an efficient means of indoctrinating the many disparate "nations" within America — the dissident South, the foreign-born immigrants, the unlettered frontier people of the expanding West — in the beliefs and values of the one, federally reunited Union. Free public education was prescribed by state conventions in 1868 and 1870, and literacy began to emerge as a more inclusive public value. Nevertheless, literacy was not a prerequisite for manual laborers in the Second Industrial Revolution, and much of the "brawn over brain" mentality that characterized this period is still apparent as we move into the Information Age.

Farming, marketing, and keeping the family accounts required an ability to read and write, however, and as hundreds of thousands of immigrants poured into the United States at the turn of the century, legislation (the Smith-Lever Act, 1914) was passed to provide public education for the masses. Instruction in the English language and in U.S. history, government, and citizenship was deemed especially necessary for new Americans (Cook, 1977). During World War I, citizenship classes became a priority. Political need had made literacy expedient. Democracy works best and can be protected only if the people can read and write. Literacy training for the military made great strides during both World Wars.

In the 1960s a new social consciousness flowered in America, prompting a reordering of society's primary institutions. Equal rights for all, valued in theory since Lincoln had spoken 100 years before at Gettysburg, became the pillar of fire that led a generation of civil rights workers to try to finish "the work which they who fought here have thus far so nobly advanced." In proclaiming "government of the people, by the people, and for the people," Lincoln was promising greater freedoms for more people than he imagined.

Beliefs and values intermingle in human experience. As we ponder American values and Constitutional beliefs, we come face to face with the inevitable logic of democracy: as basic democratic values have been extended to more people, concomitant beliefs have followed about extending democratic education, including the basic skills of reading and writing. The idealism of the 1960s was no mere youthful dream. It was the same kind of new-world ideal about natural rights and human freedom that had informed the founders of the American experiment; only in the 1960s, democracy was intended for more than white male property owners. The outflowing of that idealism into the literacy movement of the 1970s, and the formation of the National Coalition for Literacy in the 1980s, was the consistent expression of these American values and beliefs:

- Public education is worth working for.
- Legislation can make a difference.
- Public awareness of the adult illiteracy problem is the first step in making a difference.

- Public sector involvement and volunteer recruitment can make a difference.
- Coordination, networking, collaboration, and coalitions can make a difference.
- State literacy commissions can make a difference.
- The learning of English, history, government, and citizenship is meaningful to, and needed for, new citizens.
- Adult learning can and should take place at times and places convenient and accessible to the adult learner.

We have not yet turned each of these beliefs into working policies, but we are closer to the "long-range, ongoing, consistent planning [needed] in program development, assessment, and evaluation" (Coy, 1988, pp. 13-14) than we were before the Literacy Decade of the 1980s.

The United States was founded on the precept that political liberties are natural human rights. Freedom of religion, freedom of speech, freedom of the press, the right to assemble peaceably, and the right to petition the government for redress of grievances are all liberties innate in each citizen's life, and are not derived from the government. Literacy is implied with each of these liberties.

The Constitution's framers understood that literacy was a condition both useful and desirable to the establishment of the new nation. For example, Article 1, Section 8, of the Constitution reads: "The Congress shall have power...to promote the progress of science and useful arts, by securing for limited times to authors and inventors the exclusive right to their respective writings and discoveries." The protection of copyrights and patents was built into the foundation of the democracy because the implied literacy skills, reading and writing, were perceived as fundamental to the common wealth. The founders were educated, university-minded men who knew that the educational wherewithal to develop authors and inventors must be fostered in a society that is to be free, strong, happy, and rich. Although literacy and education per se are not defined as rights in the Constitution, the learning of those literate men was something they assumed, a value they would have parted with even more reluctantly than they would have parted with the right to vote. They could not imagine the absence of literacy in their political and economic enterprise. In the absence of literacy, they could not have conceived their political or economic enterprises.

The United States has taken 200 years to realize that literacy is a natural human right and, therefore, a moral obligation—a long time in terms of one human life, a twinkling in the overall scheme of things. The U.S. government depends on the participation of the people in the democratic process; the participation of uneducated illiterates is dangerous to democracy. The Preamble to the Constitution promised to "promote the general welfare" of all our generations. Because the welfare of our citizens rests on their ability to read and write, we must declare anew the independence of our people from ignorance and illiteracy.

References

Bedenbaugh, E.H. (1985). Education is still a good investment. *Clearing House*, *59*(3), 134-136.

Bhola, H.S. (1988a). At issue: Universal literacy by the year 2000. *Chalkboard*, *37*, 23.

Bhola, H.S. (1988b). A policy analysis of adult literacy education in India: Across the two national policy reviews of 1968 and 1986. *Perspectives in Education*, *4*(14), 212-228.

Bhola, H.S. (1984). *Campaigning for literacy: Eight national experiences of the twentieth century with a memorandum to decision makers*. Paris: UNESCO.

Bhola, H.S. (1989, Spring). International literacy year: A summons to action for universal literacy by the year 2000. *Education Horizons*, *67*, 62-67.

Bowen, H.R. (1977, November). The residue of academic learning. *The Chronicle of Higher Education*.

Cook, W.D. (1977). *Adult literacy education in the United States*. Newark, DE: International Reading Association.

Cornelius, J. (1983). "We slipped and learned to read": Slave accounts of the literacy process, 1830-1865. *Phylon Journal*, *44*(3), 171-186.

Coy, J. (1988). *Adult literacy from a sociocultural perspective*. Paper presented at the Florida Reading Association Annual Conference, Orlando, FL.

Elkins, S.M. (1968). *Slavery: A problem in American institutional and intellectual life* (2nd ed.). Chicago, IL: University of Chicago Press.

Fingeret, A. (1987, May). *Directions in ethnographic adult literacy research*. Paper presented at the Thirty-Second Annual Convention of the International Reading Association, Anaheim, CA.

Fingeret, A. (1985). *North Carolina adult basic education instructional program evaluation*. Raleigh, NC: North Carolina State University, Division of Adult and Continuing Education.

Freire, P. (1985a). *The politics of education: Culture, power, and liberation*. South Hadley, MA: Bergin & Garvey.

Freire, P. (1985b). Reading the world and reading the word: An interview with Paulo Freire. *Language Arts*, *62*(1), 15-21.

Goldberg, S. (1951). *Army training of illiterates in World War II.* New York: Publications, Teachers College, Columbia University.

Harman, D. (1985). *Turning illiteracy around: An agenda for national action.* New York: Business Council for Effective Literacy.

Harste, J.C., & Mikulecky, L.J. (1984). The context of literacy in our society. In A.C. Purves & O. Niles (Eds.), *Eighty-Third Yearbook of the National Society for the Study of Education* (pp. 47-78). Chicago, IL: University of Chicago Press.

Heath, S.B. (1980). The functions and uses of literacy. *Journal of Communications, 30*(1), 123-133.

Heath, S.B. (1984). *Issues in literacy: A research perspective.* Keynote address, National Reading Conference, St. Petersburg, FL.

Heath, S.B. (1983). *Ways with words.* New York: Cambridge University Press.

Hey, R.P. (1989, August). Congress studies aid to black males. *Christian Science Monitor, 81.*

Karier, C.J. (1975). *Shaping the American educational state: 1900 to the present.* New York: Free Press.

Kazemek, F.E. (1985). An examination of the adult performance level project and its effects upon adult literacy education in the United States. *Lifelong Learning, 9*(2), 24-28.

Kazemek, F.E. (1988a). Necessary changes: Professional involvement in adult literacy programs. *Harvard Educational Review, 58*(4), 464-486.

Kazemek, F.E. (1988b). The self as social process: The work of George Herbert Mead and its implications for adult literacy education. *Adult Literacy and Basic Education 12*(1), 1-13.

Kelly, M.F. (1989). *Addressing literacy in the military workplace.* Presentation at the Adult Literacy and Technology Conference, Louisville, KY.

Kullander, J. (1989, June 29). Bound to China. *Christian Science Monitor, 17.*

Mikulecky, L. (1988). *Literacy for the workplace.* In L. Mikulecky & R. Drew (Eds.), *The work education bridge.* Bloomington, IN: Indiana University.

Newman, A.P. (Ed.). (1980). *Working in construction.* Bloomington, IN: Indiana University.

Park, R.J., Davis, R.V., Rengel, E.K., & Storlie, R.L. (1985). The selection and validation of a reading test to be used with civil service employees. *Public Personnel Management, 14*(3), 274-284.

Schwartz, J. (1988). Learning and earning. *American Demographics, 10*(1), 12.

Stein, S.G. (1989). *What we have learned and are still learning.* Paper presented at the Annual Conference on Adult Basic Education of the American Association for Adult and Continuing Education, Atlanta, GA.

Sticht, T.G. (1988). Adult literacy education. In E. Rothkopf (Ed.), *Review of research in education,* 59-95.

Thimmesch, N. (1984). *Aliteracy: People who can read but won't.* Conference sponsored by the American Enterprise Institute for Public Policy Research, Washington, DC.

2

What Literacy Has Come to Mean

T he idea of literacy for all the people has matured during the
twentieth century. With that maturation have come new definitions that lead us beyond rudimentary notions of the mere ability to
read a simple sentence and make our mark (X) or sign our name.
The term *literacy* has come to be associated with everything from
cultural literacy to computer savvy.

When literacy workers get together in state coalition meetings and at conventions, we sometimes get stalled over definitions.
We have to remind one another that our main purpose is to do something about the illiteracy problem, not to spin our wheels in the
shifting sand of defining terms. Cervero (1985) argued against a
single definition, saying that we are not interested in promoting "a
technical process aimed at discovering the objectively best definition of literacy." Rather, we are taking part in the "clash of compet-
ing value positions, ideologies, and power structures" to ensure that
whatever definitions win the struggle, they will not be those that
merely "reproduce the existing social distribution of knowledge.
The question...is not whether there is a need for a common definition of literacy, but whose needs will be served" (p. 54).

The debate over the nature of literacy can turn into a political
harangue over the uses of literacy, especially the elitist uses of literacy to keep the underclass "in their place" or to let them into "our
place" but only on "our" terms. Giroux (1987), who published a critical theoretical analysis of literacy in the United States, categorized
the interests served in this way as tied to "narrowly conceived eco-

nomic interests" and to the initiation of the poor, the under-privileged, and minorities into a unitary and dominant cultural tradition.

Giroux disputed the notion that there is a literacy crisis, saying that the adult literacy movement in part is "predicated on the need to train more workers for occupational jobs that demand 'functional' reading and writing skills" and intended to "legitimatize school as a site for character development." Concerning the latter, Giroux said, "Literacy is associated with transmission and mastery of a unitary Western tradition based on the virtues of hard work, respect for family, institutional authority, and an unquestioning respect for the nation" (p. 149). Frankly, we consider the movement to teach people to read and write to be more benign. However, in the following documentation of the evolution of literacy in all of its many meanings, we proceed with our eyes wide open. The threat of illiteracy is second in power only to that of the promise of literacy.

To present the following outline history of the development of literacy, we have appropriated the samplings of definitions in Costa (1988), the discussion of Resnick and Resnick (1988), and the carefully developed essay, "Illiteracy in the United States: Definitions and Statistics" (PIVOT, 1976). With the exception of the 1980 citations, the boxed information was derived from Cook (1977). Drawing on these surveys, and the resources of many other writers, we present a context, an array, a matrix for definition, rather than supposing that we have attained a final definition.

According to the U.S. Census Bureau, from 1870 onward the difference between illiterate persons and literate persons was that illiterates could only make their mark (X), and literates could sign their name and read and write a simple sentence. Not quite 90 percent of the population surveyed was deemed to be literate according to that iffy standard.

This definition is similar to the one that was used by most other countries, and to the one adopted by UNESCO in 1951.

By 1910, the portion of the population said to be literate had gone above 93 percent, but the definition of literacy had sagged. The Census Bureau no longer inquired about someone's ability to read.

1900 U.S. Census Bureau Literacy Definition

Definition

Any person 10 years of age or older who can read
or write in the individual's native language.

Criterion

Literacy determination based on a question so phrased as to require
only a *yes* or a *no* answer.

*Percentage
Literate*

89.3

1951 UNESCO Literacy Definition

"A person is literate who can with understanding both read and write
a short, simple statement on his everyday life."

1910 U.S. Census Bureau Literacy Definition

Definition

Any person 10 years of age or older who can write
in any language.

Criterion

Literacy determination loosely defined; included those persons
barely able to write their names or read a few words.

*Percentage
Literate*

93.3

By 1930, reading had been restored to the definition of literacy, and the percentage of literates was nearly 96 percent. However, the criterion for determining a person's literacy was a simple question that required only a *yes* or *no* answer. (This was the last time an actual literacy question was asked.) The census taker did not ask anyone to write a sentence or read a book.

By 1940, defining literacy had become more tricky. The census taker no longer asked if people could read or write, but rather whether they had been to school, and for how many years. World War II interrupted the census taking in 1940, and a retrospective estimate was developed by the Census Bureau in 1947. Two age

1930 U.S. Census Bureau Literacy Definition

Definition

Percentage Literate

Any person 10 years of age or older who can read as well as write in any language.   95.7

Criterion

Literacy determination returned to the criterion used for the 1900 census. Question so phrased as to require only a *yes* or a *no* answer.

1940 U.S. Census Bureau Literacy Definition

Definition

Percentage Literate

Any person 10 years of age or older who has completed 5 or more years of school.   97.1

Any person 14 years of age or older who has completed 5 or more years of school.

Criterion

Literacy determination for Army induction based on the ability to pass an examination written on a fourth grade level.

groups were distinguished, and the term *functional literacy* was used for the first time. Moreover, in 1942 the Armed Forces had relaxed literacy requirements from the ability to pass an exam written at the fourth grade level to an understanding of enough English to absorb military training. On this generous and speculative basis, America congratulated itself for being 97.1 percent literate.

Essentially the same definitions were employed during the 1950 census. In 1960, the standards were even more lax ("some formal schooling"), and the percentages even more grand. The census asked only for grade completion information.

Meanwhile, through their U.N. representatives in UNESCO, the other nations of the world were toughening their definitional standard of literacy.

By 1962, UNESCO was placing emphasis on practical functionality in everyday life.

1960 U.S. Census Bureau Literacy Definition

Definition	*Percentage Literate*
Any person 14 years of age or older who has some formal schooling.	98.1
Any person 25 years of age or older who has some formal schooling.	97.7

Criterion

Literacy determination percentage and definition based solely on manipulation of figures from information about grade completion provided by the Census Bureau; the terms "illiteracy" and "functional illiteracy" not defined by the census.

1958 UNESCO Literacy Definition

"A person is illiterate who cannot with understanding both read and write a short, simple statement on his everyday life."

1962 UNESCO Literacy Definition

"[Literacy is] the possession by an individual of the essential knowledge and skills which enable him or her to engage in all those activities required for effective functioning in his or her group and community and whose attainments in reading, writing, and arithmetic make it possible for him or her to use these skills toward his or her own and the community's development."

By 1978, although the emphasis was still on practicality and functionality, the evolving definition had begun to include an awareness of the individual's "own development."

In 1980, sounding more like a national Chamber of Commerce than the Census Bureau, the U.S. government reported a 99.5 percent literacy rate, using a definition of literacy not much different from the one it had used a century before.

Before the literacy decade of the 1970s and the adult literacy decade of the 1980s, the United States—content with the census figures—was unaware as a nation that the official definitions of literacy were hopelessly antiquated and that one-fifth of the citizenry (according to the more enlightened international standard) was functionally illiterate. UNESCO's cultural revolution efforts and its perception of greater need in the Third World enabled the United Nations to keep its finger on the pulse of the population and diagnose endemic illiteracy.

Taking the Measure of the Nonreader

There was an inherent flaw in the Census Bureau's approach to determining literacy. Illiterate people often will not admit they are illiterate. Census data were collected from any member of a household, and were not verified by the census taker. No proof of reading or writing ability was required, and many a nonreader kept the family secret safe.

By the 1960s, many educators had seen that both the definitions of literacy and the methods of testing for illiteracy were inadequate. The optimistic statistics published by the Census Bureau had never described the situation accurately, and the seriousness of the problem had only been glimpsed. Being able to sign their name or read a simple sentence did not make people literate in a functional sense, as the U.S. Army had discovered during World War II. In one of the first allusions to what we now call *functional literacy*, the Army defined many of its new recruits as illiterates—people who were "incapable of understanding the kinds of written instructions needed for carrying out basic military functions or tasks" (U.S. Bureau of the Census, 1963, p. 1).

About the same time that UNESCO was working out its definitions of functional literacy, Robinson (1963, p. 417) devised a Stairway of Literacy:

Step 1: Complete illiteracy—unable to read English.

Step 2: Low-level literacy—reads between grades 1 and 4; barely able to contend with adult reading material.

Step 3: Partial literacy—reads on a fifth to sixth grade level and can read essential information.

Step 4: Variable literacy—reads materials at a number of reading levels but has specific problems that prevent full literacy.

Step 5: Complete literacy—can read effectively all materials required. Can evaluate and draw concepts from them.

Robinson's inclusion of ability with the English language as a criterion of literacy foreshadowed debates about the establishment of an official language in some U.S. states, especially where Spanish also

Newman and Beverstock

is used. The narrower definition obscures the fact that a person may be literate in any number of languages, whether or not one of them is English.

Others also thought of literacy in stages or levels. Included in this group were the Survival Literacy Study (Harris, 1970) and the Adult Performance Level (APL) study (Northcutt, 1975). Harris surveyed a randomly selected sample of the population and described illiteracy under three ambiguous headings in terms of a person's inability to read well enough to survive in American culture. These headings were low survival, questionable survival, and marginal survival. (One wonders how the interviewees had managed to survive long enough to be surveyed!) The APL study divided people into three categories: functionally incompetent, marginally functional, and functionally proficient (Northcutt, 1975).

The APL study then combined the concept of functional levels of illiteracy with a staged understanding of literacy. The purposes of the study were "to define literacy in terms of actual competencies performed in everyday life tasks" and "to assess these competencies for the adult population [ages 18-65 years] of these continental United States."

Chall (Chall, 1990; Chall, Heron, & Hilferty, 1987) proposed a levels approach "to bring greater understanding of the qualitative measures of reading." At first she suggested a six-stage categorization, which she later collapsed into three levels: below functional literacy, functional literacy, and advanced reading level. Resnick and Resnick (1988) described four stages: signature, recitation, comprehension, and analysis. Georgia was one of several states to base its programs on a definition of literacy in levels: basic literacy, general literacy, and specialized literacy. *Stages* and *levels* had become ideological orthodoxy among American intellectuals during these years, and whether a set of three or five or seven such orderly categories adequately described the many dimensions of literacy, the labels tended to stick.

The Many Dimensions of Literacy

With the growing awareness that literacy and illiteracy were neither simple nor monolithic concepts, in the 1970s students of literacy began to describe the sides of literacy that had been ignored. UNESCO added the element of relativity to its definition of literacy by recognizing that reading and writing "adequate to one community or country at one time would be inadequate in another country or in the same country at another time." The evolving UNESCO definition also included the element of mastery, by saying that "the skills must have been sufficiently mastered so that the individual can continue to use them" (PIVOT, 1976, p. 3).

Fingeret (1988, p. 1) amplified the concept of the social relativity of literacy when she wrote:

> Literacy is not some naturally occurring object, like stone or soil or water or air. It is a social construct—it is defined and created by those in power in a society, and those definitions change as conditions change. Thus, literacy is considered historically and culturally relative; definitions of literacy depend on time and place (although they always are decided upon by those in positions of power). As the definitions shift, membership in the categories of *literate* and *illiterate* changes, and the rewards and stigma attached to membership in each category change as well. Discussion about the relative nature of literacy usually takes place in an academic context, abstract and divorced from present practice. However, I believe that the definitions, categories, and criteria are changing right now—and that it is up to us to choose our roles, from passive viewers to active participants in the process.

Kintgen, Kroll, and Rose (1988) took a classically linguistic and historical approach to defining literacy, remarking that two distinct meanings of the term inevitably complicate its definition: they described *descriptive* literacy as a person's abilities in reading and writing, and *evaluative* literacy as a means of assessment.

> Evaluative assesses the possession of a body of knowledge, usually of literature or the "rules" of accepted usage. This

meaning apparently derives from classical Latin *litteratus*, "which meant *literate* in something like the modern [descriptive] sense and also (in the most classical usage of Cicero) described a person with *scientia litteratum*, meaning a *knowledge of letters* in the sense of literature" (Clanchy, 1988). This sense is apparent when a person who perpetrates a grammatical error or misquotes an author in a letter to the editor of a newspaper is described as illiterate by those who wish to stigmatize the writer's intelligence or viewpoint (Kintgen, Kroll, & Rose, 1988, p. xiv).

An accurate definition of the literary dimension of literacy necessarily includes awareness of the negative political and social uses of literacy by the literate to stigmatize the illiterate as inferior. However literacy is defined, its function for the census taker is different from its function for the applicant for funds (who must report literacy statistics to some authority), and different still for the illiterate person under anthropological study by a social scientist. For the literacy activist, recognition of these many dimensions of literacy has required a new direction toward a socially more tolerant and politically more egalitarian definition.

Adding the Human Dimension

Street (1984) added a novel dimension to the characterization of literacy when he distinguished between two models of literacy, arguing for the latter. He called *autonomous* literacy a culture-specific notion that assumes only a single direction for literacy development, and termed *ideological* the stress on literacy's embeddedness in its cultural and social processes, including the consequent interest in social, rather than educational, institutions.

We believe that Hunter and Harman (1985, pp. ix-xviii) in their introduction to the paperback update of *Adult Illiteracy in the United States*, added a particularly important dimension to the humanized conception of literacy when they suggested that we need to think more about whether literacy demands arise internally or externally:

External standards can only define minimum requirements; internal standards define people's hopes, choices, and ambitions. External standards can be measured and reported by statistics; internal standards are measured by the individuals who set them. Those who determine educational policy and make decisions about resources available for programs must deal with the statistics.

By separating the definition of external standards from internal ones, it is possible to eliminate the sensitive issue of different literacies for different groups....Recognition of the distinction between external and internal definitions allows us to see adult education needs along a continuum, with the starting point depending on individual requirements.

This train of thought leads to the broader sense of literacy developed by Scribner (1984). She used three metaphors to elucidate literacy as a social achievement, speaking of literacy as *adaptation*—in Bhola's sense, the ability to meet everyday needs; as *power*—in Freire and Kozol's sense, the ability to realign status and economic and power relationships; and as a *state of grace*—the power of literacy "to endow the literate person with special virtues."

Imel and Grieve (1985) pointed out that illiteracy can be understood only in relation to a culture's definition of literacy. Macro- and microsocial contexts in which meaning and interpretation of meaning (the thought processes behind the physical acts of reading and writing), as well as the social uses to which literacy is put, must be taken into consideration.

Also in this vein, Delker (1986) underscored the importance of including in the definition of literacy the other skills of problem solving required in our society besides reading, including writing, speaking, listening, and computing. Delker observed that the popular notion of literacy in America implies a broader range of competencies than does any official definition of literacy in use anywhere else. Basic skills to cope with today's uncertain world go beyond simple reading and writing to include discernment, reflection, risk taking, and openness to new perspectives. The U.S. Air Force, for example, is seriously concerned about developing higher-level thinking skills; it has begun to focus its efforts on the problem-solving aspects of literacy rather than on the achievement of more literal skills.

This emphasis on broader dimensions of literacy humanizes the familiar, rather industrial concept of functional literacy, and suggests a redefinition of the old term. Functional literacy no longer is to be equated with workplace literacy. Individuals have lives outside their workplace, and wish to function in society in many ways. People need to work, but they also need to be able to vote, get a driver's license, read their mail, look at magazines, or write to a friend. Thus, as Kintgen, Kroll, and Rose (1988, p. 263) note, "Functional literacy can be defined as the possession of, or access to, the competencies and information required to accomplish transactions entailing reading and writing [in] which an individual wishes—or is compelled—to engage." This definition appropriately balances economic necessity and social pressure with personal desire and individual initiative.

As useful as a social definition of functional literacy is in its human context, problems arise from attending relativities and ambiguities when the term is translated for purposes of assessment or policy. Functional literacy is no longer to be equated with eighth-grade ability, high school completion, or possession of a GED—even if some agencies of government still persist in the outmoded Census Bureau approach (Mikulecky, 1986; Miller, 1982). Scribner and Cole (1988, p. 25) observe that "the representation of literacy as a fixed inventory of skills that can be assessed outside of their contexts of application has little utility for educational policies." The enhanced definition of functional literacy is essentially a many-sided social one—that is, literacy implies the ability to function well at real world tasks rather than on school-based, standardized reading assignments.

This refinement of definition is meeting with acceptance in other quarters. Volunteer-based literacy organizations that work with people functioning at the lower levels of literacy have come to define literacy more comprehensively than industry once did and the Census Bureau still does.

In Michigan, the definition of literacy is being broadened through testing in five areas: written and oral communication, mathematics and related skills, problem solving, workplace attitude, and job-seeking abilities. Michigan's legislators intend to include as positive correlates of literacy such variables as improvement on the job, an appropriate frame of mind, and job-related mobility, considering them as essential to literacy in America as are reading and writing (Belsie, 1988).

Perhaps even more difficult to quantify, and to that degree also more human, is Heathington's (1987) broadened concept of literacy: "We must expand our definition of literacy to encompass aspects of affect." She made explicit the need to apply this definition to the production and use of literacy materials in ways that will result in benefits for the new reader by corresponding to the reader's emotional response. Basing her conclusions on interviews conducted over several years by the University of Tennessee Adult Reading Academy Program, Heathington elaborated six categories of persons and the negative effects of illiteracy typically associated with them:

1. Workers: embarrassment, frustration, fear
2. Consumers: embarrassment, low self-esteem, frustration
3. Parents: fear of detrimental effects on children
4. Students: frustration, feelings of inadequacy
5. People in social situations: frustration, embarrassment, shame
6. People in leisure situations: lack of pleasure, loneliness, frustration

Literacy as a cultural, social concept requires that we include within its definition all the perspectives of every community and every subculture whose people we are attempting to help become more literate (Kazemek, 1983). Each individual's literacy is a tapestry woven from the strands of cultural and temporal relativities — assumptions about real people in their own real worlds, the warp of society, and the woof of government. None of these strands can be separated from the overall design imposed by the national, intellectual, moral, and cultural climate of an era (Rigg & Kazemek, 1985). Daniell (1984) made the same point: the cultural determinants of literacy are the human values at work in religion, economics, and politics. By searching the maze of relationships among humans and their cultures, the literacy profession moves forward with its expanding definitions of literacy.

We are moving beyond limited definitions of literacy to a grasp of literacy as an all-embracing conceptual framework. As contributions to the discussion continue to be made from other social and humane sciences—for example, anthropology and critical theory (Graff, 1987)—reductionist definitions will inevitably give way. When characteristics such as diligence, work attitude, and compliance with deadlines are understood as functions of literacy, we move far beyond the etymological limits of literate defined as *learned* or *scholarly*.

The old definitions of literacy were too narrow; some of the new definitions may be too broad. The new and humane (and romantic) definitions of literacy are so profuse that we may be loading the word with burdens of meaning that will eventually negate its usefulness as a working term. Figure 1 shows some of the complexity and disparity involved in attempting to define literacy.

If everything becomes "a literacy," literacy itself is in danger of becoming lost among its hyperdefinitions. One thing is certain: the new and experimental definitions of literacy point to the individual's need to be able to implement the full spectrum of human language competency, extending beyond reading and writing (Petty et al., 1977).

Schuster (1988), developing the thought of Mikhail Bakhtin, offered a social constructionist view of literacy. According to this view, a person's position in society—measured by the perception of others—determines the strength of that person's utterance. Thus, individuals' power in one setting, where they are comfortable, well-thought of, even obeyed, may change drastically when they move into a different setting.

A film that dramatizes Schuster's idea of literacy was produced as part of the 1973 RELATE project (Newman, Harste, & Stowe, 1973). The film follows 6-year-old David through six different settings, in a parable that conveys the experiences of newly literate adults. When listening to instructions from his teacher, David, overawed, speaks no word of response. Among his peers—four other little boys for whom David was the natural leader in playing

Figure 1
The Different Terms Associated with Literacy

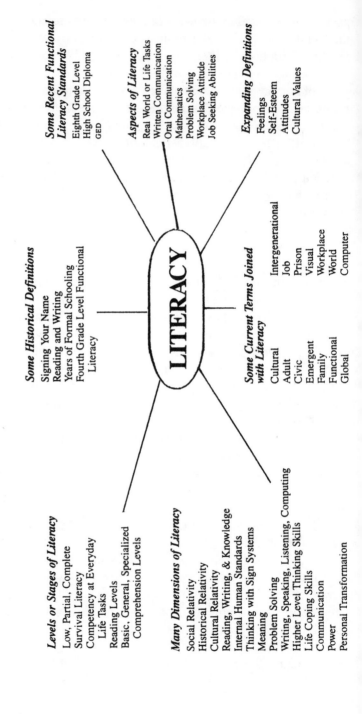

Some Historical Definitions

Signing Your Name
Reading and Writing
Years of Formal Schooling
Fourth Grade Level Functional
 Literacy

*Some Recent Functional
Literacy Standards*

Eighth Grade Level
High School Diploma
GED

Aspects of Literacy

Real World or Life Tasks
Written Communication
Oral Communication
Mathematics
Problem Solving
Workplace Attitude
Job Seeking Abilities

Expanding Definitions

Feelings
Self-Esteem
Attitudes
Cultural Values

LITERACY

Levels or Stages of Literacy

Low, Partial, Complete
Survival Literacy
Competency at Everyday
 Life Tasks
Reading Levels
Basic, General, Specialized
 Comprehension Levels

Many Dimensions of Literacy

Social Relativity
Historical Relativity
Cultural Relativity
Reading, Writing, & Knowledge
Internal Human Standards
Thinking with Sign Systems
Meaning
Problem Solving
Writing, Speaking, Listening, Computing
Higher Level Thinking Skills
Life Coping Skills
Communication
Power
Personal Transformation

*Some Current Terms Joined
with Literacy*

Cultural   Intergenerational
Adult   Job
Civic   Prison
Emergent   Visual
Family   Workplace
Functional   World
Global   Computer

cowboys—he becomes commander-in-chief, whipping out orders, placing the boys where he wants them, and devising strategy. In company with a group of bossy third grade girls, a different David emerges: helpless, he moves in and out of the action, trying to slip in a word edgewise, never quite succeeding. Six times David changes faces, depending on whom he is with and how the dynamics of the situation change.

Schuster described the ways adult new readers change and are perceived differently from one situation to another, depending on their social position. A Latino father who maintains control and exerts authority within his home—where he is the boss whether he can read or not—adapts to a more self-protective posture in his adult literacy class. A farmer, master of the fields and crops, yields to his teenage son, who reads the directions on a new package of fertilizer. A semiliterate florist, owner and manager of his shop, expert at floral design and good at public relations, must rely on his literate wife to handle the money and keep the books.

The job of defining literacy, in the new age marked by International Literacy Year, is no longer in the hands of only the bureaucrats and researchers. The newly literate, through their needs and wants, have found their voice in the literacy movement. As literacy workers, we will do our best work if we adopt definitions of our task that conform to the social and cultural demands placed on our new-reader students, that respond to their express wishes, and that satisfy them personally, aesthetically, and functionally.

References

Belsie, L. (1988, April). In Michigan, adults who want schooling just say "charge it." *Christian Science Monitor, 80*(102), 4.

Cervero, R.M. (1985). Is a common definition of adult literacy possible? *Adult Education Quarterly, 36*(1), 50-54.

Chall, J.S. (1990). Policy implications of literacy definitions. In R.L. Venezky, D.A. Wagner, & B.S. Ciliberti (Eds.), *Toward defining literacy.* Newark, DE: International Reading Association.

Chall, J.S., Heron, E., & Hilferty, A. (1987). Adult literacy: New and enduring problems. *Phi Delta Kappan, 69*(3), 190-196.

Clanchy, M.T. (1988). Hearing and seeing and trusting writing. In E.R. Kintgen, B.M. Kroll, & M. Rose (Eds.), *Perspectives on literacy.* Carbondale, IL: Southern Illinois University Press.

Cook, W.D. (1977). *Adult literacy education in the United States.* Newark, DE: International Reading Association.

Daniell, B. (1984). *Toward a definition of literacy*. Urbana, IL: National Council of Teachers of English.

Delker, P.V. (1986). *Beyond literacy in an uncertain world*. Knoxville, TN: Commission of Adult Basic Education Conference.

Fingeret, A. (1988, January). *The politics of adult literacy education*. Address to the National Urban Literacy Conference, Washington, DC.

Giroux, H.A. (1987, February). Critical literacy and student experience: Donald Graves' approach to literacy. *Language Arts, 38*(1), 61-75.

Graff, H. (1987). *The legacies of literacy: Continuities and contradictions in Western culture and schooling*. Bloomington, IN: Indiana University Press.

Harris, L., & Associates. (1970). *Survival literacy study*. Washington, DC: U.S. Government Printing Office.

Heathington, B.S. (1987). Expanding the definition of literacy for adult remedial readers. *Journal of Reading, 31*(3), 213-217.

Hunter, C.S., & Harman, D. (1985). *Adult illiteracy in the United States: A report to the Ford Foundation*. New York: McGraw Hill.

Imel, S., & Grieve, S. (1985). *Adult literacy education: Overview*. Columbus, OH: ERIC Clearinghouse on Adult, Career, and Vocational Education. (ED 259 210)

Kazemek, F.E. (1983). *Epistemology and adult literacy: An experientialist, pragmatic perspective*. (ED 236 326)

Kintgen, E.R., Kroll, B.M., & Rose, M. (Eds.). (1988). *Perspectives on literacy*. Carbondale, IL: Southern Illinois University Press.

Mikulecky, L.G. (1986, April). *A working definition of functional literacy*. Paper prepared for the International Reading Association's Adult Literacy Committee.

Miller, J. (1982). *Competency education for adult literacy overview*. Columbus, OH: ERIC Clearinghouse on Adult, Career, and Vocational Education. (ED 237 798)

Newman, A.P., Harste, J.C., & Stowe, R.A. (1973). *Project Relate: Student guides I-IV and V-XI* (two volumes). Bloomington, IN: Indiana University, Division of Teacher Education.

Northcutt, N. (1975, March). *Adult functional competency: A summary*. Austin, TX: University of Texas.

Petty, W.T., Petty, D.C., Newman, A.P., & Skeen, E.M. (1977). *Language competencies essential for coping in our society* (pp. 66-95). Seventy-Sixth Yearbook of the National Society for the Study of Education. Chicago IL: University of Chicago Press.

PIVOT (1976, February, April). *Illiteracy in the United States: Definitions and statistics*. Philadelphia, PA: Reading Development Program.

Resnick, D.P., & Resnick, L.B. (1988). The nature of literacy: A historical exploration. In E.R. Kintgen, B.M. Kroll, & M. Rose (Eds.), *Perspectives on literacy*. Carbondale, IL: Southern Illinois University Press.

Rigg, P., & Kazemek, F.E. (1985). *Adult illiteracy: America's phoenix problem* (Occasional paper no. 12). The Program in Language and Literature, University of Oregon.

Robinson, H.A. (1963, May). Libraries: Active agents in adult reading improvement. *American Library Association Bulletin, 47*, 416-420.

Schuster, C.I. (1988, September). *The ideology of illiteracy: A Bakhtinian perspective*. Speech given at the Right to Literacy Conference, Columbus, OH.

Scribner, S. (1984, November). Literacy in three metaphors. *American Journal of Education, 93*, 6-21.

Scribner, S., & Cole, M. (1988). Unpackaging literacy. In E.R. Kintgen, B.M. Kroll, & M. Rose (Eds.), *Perspectives on literacy*. Carbondale, IL: Southern Illinois University Press.

Street, B.V. (1984). *Literacy in theory and practice*. New York: Cambridge University Press.

United States Bureau of the Census. (1963). *Current population reports—Estimates of illiteracy by state: 1960*, Series P-23, No. 8. Washington, DC: U.S. Government Printing Office.

United States Bureau of the Census. (1983). *Statistics and abstracts of the United States, 1982-1983*. Washington, DC: U.S. Government Printing Office.

3

Measuring America's Literacy

N ot since the 1950s, when the U.S. Supreme Court ordered the schools desegregated and the Russians launched Sputnik, has there been such an outcry over the state of literacy as there has been in the 1980s, continuing into the 1990s. Illiteracy has been declared a crisis by some, and literacy has gained a place on the national agenda.

American society is undergoing enormous changes: immigration, population shifts, and new technologies are affecting our lives. The 1985 awareness campaign waged by the National Coalition for Literacy added more stress when it caught the nation's attention with the image of a father reading to his daughter. The caption read: "To 27 million Americans, this scene is a fairy tale." The accompanying slogan read: "Volunteer against illiteracy. The only degree you need is a degree of caring." Articles in newspapers and magazines, as well as public service announcements on television and radio, caught the public's attention with alarming statistics about illiteracy. Project Literacy United States (PLUS) brought dramatizations and discussions of literacy issues to national television. This unprecedented public attention caused illiteracy to be perceived as a national crisis.

People often ask us if illiteracy is as bad as everyone says, and then, without waiting for a reply, begin telling stories: "At my company, I can't believe the poor writing that crosses my desk." "I'm amazed at the number of people with high school diplomas who can't complete a job application." "How do these people function in society?"

To 27 million Americans, this scene is a fairy tale.

That's because 27 million American adults can't read a child's bedtime story, can't read a street sign, can't read...period.

Functional illiteracy has become an epidemic, an epidemic that has reached 1 out of 5 American adults. It robs them of a decent living, it robs them of self-respect, it robs them of the simplest of human pleasures...like reading a letter from a friend or a fairy-tale to their children.

Tragic as that is, it's not the worst part. Because people like this could be taught to read, if we had more tutors to teach them. Sadly, we don't. Today, the waiting period for a tutor can be up to a year.

You can change that by joining the fight against illiteracy yourself. It takes no special qualifications. If you can read, you can tutor or help us in countless other ways. You'll be trained to work in programs right in your own community. And you'll experience the greatest satisfaction of all...the satisfaction of helping people discover whole new lives.

So join the effort. Call the Coalition for Literacy at toll-free **1-800-228-8813.** Helping takes so little. And illiteracy robs people of so much.

**Volunteer Against Illiteracy.
The only degree you need
is a degree of caring.**

 Ad Council Coalition for Literacy

This advertisement appeared as part of the National Coalition for Literacy's 1985 awareness campaign.

Then comes the real question: "How many illiterate people are there, anyway?" People usually want statistics to help them understand the magnitude of the problem.

Literacy is not an on/off characteristic, and it is more than the ability to read and write a little. Literacy describes a wide variety of communicative acts, interpersonal strategies, and survival skills. It is more appropriate to picture a spectrum of literacies across a variety of specific needs and communities, from barely able to write or recognize your own name to highly and multiculturally educated. It is more accurate to ask whether people are *sufficiently* literate to meet their own needs and what society expects of them than to ask if they are literate.

A precise answer about past literacy is hard to give. Historians have examined evidence that only hints at degrees of literacy. Signatures provide a limited hint; the census supplies elusive clues, limited by sketchy responses to unsophisticated questions about literacy; and the number of years in school offers some sense of a person's potential for literacy.

An answer to the question about America's present degree of literacy is somewhat easier. Although recent attempts to test for and describe functional literacy (or lack of it) were not aimed at describing the many complexities of the full range of literacy contexts, they did document the extent of the basic ability to read and write. Studies done in the 1970s and 1980s used real world material, such as job applications or questions about benefits. However, none of the studies tracked people through the actual literacy demands of their daily lives.

Many people did not do very well when tested on real world items. The studies varied, and so did their results. The estimates ranged from 13 percent to over 50 percent of the adult U.S. population having some difficulty with basic literacy. Depending on who is talking, and which study is cited, the United States has a low literacy rate, a high literacy rate, or a rate somewhere in between.

The answer to the question "Is illiteracy really a crisis?" is both "yes" and "no." As a nation, we must consider the need for ever-increasing literacy, and we must find increased resources to allow more people to acquire needed reading, writing, and other literacy skills. Lack of sufficient literacy constitutes a crisis for many individuals; lack of sufficiently literate employees constitutes a crisis both for the government and for business. But we resist the notion that the United States has suddenly fallen into an unprecedented literacy tailspin. Americans are not less literate today than they were

100 years ago; in fact, we are more literate. However, too many members of our economic underclass remain insufficiently literate to keep up with rapid change. If a crisis exists, it is proportional. Demands for increased literacy seem to be outracing the educational system's ability to teach; and the historically illiterate underclass, larger in numbers because of population growth, remains stuck in illiteracy.

How Literate Was America in the Past?

American folklore enshrines many images of the struggle for literacy. Abraham Lincoln walking to school through drifts of snow and studying for hours by the flickering light of the fireplace. Barefoot school children hunched over desks in a one-room schoolhouse. Thomas Jefferson, founder of a university as well as of our democracy, maintaining his strong advocacy of education even in his epitaph (Here was Buried Thomas Jefferson Author of the Declaration of American Independence of the Statute of Virginia for Religious Freedom and Father of the University of Virginia). People who labored all day and worked their way through school at night. Self-sacrificing parents who worked hard so their children could have what they had been denied. Harvard opening its doors to women. Horace Mann and others convincing the American public of the need for free and compulsory education. The Lakotas and Pawnee using syllabaries developed within their tribes to achieve widespread literacy in the middle 1800s. The Choctaw, forcibly removed from their native Southeast to Oklahoma, irritating the white population by being more literate and thus frustrating officials who wanted to see Indians as "somehow less than themselves" (Brescia, 1988). We Americans see ourselves as having valued education and as having made a public commitment to reading and writing long ago. But these images, from the folksy to the presidential, tell only part of the tale.

Measuring Changes in Literacy Over Time

Each historical source of literacy data poses difficulties while also providing historical clues about the extent of literacy in the United States. Kaestle (1985, pp. 12-13) concluded that the history of American literacy is "full of surprises and reinterpretations." Not only the explanation but even the basic facts about literacy trends are uncertain. Like many emerging social history topics, the history of literacy has displayed growing pains—inadequate data, fuzzy conceptualization, uncertain topic boundaries, and the intrusions of normative debates into the historical analysis.

With these limitations in mind, we have patched together pieces of historical evidence about literacy from Kaestle (1985), Stedman and Kaestle (1987), Fisher (1977), and Folger and Nam (1965).

Signatures. Signatures and "marks" (X) are the barest fingerprints of literacy. They appear in army rolls, jury lists, birth and death certificates, wills, marriage licenses, and deeds, preserved since our beginnings. Careful comparisons of marks and signatures yield a rough estimate of the signers' literacy and serve as measures of reading ability. But this measure is susceptible both to overestimation of the numbers of people who could write something besides their name and to underestimation of those who could read but not write. At best, signature counts may constitute a crude measure of the lower limit of those who were at least marginally literate, although some historians contend that signing correlated with fluent reading ability. During the colonial period an estimated one third to one half of Americans could neither read nor write, based on signature counts (Folger & Nam, 1965). Literacy was even lower in Europe in the periods immediately before and immediately after the American Revolution. Kaestle (1985) estimated that when the Constitution was signed, 90 percent of white males could sign a document, but fewer than 50 percent of white women could read or write.

Table 1 shows signature data taken from the Army rolls between 1800 and 1880. The data clearly indicate that over this period enlistees were increasingly able to sign, rather than make a mark, when they joined the Army. The data do not, however, provide information about literacy skills beyond the ability to sign at the time of enlistment.

The limitations of signing data are clear: signatures tell us neither comprehensively nor definitively how literate Americans were in the seventeenth and eighteenth centuries.

Table 1

Signature Illiteracy, U.S. Army
Enlistees, 1800-1880

Year	Percent Not Signing
1800	42
1840	35
1850	25
1870	17
1880	7

(Kaestle, 1985, p. 30)

Census. The U.S. Census was (and is) the most comprehensive source of literacy data in the nineteenth and twentieth centuries, although the limitations of the data are severe. The census yields many kinds of information, including gender, age, ethnic origin, occupation, and years in school. It makes possible a rough comparison of literacy rates in the United States over time. If we can believe the questionable results, the census data tell the good news about basic levels of literacy from the mid-1800s to the present: literacy has been increasing steadily. The bad news is harder to hear.

Census information is collected by asking people simple "yes" or "no" questions that they often regard as intrusive and nosy. People are sometimes suspicious of the motives of the census takers and so answer their questions with what seem the most desirable answers, not necessarily the most accurate ones. Illiterate people usually are hesitant to say they cannot read and write, and many are unwilling to admit this failing to a stranger, particularly a government official. In any event, the literacy reflected in the census data is minimal literacy, based on an affirmative answer to the question "Can you read or write, or both?" The census fails to provide information on the proficiency level of the respondent.

Census questions suffer from another shortcoming: they have changed over time, which complicates direct comparisons of the data. The minimum age of people included in the literacy count is one feature that varies. It was 20 years old in 1840, 1850, and 1860; 10 years old from 1870 to 1930; and 14 years old in subsequent surveys. In 1840, the head of the household was asked how many in the household were illiterate; from 1840 until 1940, respondents were asked specifically if they could read or write. From 1870 to 1920, people were asked in separate questions whether they could read or write. The respondents were considered literate if they said they could write; reading without writing did not count for literacy in those years.

In 1940 the question about reading and writing was dropped because, according to Gray (1956, p. 35), it was thought that the "literacy standards were so low that the data secured had little value." Literacy demands had risen far above the ability to recognize or write a few words. The previous standard had allowed no conclusions about the reading levels of those counted; nor, continued Gray, did it permit conclusions about "the reading needs of adults or their ability to engage in the various types of reading essential to individual welfare or social progress." The Census Bureau switched to measuring how many years of schooling had been completed. Ironically, while the Census Bureau was dropping literacy from its list of questions, the Army was recruiting and training large numbers of insufficiently literate soldiers, many of whom required literacy instruction before they could be trained for military tasks (Goldberg, 1951).

Transformations and reinterpretation of data are required as we look back at the census data. For example, in 1840, only the literacy of white people was reported, so the literacy of the total population can only be estimated. Because of the laws prohibiting literacy among the slaves, we must assume that most of them were illiterate. On the basis of calculations from the census data—based on the question "What is the total number of illiterates in the household?"—Folger and Nam (1965) estimated that about 22 percent of the total population 20 years old and over in 1840 was illiterate. Horace Mann had compared census figures for 1840, 1850, and 1860 with signature data, and declared that "there can be no doubt that the figures of the census may be relied on as being much below the painful truth" (Folger & Nam, 1965, p. 113). Basic illiteracy in the whole population was roughly 30 percent. Even though census data for the following years are similarly suspect in underestimation of illiteracy, there is clearly an upward trend in literacy. In 1860 the illiteracy rate for the white population was estimated to be only 8.9 percent; the illiteracy rate for the total population was estimated to be 19.7 percent. Keep in mind that literacy in the census sense was of a minimal nature—being able to write a simple message.

The designers of the census recognized the difference between being able to write your name (as in the signature counts) and being able to write a simple message. However, census takers required no proof of even this minimal literacy; no writing test was given. The census taker simply asked the question and recorded the answer.

Table 2 shows the steady progression toward higher percentages of literacy documented by census reports and national sample surveys administered by the Census Bureau. Starting with the first figures in 1840, when more than one fifth of the total population was estimated to be illiterate, and moving through succeeding years, the good news about basic literacy became better. In a period of 100 years, illiteracy decreased by a factor of 10; and by 1969 only 1 percent of the total population was reported to be illiterate, *illiterate* being defined as having fewer than 8 years of school attendance. A look at the column Negro & Other Races reveals how different these figures are from those for the total population. Although overall illiteracy was steadily decreasing, illiteracy among blacks and other minority races held steady at about four times the rate of the total population. Granting the Census Bureau's definition of literacy as the ability to write a simple message, from 1840 through 1930 America had a total population that, in terms of percentages, was almost completely literate.

While the percentage of illiterates was dropping, the population was growing; thus, the numbers of illiterate people remained large. In 1959, for example, about 2.6 million people did not meet the census literacy definition of having more than 5 years of education. An additional 250,000 illiterates were in prisons, hospitals, and other institutions.

Table 2
Census Data on Illiteracy, 1840-1969
(percent)

Year	Total	White	Black & Other Races
1840	22.0	9.0	NA
1850	22.6	10.7	NA
1860	19.7	8.9	NA
1870	20.0	11.5	79.9
1880	17.0	9.4	70.0
1890	13.3	7.7	56.8
1900	10.7	6.2	44.5
1910	7.7	5.0	30.5
1920	6.0	4.0	23.0
1930	4.3	3.0	16.4
1940	2.9	2.0	11.5
1947	2.7	1.8	11.0
1952	2.5	1.8	10.2
1959	2.2	1.6	7.5
1969	1.0	0.7	3.6

Data for 1840 to 1860 are for those 20 years and older; data for 1870 to 1940, for those 10 years and older; data for 1947, 1952, 1959, and 1969, for those 14 years and older. Source: U.S. Bureau of the Census (1971); source for 1840, 1850, and 1860 data, U.S. Bureau of the Census, Historical Statistics of the United States, Colonial Times to 1970, Part 1. Figures for 1940 are census estimates.

Immigrants coming to the United States had an impact on the literacy statistics. When the migrations began in more literate areas, such as northern and central Europe, the immigrants were generally literate, at least in their first language. Immigrants from southern and eastern Europe, however, were far less likely to be literate. In the 1930 census (the last to contain a direct literacy question), about 3 percent of the people counted as literate did not speak English, but 37 percent of the illiterate population did not speak English. Even if miscommunication with English speaking census takers led to some overestimation, these figures make clear the overlap of "illiteracy" and immigrants who spoke a different language.

The relationship between literacy, educational attainment, and occupation (as illustrated with data from the census in Table 3)

Table 3
Male Illiteracy Rates by Occupation

	Percent Illiterate			
Occupation	1890	1959	1980[1]	1980[2]
White Collar	1.3	0.3	2.6	0.4
Manual/Service	10.3	2.4	10.7	1.5
Farming	20.9	8.4	23.1	6.5
Total	13.8	2.2	6.6	1.1

[1]Fewer than 9 years of school
[2]Fewer than 5 years of school
All data from the U.S. Bureau of the Census

allows us to compare literacy rates of men in white collar jobs, manufacturing and service industries, and farming. In 1959 all groups were more literate than the total for working men in 1890.

The 1980 data on occupations are based on the percentage of men with fewer than 5 years and fewer than 9 years of school, so these figures are similar, but not identical, to those from 1890 and 1959. One clear trend appears across the years: the literacy of men employed in each of the job categories remained in the same relative standing, with the highest literacy in the white collar category and the lowest in the farm category. Comparing data for men who reported fewer than 5 years of school, the men in 1980 have more schooling than in the earlier years, and may therefore be more literate.

However, jobs became more technical during this 90-year span, and because completion of the eighth grade is often used as a definition of functional literacy, we also include the data for those with fewer than 9 years of school. The total of 6.6 percent for all men in 1980 is less than the 13.8 percent of illiterates in 1890, but is greater than the 2.2 percent reported for 1959, when fewer than 6 years of school was the census standard. When we use the higher number of years of school, the statistics for men engaged in manual and service jobs and farm occupations are quite similar in 1890 and 1980. The conclusion to be drawn from both centuries is that not

Newman and Beverstock

many men can hold white collar jobs if they have fewer than 9 years of school.

According to the census data, the United States is more literate now than it was 100 years ago. This conclusion must be interpreted with the understanding that the Census Bureau documented only a minimal level of literacy. It is necessary to look further to find out how literate Americans were.

Years of schooling. For many years, estimates of literacy were made on the basis of years of schooling completed. The number of years of school required to be considered functionally literate has increased over time. In the 1930s the Civilian Conservation Corps used completion of third grade as its standard for literacy. At the beginning of World War II, the completion of the fourth grade was declared sufficient literacy for entry into the Army. However, as the war continued, literacy requirements were discontinued so that sufficient numbers of soldiers could be inducted. The special 1947 census set literacy at 5 years of schooling, and 13.5 percent of the male population could not meet that standard. The 1949 census used the fifth grade, and the 1952 census, the sixth grade. In the 1960s the United States Office of Education set literacy at 8 years of schooling. With 9 years of schooling as the minimum for literacy, the 1980 census yielded 24 million people aged 25 years and older who were illiterate — 18 percent of the people in this age group. But with 12 years of school as the minimum, the same census found 45 million people, or 34 percent, illiterate (McGrail, 1984).

The easy equation of schooling = literacy conceals a potentially false assumption that time in school necessarily equips people with needed skills. This supposition ignores the differences inherent in different schools, teachers, student abilities, and community values placed on education. It fails to take into account the different meanings placed on a "year" of schooling. Isenberg (1965, p. 46) included a story that illustrates the slipperiness of the statistics in relation to the real life of Maybelle Masters:

> At the age of 20 Maybelle — a fifth grader — got married and quit school. The U.S. Census calls her literate because she reported attending school for 5 years...yet she cannot read

and write. "When they ask me how long I went," says Masters, "I say 5 years, but the truth is I didn't go even 18 months. School was only open from January to April. Sometimes the cotton wasn't all picked in January, so you couldn't start school till the work was done. In April, the planting started. You stopped going to school when the work started in the fields. So maybe I went 2 months a year, maybe 3."

Equating schooling with literacy ignores the potential loss of skills through disuse. It also fails to take into account the potential differences between the literacy-based tasks asked of a fourth or eighth grade student and the literacy demands in the modern workplace and other adult contexts. Years of schooling is a reliable predictor of literacy in such studies as the English Language Proficiency Survey (1982) and Young Adult Literacy (1986); people who score high typically have had more years of schooling, whereas people who score low have had fewer years in school. But the confounding factors of varying educational experience, opportunity, and different literacy demands on adults at work and children in school make reliance on years of schooling alone insufficient.

If literacy is defined to be fourth or eighth grade attainment, but the job calls for twelfth grade level or better, then a person is likely to be a workplace illiterate. Mikulecky (1986) reviewed estimates of the difficulty of reading matter at work. He found that much of the material workers need to read falls between the tenth and twelfth grade levels on a readability scale. On average, workers read between 1.5 and 2 hours a day, and their reading requires more complex literacy skills—including problem solving and making applications—than is typical of reading at school. As of 1982, 5.2 million American adults had completed fewer than 6 years of school (Brizius & Foster, 1987). The millions of Americans who have attended fewer than 10 to 12 years of school are unlikely to be well prepared to use reading matter at the level of difficulty Mikulecky has documented.

Table 4

Population That Had Completed
5 or Fewer Years of School in 1980

Age	Total (thousands)	Percent of the Population
15-17	43	0.4
18-19	41	0.6
20-24	192	1.0
25-29	255	1.2
30-34	261	1.2
35-39	307	1.7
40-44	241	1.6
45-49	270	2.2
50-54	334	3.1
55-59	472	4.2
60-64	499	4.6
65-69	571	5.9
70-74	544	7.2
75+	1,202	11.2

U.S. Bureau of the Census (1987)

The amount of time spent in school increased substantially during the second half of the twentieth century. Although in 1910 only 8.8 percent of the population had graduated from high school, nearly 75 percent graduated in 1990. Table 4 shows that the percentage and numbers of people with 5 or fewer years of schooling has decreased steadily with each succeeding age group. As education expanded to include more people, fewer have been left in the lowest group with few years in school. For example, while 11.2 percent of the population 75 years and older had completed 5 years or less of school, fewer than 2 percent of 40- to 44-year-olds had that level of schooling.

Table 5

Schooling Completed by Persons 15 Years Old and Over, by Geographic Region, March 1987 (percent)

Years of School	Northeast	Midwest	South	West	Total United States
0-4	1.6	1.0	3.0	2.2	2.1
5-7	3.7	2.3	6.0	3.4	4.1
8	5.9	6.6	6.0	4.7	5.9
9-11	15.8	16.4	17.9	14.5	16.4
12	38.0	41.4	35.4	33.7	37.0
13-15	15.9	17.0	16.2	22.4	17.6
16+	19.2	15.2	15.5	19.2	16.9

U.S. Bureau of the Census (1987)

The census data also allow comparisons of different geographical regions of the United States in terms of educational attainment (see Table 5). Although differences among the regions have become less pronounced, the contrasts are clearest at the lowest and highest numbers of years of schooling. The South has both the largest proportion of people with an education of 8 years or less (15 percent, compared with the U.S. total of 12.1 percent) and the largest proportion of people with an education of 12 years or less (68.3 percent, compared with the U.S. total of 65.5 percent).

By contrast, the Northeast and West have the highest proportion of people with 16 years and more of education; both have 19.2 percent, compared with the U.S. total of 16.9 percent. Varying somewhat by region, about 10 to 15 percent of people have 8 years or less of schooling and may have difficulty meeting the current literacy standards of many jobs.

Efforts to award high school diplomas on the basis of proficiency or competency testing, as opposed to school attendance and grades, illustrate public concern about the reliability of estimating basic skills on the basis of X number of years of schooling. It is distressing to realize that students can attend school through the twelfth grade, get a diploma, and still lack the literacy skills required by many employers. Dissatisfaction with public education has led to increasing demands for accountability from educators and others in authority. This perceived decline in the quality of public education has left many people with the questionable belief that public instruction in the past was far superior; but whether education has declined or has not kept up with expanding needs, students now are underprepared for many tasks.

Testing. Competency testing and basic skills testing have been instituted in many school districts as alternative measures of functional literacy. Competency testing has not been universally accepted, and has been legally challenged (*Debra P. v. Turlington*). The courts had to consider the effects of previous racial segregation in producing inferior educational opportunities for minorities (an extension of *Brown v. Board of Education*), and whether the test used was fair and had curricular validity. In other words, did the test cover material not only listed in the school curriculum, but actually taught in the schools? (Popham & Lindheim, 1981)

In some cases, students have been able to obtain diplomas despite their inability to pass the competency examination, so that the possession of a recently issued high school diploma may or may not certify the basic skills achievement of its holder. In many areas, high school graduates have had to demonstrate some level (usually, eighth grade) of basic skills. Many people are dissatisfied with requirements they think are too easy. These contested competency tests and their deflated standards will continue to be a point of contention as the public requires more accountability from schools and their graduates.

How Literate Were We?

Reaching back in time with the help of historians and census takers, we find no answer to the question of America's literacy past, only an impression. The definitions used both enable and limit our understanding of earlier times. Signature data and census data on literacy both point only to an estimate of the literacy minimums, without supplying much information on the literacy uses and abilities of our ancestors. As Kaestle (1985, p. 45) pointed out:

Even where we have some evidence about the uses of literacy, there is no way to summarize for a whole society the significance of so commonplace and pervasive an activity as reading. There will be, then, no comprehensive social history of the uses of literacy.

Even years spent in school and the possession of a high school diploma, although potentially more useful than either signatures or the question "Can you write a simple message?" yield ambiguous information about the extent of literacy. Over time, U.S. residents have been counted as increasingly, if minimally, literate. The facts do not support the idea that illiteracy is a new problem. As Kaestle (1985, p. 33) pointed out:

> The problems of today's illiterates, the dearth of writing practice in the schools, the absence of critical reading skills on the job, and the negative effect of the electronic media on reading activities, are all matters of legitimate concern and have some basis in fact; but they should not lead us to invent a golden age of literacy in some earlier decade.

An educated guess concludes quite the opposite: more Americans are literate today than ever before. The harder question is: Are enough Americans today literate enough?

How Literate Is America Now?

Beginning in 1970, seven attempts have been made using nationally representative samples to estimate rates of functional illiteracy in the United States. Designing and implementing a study of the functional literacy of U.S. adults is a difficult task. Unfortunately, in a society that is permeated with testing and that rushes to publish the results of various tests in the daily papers, the differences between test results and the real world often are forgotten. Even though a test may purport to measure functional literacy, it may be several steps removed from the actual demonstration of the respondent's functional literacy.

In an ideal and luxuriously funded world, researchers might approach the description of functional literacy by following people through the complexities of their daily lives, observing their literacy skills in action. When the intent is to characterize large portions of the national population, cost and time considerations preclude such an intensive study.

Simulations of functional literacy tasks offer the next closest look at literacy, but they, too, are expensive to conduct on a large scale. Researchers must not only observe how the respondents perform the tasks but also select tasks that are as close as possible to the real thing.

Large-scale simulations also suffer from the lack of actual products of respondents' uses of literacy. Interpreting a collection of materials that required reading and writing would present problems: it would be difficult to determine how much had been accomplished by the respondent alone, conditions could not be standardized, and scoring would be difficult.

Paper-and-pencil tests remain the easiest alternative. These tests offer several advantages. They can be administered to large numbers of people, and they are both fast and inexpensive. But these advantages are coupled with the disadvantages of increased distance from actual reading and writing, as well as from the context-specific literacies of the respondents. Fisher (1977) listed several problems with standard tests, including possible fatigue of the respondents, poor match of test tasks with actual challenges in the respondents' lives (rural people, for example, tend to be less familiar with bus schedules than city people), and the probability that people who could master the task would nonetheless make errors. Gadway and Wilson (1976, p. 19) also make this point in their discussion of common items used in their study (an automobile insurance policy, a book club form, a traffic ticket) that were troublesome even for "superior readers."

> These exercises...point out that there are reading materials that we encounter in everyday life that stymie even some of the best readers, yet we would not say that they are functionally illiterate.

Completion of forms and applications may require a surprisingly sophisticated demonstration of literacy, an effort even for educated people. When forms and applications serve as test items, those being tested may be unable to complete a particular task despite levels of education that would seemingly predict success.

Seven National Studies of Literacy

With these test design factors in mind, we can consider the seven studies of national functional literacy, each of which attempted to assess the ability to perform the basic literacy tasks required of adults in our society. This grounding in the daily requirements of literate living gave the measures greater credibility than, for example, standardized tests originally designed for elementary school students.

Analysis of the performance of a large sample on individual items may be more useful in understanding functional literacy than overall conclusions about the numbers of the functionally illiterate. Such broad conclusions must be based on the slippery basis of cutoff scores designating who is "literate" or "illiterate." Setting up this dichotomy introduces the conceptual difficulty of reducing literacy to a single literacy-is-present or literacy-is-absent judgment, which does not fit our understanding of the spectrum of literacies. The arbitrary labeling of literate/illiterate sets up a stumbling block in the use and interpretation of many of these studies. Among the seven studies, only the Young Adult Literacy and the Adult Functional Reading avoided the literate/illiterate dichotomy.

Survival Literacy Study (Harris, 1970). In July 1970, the National Reading Council was appointed by President Nixon to "combat illiteracy and develop a national reading program" and to assess the extent of "reading deficiencies" in the United States (Heckler, 1970, p. 38036). This council, with a 5-year budget of $1.5 million, set up a National Reading Center in Washington, DC, as its working and research division, and commissioned two literacy studies by Louis Harris and Associates.

Through the first of these studies, the Survival Literacy Study, the council sought to determine how many Americans lacked enough literacy to complete common applications such as for Social

Security numbers, public assistance, loans, driver's licenses, and Medicaid. Five applications were prepared, similar to the applications for each of these, although they were simplified to ensure that the study evaluated reading ability and not the layout of the form itself. The word *survival* exemplifies the naming and conceptual dilemmas inherent in studying functional literacy. Obviously people do survive in spite of illiteracy, so survival in this sense refers to the ease with which people will be able to conduct basic transactions in a print-based and bureaucratic society.

Four criterion levels were set: *likely survival*, 90 percent or more of items correct; (2) *marginal survival*, 80-90 percent correct; (3) *questionable survival*, 70-80 percent correct; and (4) *low survival*, less than 70 percent correct. The last three levels were designated as the "range of illiteracy." Harris estimated that 87 percent (123.8 million people) completed the forms with 90 percent or more correct, and 3 percent (4.3 million) correctly completed 70 percent or less of the items. People with greater levels of education made fewer errors. However, even among those who had a college level education, 8 percent had less than 90 percent correct. The difficulty levels of the five forms varied considerably, as reflected in percentages of people who had trouble with them: public assistance, 3 percent; driver's license, 8 percent; bank loan, 11 percent; and Medicaid, 34 percent. These percentages probably would have been higher if the forms had not been simplified for the study.

The attempt in this study to distinguish between reading running text and reading text in forms produces another questionable dichotomy. Tests that use text in forms measure what we would call application literacy—the ability to read, comprehend, and respond to forms.

Reading Difficulty Index (Harris, 1971). This study, commissioned by the National Reading Council and also conducted by Harris, used an approach comparable to that taken in the Survival Literacy Study. Respondents filled out a written application and answered oral questions concerning classified ads and telephone use. Four percent (extrapolated 5.7 million) scored less than 80 percent correct and were characterized as seriously deficient in functional reading. Eleven percent (extrapolated 15.5 million) scored between

80 and 90 percent correct and were characterized as needing to make a "serious effort" to manage real world functional literacy demands.

The questions about income and medical information were the most difficult for all the respondents, while personal identification, housing, and citizenship were the easiest.

Miniassessment of functional literacy (Gadway & Wilson, 1975). The federal Right to Read program commissioned the National Assessment of Educational Progress (NAEP), through the Education Commission of the States, to make a miniassessment of functional literacy along with the NAEP's periodic assessments of the educational progress of students. In 1975, Gadway and Wilson administered 64 items from the 1971 NAEP reading test to 17-year-old students to assess the trend in their functional literacy over a 4-year period. The items included reading prose passages, charts, maps, pictures, coupons, and forms.

Seventy-five percent correct was declared the minimum for functional literacy; 12.6 percent of the students failed to reach that level. However, the average performance rose from 83.7 percent correct in 1971 to 85.9 percent in 1975. While Gadway and Wilson were confident about the representativeness of their sample of students, they were more cautious about the representativeness of the tasks used in the miniassessment. The exercises were selected and categorized by panels of reading specialists, but no steps were taken to ensure the validity of the selected tasks.

Stedman and Kaestle (1987) pointed out that the results of the miniassessment depended on the cutoff scores, which were selected to represent the presence or absence of literacy skills. If the cutoff had been 60 percent, only 2.9 percent would have failed to meet the literacy standard. Stedman and Kaestle suggested that the designers probably considered 60 percent too low because they had selected items they thought all students could answer correctly. These authors also stated that the miniassessment estimate of 12.6 percent functionally illiterate must be revised upward because the test was taken only by enrolled students; the results did not include students who had dropped out or non-English-speaking students. Stedman and Kaestle concluded that these revisions would raise the miniassessment illiteracy rate to about 18 percent. They further maintained that estimates of both the Harris studies should be raised by 2 to 3 percent to include the non-English speakers. This would put the national illiteracy rate in 1975 at above 20 percent.

The miniassessment represented the performance of students only, not of the general public. Students might be expected to be better prepared to take a test than would people not in school. If nonstudents had been tested, the percentage of estimated illiteracy probably would have been higher.

Adult Functional Reading (Murphy, 1975). Conducted by the Educational Testing Service, the Adult Functional Reading study was the first that did not set a single criterion of literacy/illiteracy. Rather, the study specified the domain as the reading tasks of day-to-day living, and set three bases of judgment: 1) the percentage of people who actually performed the tasks, 2) the time spent on performing the tasks, and 3) the importance of the tasks.

In 1971, 5,073 people 16 years of age and older were asked to answer questions about the time they spent reading, the kinds of materials they read, and how important they felt the materials were. As Murphy (1975, p. 52) reports, the most important reading tasks performed by adults, in order of importance, were:

- Price, weight, and size information
- Street and traffic signs
- Main news in the newspapers
- Writing on packages and labels
- Manuals and written instructions
- Forms, invoices, and accounting statements
- Tests, examinations, and written assignments
- Letters, memos, and notes
- Order forms
- Local news in the newspaper
- School papers and notes
- Bills and statements

Using these data, test developers at the Educational Testing Service developed reading tasks using different forms of reading (books, periodicals, legal documents, listings, instructions, advertisements, forms, letters, signs, and labels) and different benefits (economic, occupation, education/culture, recreation, health, maintenance, personal relationships, and citizenship). The tasks were reviewed by a panel that generally approved the effort but recommended multiple-choice items not be used. After field tests, the 170 reading tasks were administered to 8,000 adults, each of whom completed 17 of the items with interviewers, who gave oral instructions. The respondents marked directly on the reading materials by checking, underlining, or circling. The researchers found that about half of the items were answered correctly by 80 percent of the people, and 20 percent of the tasks were answered correctly by 90 percent. Total scores were not calculated, nor did the researchers "set a standard for evaluating good or bad performance in general." Instead they recommended interpreting the results as "reasonable estimates of how well American adults, and various subgroups of American adults, can read specific tasks intended to represent the kinds of reading tasks performed by adults who function adequately in normal day-to-day life" (Murphy, 1975, p. 56).

Later, Kirsch and Guthrie (1978) analyzed the data, categorizing "maintenance items" (such as a table of contents or a train schedule) as difficult for 18 percent of the population, and "occupational items" (such as employment applications, sick leave forms, and company antidiscrimination policies) as difficult for 25 percent. Both the original study and its later analysis brought a welcome focus on specific literacies and a rejection of blanket labeling of respondents as either literate or illiterate. Consequently, no general statement about the illiteracy rate was made in this study.

Adult Performance Level Study (Final Report, 1977). Funded by the U.S. Office of Education in 1971, the APL study was designed to define functional competency. In the memorandum that invited proposals for the project, an ambitious goal was set:

> The challenge is to foster through every means the ability to read, write, and compute with the functional competence needed for meeting the requirements of adult living.

The emphasis of this definition is in its final phrase, "requirements for adult living." These requirements must be determined by an analysis of adult living rather than the common practice of attaching a grade equivalence to them. Existing grade equivalents cannot be effectively adapted to adult needs....A system of adult education must derive its own specific aims and have its own adult based curricula, methodologies, and materials (Final Report, 1977, p. 2).

The project began with a review of the literature, conferences, interviews with state and federal officials to identify what skills should be taught in adult education classes, and interviews with undereducated and unemployed adults. This process generated a taxonomy of skills (reading, writing, speaking, listening, computing, problem solving) and knowledge areas (consumer economics, occupational knowledge, health, community resources, government, and law). The researchers then developed 65 specific competency objectives based on these skill and knowledge areas. They also developed what they called small simulations (as opposed to test items), and field-tested them on 3,500 people in Adult Basic Education classes in 30 states. Then five nationally representative samples were drawn, and 7,500 adults were tested in their homes for about an hour. Measuring on the basis of the results of this test and on indicators of "success" (income, job status, education), the researchers defined three Adult Performance Levels.

APL 1   Functionally Incompetent
- mastery of skills that are associated with, but do not determine, inadequate income (at or below the poverty level)
- inadequate education, equivalent to 8 years or less of schooling
- unemployed or with occupations of low job status

APL 2   Marginally Functional
- mastery of skills associated with income at about the poverty level (but no discretionary income)
- completion of 9 to 11 years of school
- occupations with medium status

APL 3   Functionally Proficient

- mastery of skills associated with high levels of income
- completion of at least 12 years of school
- occupations with high status

Table 6
APL Estimates of American Competence

APL Level	Percent of Population
1 Functionally Incompetent	19.1
2 Marginally Functional	33.9
3 Functionally Proficient	46.3

As Table 6 shows, the APL project researchers concluded that 19.1 percent of American adults were functionally incompetent, 33.9 percent were marginally functional, and 46.3 percent were functionally proficient. The authors of the *Final Report* (1977, p. 17) claimed that the sample data were nationally representative and that it was possible to estimate the proportion of the U.S. adult population at each APL level. The percentages for APL 1 and APL 2, combined with 1983 census data, produced an estimate of 100.4 million Americans who were less than functionally proficient. Kozol used these figures in *Illiterate America* (1985), and they also were cited in the federal Adult Literacy Initiative literature.

Sample results from the general areas of occupational knowledge and consumer economics follow:

- Given a series of four newspaper help wanted ads, 17 percent of the sample were not able to determine which one was placed by a private person rather than a corporation or public institution. This result yielded an estimated figure of 20 million adults who were unable to perform this task.

- When given an incomplete business letter, only 20 percent

of the people were able to complete the return address section with no errors in form, content, spelling, or punctuation.

- Given odometer readings and fuel consumption, a surprisingly high 73 percent, or a projected 86 million adults, were unable to calculate accurately the gasoline consumption rate of an automobile (Northcutt, 1975, p. 48).

Other tasks included addressing an envelope well enough to ensure that it would reach the desired destination (failed by 22 percent), placing a return address on an envelope (failed by 24 percent), reading a mock airline schedule (failed by 30 percent), determining amounts of deductions from a gross salary (failed by 33 percent), computing the number of allowable deductions on the Internal Revenue Service's W-4 form and entering the number in the correct block (failed by 36 percent), and matching personal qualifications to job requirements (failed by 44 percent).

The APL had a tremendous impact on adult literacy instruction. "The 65 objectives...became the basis for curriculum and materials development, testing strategies, staff development, and delivery systems....They became the foundation for the evolving adult education system" (Delker, 1984, p. 2).

Proponents of the APL approach asserted that the study improved standards for identifying functional literacy by using criteria that replaced grade equivalents as the test of functional literacy and by including performance on real world tasks that reflected adults' literacy demands (Hunter & Harman, 1979).

The APL study was by no means universally accepted (Fischer, Haney, & David, 1980; Griffith & Cervero, 1977; Irwin, 1985; Kazemek, 1985, 1988). Griffith and Cervero asserted that the APL method was not new, that it "exemplifies a philosophy of adjusting to the status quo rather than an active, inquiring attitude compatible with the notion of responsible citizenship in a free society," and that its validity was in serious question since "all claims for the utility of the approach rest upon the credibility of its advocates and not upon the results of rigorous research" (p. 221).

Roger Farr concluded that proof of the validity of the items and of the criterion levels are missing from this study, making it "worthless." He continued, "The study was done to plan curriculum and to determine who was functionally incompetent. I don't think those goals are both possible with the same test" (personal communication, February 26, 1989).

One point of contention was the criteria by which the APL designers defined success: occupational prestige, weekly income, and years of formal schooling (Final Report, 1977). Irwin (1985, p. 8) objected to this approach:

> The researchers appear to have failed to consider that everyone cannot hold a high status job or that everyone cannot be highly paid. Literacy problems appear to be closely related to low income, low job status, and other social and economic disadvantages, but it is not a logical necessity to ascribe these conditions solely to educational failure.

Critics also have charged that the APL is vulnerable on a number of other bases. It emphasizes one set of competencies by assuming that they are the only ones worth having, that all Americans face the same problems, and that problems can be solved in only one way (Fischer, Haney, & David, 1980).

Acland (1976) questioned the measurement validity of the APL, noting that the test takers who failed the item based on the mock airplane schedule (30 percent) may have had a good reason. At the time of the study, Acland said, only 50 percent of Americans had flown. "This makes the 'bad' result look a lot less depressing; it [the APL finding] now seems to reflect differences in the tasks people face rather than differences in their problem solving skills" (p. 26). In another example, an item based on federal income tax form 1040 calculations, Acland noted that taxpayers rarely face such problems without help from tax preparers. The social nature of problem solving was thus ignored in the APL.

Similarly, Fischer, Haney & David (1980, p. 64) pointed out:

Newman and Beverstock

It cannot necessarily be inferred that a person lacks a partic- ular skill simply because he or she is unable to demonstrate it in a particular situation or type of situation. Second, just because someone lacks a particular skill does not mean that he or she will be unable to deal with a problem in a particu- lar real life situation. In real life, and even on tests, people may bring very different skills to bear in solving the same problem.

Whatever its flaws, the APL study was the first national at- tempt to corral the field of adult literacy, impose some definition, and determine where the nation stands with respect to a set of tasks. The study has been influential and widely quoted, and has spawned the competency-based education movement. The APL study's esti- mates of literacy rates have been quoted often, while the specific item-by-item results have been much less publicized. The APL has not been replicated nationally and "is still a primary influence on other research, whether or not the premise and results are accepted" (Fischer, Haney, & David, p. 4). APL simultaneously broadened ideas of the organization of adult education and "enriched the body of curriculum materials," while constricting assessment of adult competence with a "questionably narrow approach" (p. 75).

English Language Proficiency Survey (Barnes, 1986). In 1986, the U.S. Department of Education (DOE) established esti- mated adult illiteracy rates for each of the states and the District of Columbia. The DOE applied the findings of the Census Bureau's 1982 English Language Proficiency Survey (ELPS) to the 1980 cen- sus data on the composition of each state's population, including such factors as ethnicity, amount of education, and native speakers of other languages. The risk factors were applied to the 1980 census data to develop an estimate of the number of illiterates in each state.

The Census Bureau administered the Measure of Adult En- glish Proficiency (MAEP) to 3,400 people in a representative sample of adults. The test is composed of 26 items that require the respon- dent to answer questions, identify key words and phrases and match them with one of four possible answers that have the same meaning, or choose the best word to fill in blanks in passages. There are no graphics other than test direction stop signs. Robert Barners, supervisor of the project, characterized the test as "read-and-recognize" in contrast to those measures that might be called "read-and-perform" or "read-and-write."

Of the 4,200 people selected to take the test, 81 percent complied. For those who refused, the administrators estimated scores using membership or nonmembership in high-risk groups that were represented in the 1980 census data. Risk factors (or correlates) for failing scores had to do with age, country of birth, recentness of immigration for nonnatives, race, income, amount of schooling, and reported English speaking ability (of persons who use a non-English language at home).

Years of schooling was by far the most successful predictor of scores. Based on the study's findings, it was concluded that 13 percent (or 18.7 million) of the adults living in the United States were illiterate. This figure does not distinguish between functional and total illiteracy.

The developers of the survey listed some possible difficulties in the study. The passing literacy score was set at 20 correct items, although the developers considered this to be a conservative score; in their opinion, the number of illiterates may have been underestimated. Other factors also may have contributed to error in this estimate. For one thing, adults literate in a language other than English were labeled as illiterate. For another, migrations since the 1980 census have changed the proportion of high-risk groups in different locations. Finally, some who were estimated to be illiterate in the ELPS later became literate.

The developers of the ELPS regarded the test as superior to other estimates for the following reasons (DOE, 1982, p. 2):

- *Direct testing.* This is superior to "impressionistic evidence or inferences from a single variable such as years of school completed."

- *Coverage and uniform methods.* "Superior estimates may be found for segments of the U.S. adult population, but we know of none that covers adults of all ages and is based on the application of uniform methods to all states."

- *Reliability*. The study's estimates are considered reliable because "state rankings are determined by the differences in the composition of the adult population as reflected on the 1980 census."
- *Relevance for literacy programs*. These data show that "illiteracy is now predominantly a problem of our center cities, and that among native English speaking adults in their 20s and 30s, it is 10 times more prevalent than one would estimate using the traditional criterion of completion of fewer than 6 years of school."

The ELPS study can be questioned on two points. First, it is increasingly apparent that literacy is not a single characteristic that can be said to be present or absent. The designation of an arbitrary cutoff score is a questionable practice if literacy is defined as a constellation of abilities. Second, the tasks required by the test are test-specific and are not related to specific literacies the examinees may possess.

Young Adult Literacy (Kirsch & Jungeblut, 1986). In 1985, the NAEP conducted a study of the literacy of adults aged 21 to 25, using materials selected to represent the common demands of adult reading. From the 40,000 contacted in a nationally representative sample of households in the contiguous 48 states, 3,600 young adults were chosen for the study. The data in this study were collected by 500 interviewers who spent approximately 30 minutes collecting background information—such as occupation and aspirations, school experiences, current uses of reading and writing, and language background—to relate to the respondent's performance on the assessment task. The interviewers then spent 60 minutes assessing each subject.

In contrast to other literacy assessments, this study allowed the interviewees to respond to the task as they would in the real world, rather than requiring them to choose a correct answer or fill in the blanks of a test form. Tasks included writing a letter, writing a check, filling in an order form, and orally explaining differences in job benefits. Criteria for judging the adequacy of the responses were developed by interviewing people who worked in the fields being tested—for example, bank tellers were interviewed to find out what criteria are applied in accepting or rejecting a check. The test designers wanted a more effective literacy assessment than previous measures. They aimed to "preserve the integrity of stimulus materials, response procedures, and scoring criteria associated with these types of tasks as they occur in various adult contexts" (Mosenthal & Kirsch, 1987). For example, the testers provided paper and pen for writing a letter rather than presenting a prewritten letter and asking questions about the meaning of the letter or the correct form.

The designers rejected both the idea of using a single scale and of using one for each of the 100 tasks. Instead, they classified the tasks into three categories. Each task was scaled from 1 to 500 in terms of levels of difficulty (Kirsch & Jungeblut, 1986). Using Item Response Theory, a model of estimating the likelihood of a correct response based on the proficiency of the person and the properties of the task (including difficulty, task discrimination, and possibility of guessing), comparable tasks were generated and the numbers representing difficulty were attached. The designers also identified what they considered to be the underlying psychological constructs, and separated them into three levels of difficulty. Tasks that required matching a known item (a person's name) with information requested (a blank for signature), were considered to be quite easy (110 on the NAEP scale). Nearly 100 percent of respondents could complete this task. The next level of difficulty required choosing information when several possible items, both correct and distractors, were present (finding a location on a map [249], using a table to calculate eligibility for benefits [262]). About 84 percent of respondents could complete these tasks. At the third level of difficulty, readers needed to match more features, infer information stated in different terms from the question, and deal with more distractors (using a chart to locate the appropriate grade sandpaper given certain specifications [320]). Only 20 percent of respondents were judged to be operating at this level.

These levels of difficulty also applied to the conclusions drawn from the study. The findings showed that young adults are literate if judged by previous standards of literacy such as signatures (virtually all), fourth grade reading (95 percent), eighth grade reading (80 percent), and eleventh grade reading (60 percent). But the scales of difficulty also demonstrated that complex and demanding tasks—those that are expected to characterize work in coming years—may be beyond the current skills of many young adults. For example, workers often will be expected to use information on computer screens, make calculations, consult documentation, and then type new instructions. This requires thinking and problem solving at the 275 level and above on the NAEP scale.

The data also demonstrate that minority groups do not score as well as whites. Table 7 (Kirsch & Jungeblut, 1986) displays the percentages of young adults at or above the 200, 275, and 350 levels. At each of the levels, the percentage of white students exceeds that of Hispanic students, which in turn exceeds that of black students. Statistics on other ethnic groups were not reported.

Mikulecky (1986) has noted that the line between who has and who has not acquired enough literacy to function and thrive is, to a great extent, drawn along ethnic lines. This division implies an alarming trend, considering the fact that minorities who have been economically and educationally disadvantaged comprise an increasingly large percentage of the population. The data also suggest that levels of education are increasingly important as the difficulty of tasks increases (see Table 8). While amount of education makes very little difference in the ability to complete the items at the 200 level, few people with little education operated well at the higher levels (Kirsch & Jungeblut, 1986).

Table 7
Comparative Performance on the NAEP Scale of Racial and Ethnic Groups

| | Percent at or Above Level | | |
	200 level	*275 level*	*350 level*
White	95	78	25
Hispanic	90	57	10
Black	82	39	3

Table 8

Comparative Performance on the NAEP Scale of Adults with Different Levels of Education

	Percent at or Above Level		
	200 level	*275 level*	*350 level*
0-8 Years of Education	NA	less than 30	1
Some High School	84	40	4
High School Graduate	97	68	12
Postsecondary Degree	99	91	40

The NAEP study also considered oral language test performance. The oral test was administered to two groups whose skills were judged to be too limited to take the regular exam, as well as to a random sample of those who did complete the exam. This approach tested whether the oral language skills of the two groups would be comparable on 10 items construed to be within the experience of a wide variety of people. The tasks included interpreting pictures, giving directions, describing a movie or television show, and communicating persuasively. Responses (which were taped) were scored on comprehensibility, overall task accomplishment, delivery problems, and language problems.

Results indicated that individuals characterized as limited in their literacy proficiency had similarly limited oral language skills. Some even had difficulty completing the tasks. The people who had difficulty were likely to have come from homes where a language other than English was spoken, where there was less income, and where educational backgrounds were limited. Individuals who showed higher levels of literacy also performed better on the oral language measure.

The Young Adult Literacy study was characterized by Mikulecky (1986, p. 8) as "the most accurate currently available estimation of the literacy abilities of young adults." Sticht, who was invited by NAEP to write the introduction for the report, described it as "the most conceptually and analytically sophisticated study of adult literacy ever conducted in this country" (Kirsch & Jungeblut, 1986, p. v). Unlike some of the earlier studies, the Young Adult Literacy study did not provide a summary estimate of the number of literate and illiterate young people in the United States, but it did register information on their ability to complete tasks drawn from prose, document, and quantitative domains with differing levels of difficulty. In its analysis, the NAEP study emphasized "not only...the complex nature of literacy demands within a pluralistic society, but also of the status of people functioning in our society" (Kirsch, 1990).

Testing the Tests

In answer to the question "How literate is America now?" we can draw on these seven studies, whose results are summarized in Tables 9 and 10. Taken as a whole, the studies—with their varied aims, approaches, and results, and the responses they generated—

Table 9
Summary of the Format of
the Literacy Studies

Study	Year	Ages	Tasks
Survival Literacy	1970	16+	Application forms
Reading Difficulty Index	1971	16+	Application forms, classified ads
Adult Functional Reading	1973	16+	Everyday reading
Adult Performance Level	1974	18-65	Functional competence
Miniassessment	1975	17	Everyday reading
English Language Proficiency	1982	20+	Multiple choice from applications, official notices
Young Adult Literacy	1985	21-25	Prose comprehension, documents, quantitative, oral language

Stedman and Kaestle (1987, p. 28)

dramatically illustrate that a seemingly simple, reasonable question can defy a simple, satisfying answer.

How literate is America? The seven studies do not answer the question either simply or completely. They are instructive, nonetheless, both for their content and for their potential as historical artifacts. The studies span the years 1970 through 1985 and reflect the changes in thinking about adult literacy that have occurred during that period. Those changes are illustrated by the styles of the tests. The first of the studies (Survival Literacy Study) was conducted as a poll, whereas the most recent (Young Adult Literacy) was a more involved attempt to study literacy from a number of perspectives, including the kinds of literacy tasks and their relative difficulty. However, the Survival Literary Study did try to use real world materials; and, to their credit, all the researchers in the seven studies

Table 10
Summary of the Findings of the Literacy Studies

Study	Criteria	Lower Criterion %	Higher Criterion %
Survival Literacy	70%, 90% correct	3	13
Reading Difficulty Index	80%, 90% of weighted items	4	15
Adult Functional Reading	None set	—	—
Adult Performance Level	APL 1, APL 3	19.7	53.6
Miniassessment	75% correct	12.6	—
English Language Proficiency	20 of 26 correct	13	—
Young Adult Literacy	None set	—	—

Stedman and Kaestle (1987, p. 28)

tried (in different ways and with different outcomes) to design studies that would reflect the real world of their subjects. These were honest attempts to answer a challenging question about the ability of Americans to handle the everyday demands of literacy.

As Table 10 shows, the answers of the seven tests differ substantially. The percentage of subjects who failed to reach the higher criterion ranged from 13 to 53.6 percent, and the percentage who failed to reach the lower criterion ranged from 3 to 19.7 percent. In addition, at first glance there appears to be a trend toward lower literacy with the passage of time.

A closer examination of the studies yields a different, more complicated conclusion. Some of these studies set single criterion scores to separate literates from nonliterates, while others avoided this dichotomy. When multiple levels were set, they tended to be defined on different bases from study to study. The studies also varied in testing conditions, from testlike to lifelike situations. The operational definition of literacy ranged from narrow to broad. When these differences are noted, the seeming trend toward lower literacy becomes muddy. Broad conclusions are dangerous to attempt when treading such slippery terrain. Stedman and Kaestle (1987, p. 34) accepted the challenge in their review of the seven studies:

> We find it reasonable to estimate that about 20 percent of the adult population, or around 35 million people, have serious difficulties with common reading tasks. Another 10 percent or so are probably marginal in their functional literacy skills.

Some critics reject the entire notion of setting a minimum score for literacy and declaring illiterate those who fall below their single standard. Kazemek (1988, pp. 470-471) asserted:

> Assessment instruments like those used in the APL study can never give us an adequate understanding of illiteracy or an accurate count of adult illiterates in the United States. Such instruments attempt to measure a relative, particular, and situationally specific process in a universal and quantifiable manner.

The Young Adult Literacy study came the closest to categorizing tasks on the basis of relative difficulty and the relative performance of young adults on those tasks. It approached the diversity of literacy skills through multiple scales rather than a single one, and furnished a sense of the relative challenges of different tasks and the reasons they may be easy or difficult.

Despite the disagreement among reading professionals about the relative merits of all these studies, the results are commonly used by federal, state, and local governments. Several years ago, the National State Boards of Education (1986) prepared a list of reported measures of illiteracy in each state. Definitions, identification criteria, and the estimates of the problem were borrowed from some of these tests. Among the definitions, *functional* literacy appeared frequently. Identification criteria of illiteracy were said to vary locally or were expressed in a combination of age (over 15 or 16) and below a certain grade level. Among the different state criteria, one was derived from the Adult Performance Level Study, one from projections from the 1980 census (perhaps ELPS), and the rest on the amount of schooling completed by state residents.

In their policy guide for state governments, Brizius and Foster (1987) pointed out that the prevalent practice within state politics is to set "arbitrary definitional distinctions and count the 'literate' and 'illiterate'." They commented further (pp. 38-39):

> Most officials are uncomfortable with this approach, but like other facts of state life, they live with it....This approach is justified by the fact that even arbitrary distinctions between "illiterate" and the "literate" generate such large numbers of adults who need assistance that current service programs only serve a small percentage. Methodological purity gives way to practicality.

Brizius and Foster proposed as a better approach the use of combinations of ELPS, NAEP scores, and more recent state demographics to portray a continuum of literacy skills. They suggested that this combination would yield the clearest picture for the governors, and would allow them to target population groups for specific literacy assistance. We agree that the best estimates of literacy are those that take into account the wide spectrum of literacies and literacy demands.

Challenges in Measuring Adult Literacy

Measurement of adult literacy is undertaken with a variety of purposes in mind. The seven large-scale studies were aimed at drawing a national estimate of literacy or lack of literacy. Funding agencies want to be able to evaluate the progress of learners in their programs. Researchers and practitioners want to compare the effectiveness of various approaches to literacy learning. Instructors and learners need dependable ways to measure literacy gains and to gain information that will influence the course of instruction. Employers want to know whether prospective employees have the literacy skills needed for the advertised position.

Kirsch (1990) categorized the approaches to estimating adult literacy into three groups: traditional (standardized achievement tests), competency-based (tasks based on nonschool materials and a single score), and profiles (a range of real world tasks and multiple scores). No study researchers or pollsters have administered traditional standardized achievement tests to a nationally representative sample of adults. Despite the continued use of standardized achievement tests to place adults in programs and to screen reading skills for job placement, we do not have a canonical estimate of adult literacy in the United States. Most of the studies discussed here fall into Kirsch's "competency-based" category because they all used nonschool materials to estimate adults' literacy.

Sticht (1990, p. 51) called for measurement that includes not only what the schools teach but also a prediction of how well adults will be able to function in future literacy requirements:

> I believe adult literacy should be measured in such a manner that we are able to accurately characterize how well adults have achieved in learning what the schools are teaching and that we have confidence in predicting how well the adults will be able to negotiate the demands for literacy in future

settings. Though these may sound like commonsense goals, I do not think they have guided our past efforts as well as they might.

Others have been trying out methodologies borrowed from ethnographic research and the teacher as researcher school of thought to elaborate new forms of adult literacy assessment (Fargo & Collins, 1989; Lytle, 1988; Lytle & Wolfe, 1990; Metz, 1989; Stecher & Solarzano, 1988). Fargo and Collins characterized their efforts as a "rich learning experience" that gave insights into designing and carrying out research in general, broadened their understanding of the way students learn about the learning process, enriched everyday teaching and interactions with students, and helped them to view research by others in a new light. Lytle worked with teams of literacy instructors, learners, and researchers to base instructional assessment on in-depth interviews conducted by both instructors and senior students.

An international literacy story helps to put into telling perspective the importance of which measures we use. The World Bank and the International Monetary Fund (IMF) use economic indicators such as GNP or average income to determine and target lending practices; but these figures may not be the best measures of a society's development. Means as measures can hide the great disparity between rich and poor. Literacy indicators, by contrast, seem to tell far more about the changing conditions of life.

According to H.S. Bhola (personal communication, November 1989), UNICEF found that mothers who have even a little schooling suffer a lower infant death rate than do mothers without any education. Women who have been to school also control their birth rate better than women who have not been to school. Tanzania is a case in point. Although it is among the least developed nations, and per capita income remains low, infant mortality rates have dropped substantially, as has the birth rate. Controlling for other significant factors, the best explanation of the drop in both birth rate and infant mortality rate is the relatively high literacy rate in Tanzania. Consequently, UNICEF has concluded that literacy is the most dependable indicator of progress in a society; it has recommended that the

World Bank/IMF make literacy a factor in its targeting and lending decisions for emerging nations. By contrast, the United States has an embarassingly high infant mortality rate compared with other industrialized nations—almost twice that of Japan, Sweden, or Switzerland (U.S. Bureau of the Census, 1989), which suggests the toll that illiteracy is taking in the United States in many forms.

Adult literacy requires a lot of measurement. We want to know how we are doing and what information to use in formulating better policies, programs, and instructional and individual decisions. The measurement efforts of the past form a sturdy foundation for the work to come, if we keep in mind both their strengths and their limitations.

References

Aceland, H. (1976, July). If reading scores are irrelevant, do we have anything better? *Educational Technology, 16*(7).

Barnes, R. (1986). *Adult illiteracy estimates for states*. Washington, DC: U.S. Department of Education.

Brescia, W. (1988). *Literacy among American Indians*. Unpublished manuscript.

Brizius, J.A., & Foster, S.E. (1987). *Enhancing adult literacy: A policy guide*. Washington, DC: Council of State Policy and Planning Agencies.

Delker, P.V. (1984). *Ensuring effective adult literacy policies and procedures at the federal and state levels*. Washington, DC: Office of Vocational and Adult Education.

Fargo, J.E., & Collins, M. (1989). Learning from researching: Literacy practitioners and assessment of adults' reading progress. *Journal of Reading, 33*, 120-125.

Final Report: The American performance level study. (1977). Washington, DC: U.S. Office of Education, Department of Health, Education, and Welfare.

Fischer, J.K., Haney, W., & David, L. (1980). APL *revisited: Its uses and adaptation in states*. Washington, DC: U.S. Department of Education, Office of Educational Research and Improvement, and National Institute of Education.

Fischer, D.L. (1977). *Functional literacy and the schools*. Washington, DC: National Institute of Education and U.S. Department of Health, Education, and Welfare.

Folger, J.K., & Nam, C.B. (1965). *A 1960 census monograph: The education of the American population*. Washington, DC: U.S. Bureau of the Census.

Gadway, C., & Wilson, H.A. (1976). *Functional illiteracy: Basic reading performance*. Denver, CO: Education Commission of the States. (ED 112 350)

Goldberg, S. (1951). *Army training of illiterates in World War II*. New York: Publications, Teachers College, Columbia University.

Gray, W.S. (1956). How well do adults read? In N.B. Henry (Ed.), *Adult reading*. The Fifty-fifth Yearbook of the National Society for the Study of Education. Chicago, IL: University of Chicago Press.

Griffith, W.S., & Cervero, R.M. (1977). The Adult Performance Level program: A serious and deliberate examination. *Adult Education, 27*(4).

Harris, L., & Associates. (1970). *Survival literacy study*. Washington, DC: National Reading Council. (ED 068 813)

Harris, L., & Associates. (1971). *The 1971 national reading difficulty index: A study of functional reading ability in the United States*. Washington, DC: National Reading Council.

Heckler, M.M. (1970, November). How many Americans read well enough to survive? Washington, DC: *Congressional Record*, 38036-38040.

Hunter, C.S., & Harman, D. (1979). *Adult illiteracy in the United States*. New York: Mc-Graw-Hill.

Irwin, P.M. (1985). *Adult literacy issues, programs, and options*. Washington, DC: Education and Welfare Division, Congressional Research Service. Issue Brief (Order Code IB85167).

Isenberg, I. (Ed.). (1964). *The drive against illiteracy*. New York; H.W. Wilson.

Kaestle, C.F. (1985). The history of literacy and the history of readers. In E.W. Gordon (Ed.), *Review of research in education* (vol. 12). Washington, DC: American Educational Research Association.

Kazemek, F.E. (1985). An examination of the Adult Performance Level project and its effects upon adult literacy education in the United States. *Lifelong Learning, 9*(2), 24-28.

Kazemek, F.E. (1988). Necessary changes: Professional involvement in adult literacy programs. *Harvard Educational Review, 58*(4), 464-486.

Kirsch, I.S. (1990). Measuring adult literacy. In R. Venezky, D. Wagner, & B. Ciliberti (Eds.), *Toward defining literacy*. Newark, DE: International Reading Association.

Kirsch, I.S., & Guthrie, J.T. (1978). The concept and measurement of functional literacy. *Reading Research Quarterly, 13*, 485-507.

Kirsch, I.S., & Jungeblut, A. (1986). *Literacy: Profiles of America's young adults*. (No. 16-PL-02). Princeton, NJ: Educational Testing Service.

Kozol, J. (1985). *Illiterate America*. New York: Anchor Press/Doubleday.

Lytle, S. (1988, October). *Assessment in adult literacy*. Paper presented at the Modern Language Association Conference, Columbus, OH.

Lytle, S., & Wolfe, M. (1990). *Adult literacy: Assessment and evaluation*. Columbus, OH: ERIC Clearinghouse on Adult, Career, and Vocational Education.

McGrail, J. (1984). *Adult illiterates and adult literacy programs: A summary of descriptive data*. San Francisco, CA: National Adult Literacy Project, Far West Laboratory.

Metz, E. (1989). *The issue: Adult literacy assessment*. Bloomington, IN: ERIC Digest.

Mikulecky, L. (1986). *The status of literacy in our society*. Paper presented at the annual meeting of the National Reading Conference, Austin, TX. (ED 281 182)

Murphy, R.T. (1975). Assessment of adult reading competence. In D.M. Neilsen & H.F. Hjelm (Eds.), *Reading and career education* (pp. 50-61). Newark, DE: International Reading Association.

National Association of State Boards of Education. (1968). *State adult literacy initiatives*. Report of a National Conference and a Survey of State Programs. (ED 277 871)

Northcutt, N. (1975). *Adult functional competency: A summary*. Austin, TX: University of Texas.

Popham, J.W., & Lindheim, E. (1981, September). Implications of a landmark ruling on Florida's minimum competency test. *Phi Delta Kappan, 63*, 18-20.

Stecher, B., & Solarzano, R. (1988, July). *Designing a computer system for monitoring and reporting adult learners' progress*. Paper presented at the Adult Literacy and Technology Conference, Pittsburgh, PA.

Stedman, L.C., & Kaestle, C.F. (1987). Literacy and reading performance in the United States from 1800 to the present. *Reading Research Quarterly, 22*, 8-46.

Sticht, T.G. (1990). Measuring adult literacy: A response. In R.L. Venezky, D. Wagner, & B. Ciliberti (Eds.), *Toward defining literacy*. Newark, DE: International Reading Association.

U.S. Bureau of the Census. (1989). *Current population reports: Current consumer income*, Series P-60, No. 162. Washington, DC: U.S. Bureau of the Census.

U.S. Bureau of the Census. (1987). *Current population reports: Educational attainment in the United States*, Series P-20, No. 428. Washington, DC: U.S. Bureau of the Census.

U.S. Bureau of the Census. (1959). *Current population reports: Population characteristics*, Series P-20, No. 99. Washington, DC: U.S. Bureau of the Census.

U.S. Bureau of the Census. (1986). *Current population reports: Population characteristics*, Series P-20, No. 425. Washington, DC: U.S. Bureau of the Census.

U.S. Bureau of the Census. (1976). *Historical statistics of the United States: Colonial items to 1970* (pt. 1). Washington, DC: U.S. Bureau of the Census.

U.S. Bureau of the Census. (1989). *1989 statistical abstract, table 1405, and unpublished data estimates*. Washington, DC: U.S. Government Printing Office.

Venezky, R.L., Kaestle, C.F., & Sum, A.M. (1987). *The subtle danger*. Princeton, NJ: Educational Testing Service.

4

The Emergence of Thinking about Adult Literacy

T he metaphor of a garden comes naturally to mind when we think about the development of thought in the study of adult literacy; and in our garden, we find both roots and holes. The literacy roots are healthy and tenacious in their hold, despite adverse conditions, and they support and nourish today's garden of adult literacy. These roots are the early work of the literacy pioneers who shaped our past and present literacy. We acknowledge and use their work to form our own actions and define the issues. The holes in our garden are the questions that remain unexplored or unconvincingly answered.

Pioneer Efforts

At the beginning of the twentieth century, labor unions, businesses, and community organizations directed literacy efforts toward immigrants, either to educate them or to limit their impact on society (Cook, 1977). Blodgett's 1894 review of the illiteracy statistics in the 1890 census contains a vivid sense of one attitude about the immigrants. He categorized them into "two very unlike groups."

> One group brings thrift and industry, and more or less of worldly means to add to the resources of the nation; the other is ignorant, with more brutal instincts and with scanty

possessions, imbued with prejudices corresponding to the narrowness of its information, constituting a dangerous element (p. 229).

Blodgett's concerns were not limited to the immigrants. As he compared literacy rates in the North, Midwest, and South, he asserted that the "native-born Anglo-Saxon element" and their institutions were endangered by "the negro and the immigrant" (p. 232). Finally, he closed the door on adult literacy efforts by declaring that those between 10 and 21 years old might be taught to read, but those above 21 "we cannot reach and must consider as confirmed illiterates" (p. 235).

The pioneers in adult literacy devoted their work to refuting the view of Blodgett and others like him.

Alfred Fitzpatrick

Meanwhile, Alfred Fitzpatrick, a contemporary of Blodgett's, started a lifelong crusade in Canada to "take education to the people." Not sharing Blodgett's view about "confirmed illiterates, he founded the Reading Tent Association, which later became Frontier College, in 1899. Fitzpatrick recruited students to go to work camps to assist workers with reading, writing, mathematics, and citizenship. An early incident transformed the first efforts. Angus Grey, a volunteer, was bored waiting all day for his worker-students to come to class after their shifts, so he went to work as a logger. Grey was the first "laborer-teacher"; he provided a model for self-supporting literacy workers who would, through work shared with their students, lay the groundwork for rapport, trust, and equality, and therefore be effective teachers. Both the workers and the laborer-teachers needed to learn to survive, so they developed a "learning exchange among equals" (Pierpoint, 1987, p. 279). Their teaching and programs were elaborated for a specific group of learners, and hence varied widely.

By 1919 more than 600 volunteer instructors had been trained and served all over Canada. Fitzpatrick (1919) wrote the *Handbook for New Canadians,* which became the basis for most ESL instruction. He initiated correspondence degree programs, although mail-order schooling was controversial. Another innovation was to send women "outriders" to bring educational opportunities to isolated women homesteaders. Following Fitzpatrick's vision, Frontier College concentrated on society's castaways, including isolated people throughout Canada.

Cora Stewart

In 1911 Cora Stewart, the superintendent of public schools in Rowan County, Kentucky, founded the "moonlight schools," scheduling classes on nights when there was enough moonlight to travel to and from class after a day of work. The original moonlight school was staffed by teachers who volunteered to meet adult classes several times a week from 7 to 9 p.m. These teachers were also responsible for recruiting students in their districts. More than 1,200 students enrolled for the first session, confounding other educators who were skeptical of the plan. Stewart's commentary (1917, p. 83) gives a sense of her style and leadership:

> They said the idea was preposterous. Some psychologists even said that grown people could not learn to read and write. I said to them, "In heaven's name, when a fact disputes a theory, isn't it time to discard the theory?" But they went around saying it couldn't be done, and we just went along doing it.

Since no texts were available, Stewart printed reading material in a newspaper written especially for the school. The papers contained local news, written in simple sentences with repetitive vocabulary for the new readers. The curriculum included drills in basic language, history, civics, agriculture, and sanitation. The moonlight school tablet contained the student's name to trace on layers of colored blotting paper. The colors promoted interest, and grooves for the new writers' pencil to follow in forming the letters of their names contributed to students' success.

Stewart also wrote two *Country Life Readers* that described the problems of rural life; they were written at a level between first and second grade. The books, complete with photographs and illustrations, were divided into lessons that began with a list of new words and ended with sentences to copy. One lesson, for instance, was on taxes. As "taxation is the cause of much unintelligent complaint," Stewart reasoned, "some enlightenment on the subject seemed worthwhile" (1922, p. 73). The sentences to be copied included the following:

> I pay a tax on my home.
> I pay a tax on my land.
> I pay a tax on my money.
> I pay a tax on many other things.
> Where does all the money go?
> It goes to keep the schools.
> It goes to keep up the roads.
> It goes to keep down crime.
> It goes to keep down disease.

Stewart contributed to the war effort through her moonlight classes, helping men become literate enough to join the armed forces. Special materials were written with the would-be soldiers in mind. Her books were distributed to more than 50,000 soldiers during World War I.

Stewart's moonlight schools prompted the establishment of literacy commissions; she headed one of the first of these. Since little money was available, she relied on volunteers, who made a thorough count of all the illiterates in their counties and then set out to eliminate illiteracy. Stewart asserted that illiteracy could be eradicated in Kentucky in a 6-year crusade. Such a crusade could be made successful, she said, by attaching a stigma to the inability to read:

> There is an odium attached to it today that was lacking in the years gone by. Illiteracy has been stigmatized where the crusade against it has been waged and made to seem a thing to flee as from leprosy (1922, p. 155).

The moonlight schools became the model for programs in other states, and Stewart's legacy continues in volunteer staffed literacy programs. Some newspapers still publish special sections for new adult readers. Cook (1977, p. 13) suggested that Stewart's work "might well be classified as the official beginning of literacy education in the United States."

Stewart's literacy creed (except for her traditional use of gender-exclusive language) could be a contemporary statement:

> I believe that the public school should be as liberal in its policy as is the church. I don't believe that it has any right to say to men and women, "If you did not embrace me before a certain time in life, I will close my doors to you forever." I believe that the hour of a man's opportunity should be the hour in which he awakens to his need—whether that be at the age of six or a hundred and six (1917, p. 89).

William S. Gray

William S. Gray made many contributions to the field of reading. His interests included standardized oral reading tests, diagnosis and remedial instruction, school surveys, international education and literacy, adult reading, summaries of investigations and practices, and models of reading. The International Reading Association dubbed him "Mr. Reading." In 1985, Gray was profiled in a monograph published on the centenary of his birth. Unless otherwise noted, the materials that follow came from that source (Stevenson, 1985).

Gray's attention was drawn to adult reading by test results suggesting that children were growing up without sufficient reading skills. He was a proponent of lifelong learning "that will inspire the present and future life of the reader and provide for the wholesome use of leisure time" (Gray, 1925).

In a 1929 study of adult reading habits and interests based on interviews with diverse adult readers, Gray and Monroe (1929) concluded that millions of native-born Americans were illiterate. Some had never learned to read; others had lost their reading skills through disuse after they left school. Gray and Monroe thought that much of what was being read was low quality and therefore unlikely to encourage individual growth and social enlightenment.

By 1930, Gray had written a manual for teachers of illiterates. Dissatisfied with the census question "Can you read or write or both?" and the statistics on illiteracy they produced, Gray worked to define literacy this way:

> A person is functionally literate when he has acquired the knowledge and skills in reading and writing which enable him to engage effectively in all those activities in which literacy is normally assumed in his cultural group.

Gray described the point at which reading becomes a transforming process:

> [The] crucial point along the route to maturity in reading is the time at which reading begins to inspire the reader, to give him a feeling of pleasure and satisfaction in the activity, and to exert a conscious integrative effect upon him (Gray & Rodgers, 1956, p. 237).

In 1931, Gray directed summer reading sessions in South Carolina, and engaged in a companion study to examine the potential progress of adults under favorable learning conditions. Gray found that both formal and informal training were important and that easy-to-read materials were needed.

> In teaching those who are illiterate, major emphasis should be given to those types of instruction that will provide a broader understanding of practical everyday problems, that will increase their personal and social efficiency, and that will stimulate new interests and aspirations (Gray, 1933, p. 281).

Gray's concept of adult reading proceeded from his conviction that reading contributes both to the development of the individual and to the solution of social problems. These views fit the social reconstructionist ideas of the 1930s. In his studies Gray included both marginal literates and proficient readers as he sought to improve professional practice in reading instruction. He drew vital attention to the need to educate adults as adults, and not merely to recapitulate teaching methods used with children. His definition of literacy foreshadowed the context-specific, relativist definitions that take into account the needs of individuals within their own settings and communities.

Ambrose Caliver

Ambrose Caliver, born in 1894 in Virginia, was the first employee of the U.S. Office of Education to specialize in the education of black Americans. Educated at Knoxville College, the University of Wisconsin, Teachers College Columbia, Tuskegee Institute, and Harvard University, he was an advocate of programs to improve the reading of adults. He conducted surveys, compiled bibliographies, and issued bulletins. After World War II, he was the director of the Project for Literacy Education (Ohles, 1978). Caliver's philosophy is clear in the following statement:

> The best means a person has in making sound judgments is through the written word. It follows, therefore, that in our representative form of government, where each individual is sovereign, it is imperative that he be literate enough to exercise his sovereignty with intelligence and discretion (Mobilizing for Action, 1962, p. 33).

Frank Laubach

Frank Laubach launched the worldwide "Each One Teach One" approach to literacy. He asserted that to promote literacy is to change people's conscience by changing their relationship to their environment, and that such an undertaking is on the same plane as the recognition and incarnation of fundamental human rights.

Laubach believed that everyone has a right to read and to have access to human culture through the printed word. He also believed that literate adults have a responsibility to help others become literate, and that both literacy and literacy programs function as agents of change in society.

An educator, sociologist, and minister, Laubach believed that control of the printed word would empower people. As founder of Laubach Literacy International, he developed his approach to literacy because he wanted to teach people to read life skills materials and religious books in their own (sometimes previously unwritten) languages. He first developed a written language for the Muslim Moro tribe in the Philippines. When his funds were cut, Laubach turned to volunteer teachers—thus the "each one teach one" approach was born. The magnitude of his effort is reflected in its sheer numbers: he directed literacy campaigns in 65 countries, developed the literacy charts and primers for 312 languages, and cowrote primers in more than 165 languages (many of which already had written forms, but not these beginning literacy materials).

Laubach's reading method was based on phonics, using what he called "key words" for consonant and vowel sounds. His method is now often identified as a bottom-up approach to reading instruction because of the early emphasis on decoding and structural analysis (Meyer & Keefe, 1988). Many national governments have adopted the Laubach approach to teaching reading.

Adaptation of the Laubach principles to English language materials began being tested in the 1940s and later evolved into the present *Laubach Way to Reading* series. Laubach Literacy Action (LLA) was organized in 1969 to bring Laubach's methods to the United States and Canada and to meet the needs of volunteer-based literacy programs (Kearney, 1988). Laubach's son Robert continued the literacy efforts of his father and established New Reader's Press, one of the largest publishers of materials for adult learners. In 1989, 80,000 volunteers and 100,000 learners were using the Laubach methods in 750 programs affiliated with LLA.

Welthy Honsinger Fisher

Welthy Honsinger Fisher believed that literacy made people independent and that it was a country's energizer. She tirelessly advocated literacy, even when others lost interest. She was an opera singer turned social activist who married a missionary and worked with him in China until he died. Fisher then traveled to India, visiting missions and becoming acquainted with the country. She heard Laubach speak, and commented in her diary, "He's a real find, a sweetly mystical sermon" (Swenson, 1988, p. 253). Fisher worked initially with Laubach's organization in India, but they later parted company over the aims of their literacy work. Fisher was committed to secular literacy, whereas Laubach stated, "When the religious motive is cut off, my power with audience ceases and my own enthusiasm dies" (Swensen, p. 336).

At the age of 73, Fisher founded Literacy House in Lucknow, India, at the urging of Mahatma Gandhi. She regarded India's 80 percent illiteracy rate as its most pressing problem; illiteracy prevented action against poverty, primitive conditions, and the caste system. World Education, an organization devoted to betterment of the lives of people around the world, grew out of the need to fund Literacy House. Literacy House became the center of research and development in literacy; thousands of teachers were trained there. Although her literacy work was centered in India, Fisher's theory and mission were international.

Fisher's approach to literacy was to work through local people. Her primer was based on teaching reading through whole sentences that were adult, secular, and socially relevant. Rural libraries (books carried on horses or bicycles) were established. Fisher used puppet shows to further literacy and social development. An early visitor to Literacy House reported the program in action:

> Last night I watched our trainees teaching in two villages. A brilliant starlit night, and the whole landscape dotted with lanterns and candles around which sat little rings of villagers reading loudly. The air was full of their happy chanting. Animals, always close at hand in India, listened and watched (Swenson, 1988, p. 324).

Fisher received numerous, unusual honors in recognition of her literacy work. She was the first (and the only non-Indian) recipient of the Nehru Literacy Award, and was pictured on an Indian commemorative stamp in 1980. She was given the Pioneer Award of the Adult Education Association of America and the Ramon Magsaysay Award (called by some the Asian Nobel Prize). The Dalai Lama and Mother Theresa are among its other recipients.

Moving on from Mid-Century: America in the International World of Literacy

Like Laubach and Fisher, several later literacy advocates worked in a variety of countries and established their theories in societies where print is less pervasive than in the highly literate societies of North America. Their work, combined with the efforts of those working in the United States, has advanced the field of literacy over the past several decades.

Sarah Gudschinsky

Gudschinsky provided insights with potential value for literacy work in North America as well as in the so-called developing world. As a linguist associated with the Summer Institute of Linguistics, she expected to find diverse literacy teaching approaches around the world in the mid-1950s. To her surprise, she found common features among the programs she considered successful:

- Meaningful material provided from the beginning, written in a style of language and in cultural concepts already familiar to the reader.
- Meaningful material connected in a form that fits the discourse patterns of the language.
- Frequency counts of sentence types, function words, and letters to help identify familiar sets of symbols and words that allow the use of interesting stories from the beginning of literacy instruction.
- Development of reading independence that requires learners to recognize parts of words — syllables and letters. (This usually requires drill material.)
- Introduction of elements in a controlled fashion, so the learner is not overwhelmed with too many new things at once.
- Recognition by teachers and curriculum designers that the difficulty of learning an item (such as consonant blends) is not inherent in the item or its position, but is related more to its point of introduction in the course sequence (Van Dyken, 1984).

Gudschinsky considered a learner's ability to talk about language a form of language awareness that may not be part of everyday experiences, so she included learning to talk about language as an element in the preliteracy stage before learners used the primers. She respected the learners as "competent in their culture, thought, and language" (Van Dyken), and consulted learners on their intuitive sense of how the language should be, valuing their opinion above linguistic analyses of languages for which she was inventing a writing system.

Gudschinsky is known for the sets of drills she designed to teach sound-symbol correspondences by introducing letters in syllables rather than in isolation. But she believed that the most important element in teaching literacy was the use of actual reading experiences using materials with the natural rhythms and expression of the language. She integrated what have come to be labeled top-down and bottom-up processing in the curricula she designed (Van Dyken, 1984).

Mary C. Wallace

In the late 1960s, books on how to teach illiterate adults were scarce. Robert E. Allen of the Educational Division of Follett Publishing Company characterized the situation this way:

> Prior to 1950 little interest had developed in this area, except for teaching English to the foreign-born, most of whom were not illiterate. Research in the subject was practically nonexistent and, even more important, practical experience — the experience that comes from trial and error in life situations — was also nonexistent; or at least such records were not readily available. The teaching fraternity, busy with school problems, had no time for illiterate adults and, like the rest of the community, pretended they did not exist (Wallace, 1965, p. vii).

After 2 years of traveling around the United States in search of programs designed especially for the adult illiterate and the culturally disadvantaged, Allen discovered Mary C. Wallace, who had started her work among the migrant workers in the fruit orchards of Washington. Allen was particularly impressed because Wallace not only had learned how to teach the illiterate and the culturally disadvantaged by trial and error, but she also had carried out a careful testing program. Her students became evangelists for the program, plunging in with little training, but obviously fired up by Wallace's enthusiasm.

Wallace was respected in the community because of what she had done for the disadvantaged. She made sure that her Literacy and Related Knowledge (LARK) schoolteachers did not fail or permit their students to fail. She said they "cannot fail today and succeed tomorrow; for if they fail today, they will not be back tomorrow" (p. ix). Her students kept coming back.

Wallace had a directness of approach that included anyone who would help. She believed that starting a literacy program was as simple as calling friends, giving them some quick training, and getting on with the class. Her teachers soon wanted further instruction, and once they got to know their students, they became promoters of the literacy program. "With very little publicity and effort, more teachers will be forthcoming. Don't be afraid to make a start. Many people are glad to help in any way they can" (p. 46).

Wallace's teaching of literacy was strongly flavored by her commitment to showing her students what she wanted them to do and be. She taught by example. "Courtesy and tolerance are the marks of a good citizen—as the good teacher will try constantly to demonstrate" (p. 114).

Wallace believed that something could be done about the literacy problem, and she did it. Hundreds of adults came out of her classes reading, holding jobs, and leading fruitful family lives.

Myles Horton

Myles Horton was a talented community organizer who believed that people who worked together could solve their own problems. He attended Columbia University, took courses from many of the progressive thinkers of the time—including Reinhold Niebuhr, John Dewey, and Eduard Lindeman—and made a trip to Denmark to see folk schools in action (community-based schools for the preservation of local culture and solution of local problems). When Horton decided he was ready to open his own school, he returned to Tennessee and set up the Highlander Folk School.

The first Highlander agenda was to help local workers unionize and demand higher wages and better working conditions. Groups of workers would meet at Highlander, search for strategies, and put them into action. They dodged bullets, rallied people with music composed for specific fights ("We Shall Overcome" was modified by Zilphia Horton and Pete Seeger into its present form from a song taught to her on a picket line), and confronted the legislated racism of the time. Rosa Parks attended a problem-solving session at Highlander the week before she became the center of national attention by refusing to move to the back of the bus in Birmingham.

In the 1950s, Septima Clark, a black teacher, came to Horton's attention when she was censured and then fired by her school system for attending racially mixed socials. Horton encouraged her to put her educational talents to work in other ways by becoming Highlander's director of education. She was drawn to the difficulties of rural blacks, so she and Horton analyzed the literacy needs of residents of John's Island, off the Georgia coast. They found that adult education programs were not effective in reaching the residents of rural communities unless they were taught by people of that community. Clark and others from Highlander trained local teachers and supported them in their instruction. It was found that outsiders, however, destroyed the learning environment when they attended the classes.

These "Citizenship Schools" focused on teaching adults what they needed to know as members of the political community—this was not a children's curriculum. Would-be voters learned how to read state constitutions, election laws, and the United Nations Declaration on Human Rights. For the most part, classes focused on neither workplace skills nor conventional academic skills but on obtaining political power and on mastery of life's daily needs. Costs were low since teachers were volunteers, and classes were held in community locations. Education professionals were used as advocates and supporters. Highlander turned over the support of these classes to the Southern Christian Leadership Conference (SCLC) when Tennessee state officials, in their drive to close Highlander, imperiled the program. The Citizenship Schools taught an estimated 100,000 black people to read and write so they could register and vote, making it one of the major literacy efforts in U.S. history. Citizenship Schools continued until the 1970s (Adams & Horton, 1975; Hunter & Harman, 1979).

Don Brown and Anabel Newman

In the mid-1960s, Don Brown and Anabel Newman undertook a study in Buffalo, New York, to look at experimental factors pertinent to adult reading instruction. At the time, Buffalo was a city in transition. The downtown area had been largely demolished and not yet rebuilt; its population was largely black, and 72,000 of its innercity residents were said to be functionally illiterate. The summer of 1967 was marred by racial disturbances; the youth of the city were in turmoil.

It was against this backdrop that Brown and Newman worked. They wanted to find out where adult basic education (ABE) students came from, what education they had, the effects of their deprivation, the kinds of experiences they had (farm, factory, housework), their interests, and their abilities and academic skills. What kinds of things did they need to know? How well had they learned to function within their environment?

Brown and Newman's final report turned up information that has kept its significance. The 207 adults they studied who read below third grade level (all from Buffalo and Niagara Falls, New York) were:

- Less likely to show gains in reading achievement if they were on welfare.
- More likely to be stimulated in an educational experience if they had been stimulated in a previous school experience.
- More easily taught to read if their parents' occupations involved some degree of communication, and if they had family members who read to them.

- More likely to make gains in reading if they possessed a radio or phonograph or if they could use the telephone.
- More likely to make gains in reading if their book preferences related to science, travel, or social or utilitarian topics.
- More likely to profit from reading instruction if their time sense (i.e., knowledge of days, months, seasons) was developed to some extent. Also, map skills such as identifying railroad markings and finding shortest routes correlated with success in reading (Brown & Newman, 1968).

Brown and Newman's recommendations concerning adult illiterates are as valid today as they were in 1968.

1. Provide greater stimulation and communication in classes to improve the reading learning rate of adult illiterates. Include relevant discussions in every class period. Involve nonverbal students in daily discussions. Provide warranted praise and recognition. Engage family members in support of literacy training. Build ties between libraries and adult students. Develop book centers in schools, especially in classrooms.
2. Improve attendance. Encourage adults to improve their educational status. Locate adult programs within walking distance of students or in areas easily accessible by bus. Subsidize attendance, especially for welfare recipients. Cover bus fare and break-time refreshment costs for financially marginal families. Make child care available. Include more adult-centered materials dealing with home, employment, and personal and family needs. Follow up on students who drop out of class. Communicate genuine interest in the needs of the student and suggest solutions to problems that may inhibit attendance.
3. Check the student's general knowledge.
4. Provide materials and experiences with utilitarian values. Adults want more education to get a job, learn special

skills, or be able to read the newspaper or the Bible. Adult learners want experiences that make their time investment worthwhile.

The recommendations for method that grew out of the study were as follows:

1. Construct standardized measures of beginning reading ability from adult vocabulary, adult concepts, and with adult pictures. For more informal inventories, use test materials from what adults are reading.
2. Teach adults how to follow written and spoken directions.
3. Use relevant adult materials: how to make home repairs, figure mortgage interest rates, use credit cards, write checks, balance a check book, use a telephone book, or read a map.
4. Pace learning to the needs of adults, including low-level materials that will ensure success from the beginning. Adults need meaningful repetition.
5. Include frequent reinforcement and short range goals.
6. Upgrade teacher competencies. Expose them to a broad cross section of materials, including demonstrations and practice in how to evaluate materials. Include observation and conference time. Ensure competence with various media, including computers.
7. Assign a special teacher to work with small groups of incoming students, orienting them to class work, the educational situation, and the building.
8. Explore variables that may predict reading success.
9. Develop other instruments to differentiate the learning capacities of adult city-core populations.

H.S. Bhola

H.S. Bhola grew up in India, took his higher education in the United States, and divided his working life between America and the Third World. In his personal experience he bridged the world of literacy. After working for more than 12 years in India, he joined a

UNESCO team working on a pilot literacy project in Tanzania. Through his research at Indiana University and his work as a literacy consultant, Bhola influenced the development of literacy policy at the United Nations Development Program (UNDP), UNESCO, the United States Agency for International Development (USAID), and the German Foundation for International Development.

An ardent champion of literacy, Bhola asserted, "You can do no wrong by doing literacy. Even if it appears to serve narrow purposes in the short run, literacy ultimately liberates" (personal communication, October 1989). Bhola (1988, p. 670) classified efforts for literacy development into three dominant, continuous categories (see Table 1). In his motivational-developmental model, individual motivations are emphasized. The planned development model concentrates on institution building for reform in nationwide programs aimed at development and quality of life in the society. The structural-developmental model focuses on revolutionary change and mass participation to promote growth with equity. These three categories apply to school systems as well as political systems: "Revolutionary societies favor universalization of primary education, reformist societies talk of manpower training, and gradualists continue with elitist systems of education free to the privileged" (1988,

Table 1
Political Model of Literacy Development Efforts

Motivational- Developmental Model		Planned Development Model		Structural- Developmental Model
Gradualist	➡	Reformist	➡	Revolutionary
Organic growth		Growth with efficiency		Growth with equity
Project approach to literacy		Program approach to literacy		Campaign approach to literacy

p. 670). Bhola favors the campaign approach to literacy, thinking it the strategy most commensurate with current needs. He supports the role of the state in sustaining literacy work, especially in the Third World, where the state may be the only agent of social transformation.

Bhola's observations of change over time in countries around the world bolstered his staunch advocacy of literacy. In 1989, he evaluated the national literacy program in Zimbabwe. Acquainted with the country for 20 years, he was struck by the differences increased literacy was making in society. He noted that the effects of literacy appeared in everyday life. When husbands became literate, they began to view their wives as important. Once wives became literate, they shared in family decisions and became active users of the information around them. In economic realms, people became vendors, started poultry farms and vegetable gardens, and set up a credit society.

Bhola has found that, in all the languages, the metaphors of literacy are *freedom* and *light*. Newly literate people say they have come out of the shadows and have seen the light.

Paulo Freire

Paulo Freire's analysis of literacy has had a powerful impact on the thinking and practice of adult literacy instruction around the world. Two interwoven strands of his work—his theoretical analysis of literacy education and his critical pedagogy for literacy acquisition—are the most telling for adult literacy.

Freire, a radical social tranformationist, was seeking to change society through assailing the political, economic, and legal institutions that he saw as oppressive. He proposed revolutionary, rather than evolutionary, change. Adult educators, in his view, must be instrumental in this revolutionary process and must not delude themselves into thinking that adult education is a value-neutral activity.

Empowerment and *emancipation* are at the heart of Freire's work. According to Freire, education must illuminate the power relationships in society and teach the learner how to participate in and change those power structures. As Freire developed his theories, he moved from disconnecting politics and education to seeing education as an aspect of politics to affirming that "education is politics" (Shor & Freire, 1987).

Freire saw that illiterate, oppressed peoples live in a "culture of silence." He talked about "marginal men" but argued that the excluded people have not chosen to be marginal; they have been "expelled from and kept outside of the social system" (Freire, 1970, p. 402). Marginal people, he said, are dependent on a dehumanizing social structure, and the only way out of it is to transform it—not to enter into it. The oppressed understand that they are oppressed but do not understand the causes of their oppression. Fostering this understanding of the reasons for oppression is the role of critical consciousness. Reflective dialogue is not enough; it must be coupled with action to produce transformations in society. Power to transform the world comes from being literate; that is the motivation for learning to read and write.

> Thus...teaching men to read and write is no longer an inconsequential matter of *ba, be, bi, bo, bu,* or memorizing an alienated word, but a difficult apprenticeship of naming the world (Freire, p. 402).

When educators participate as equals with adult learners in the "true dialogue" of problem-posing sessions, they facilitate greater understanding of the reasons for oppression. In Freire's view, this mode of social learning is in contrast to the typical approach he calls "banking education," wherein the teacher deposits information in the passive student. "This teaching cannot be done from the top down, but only from the inside out, by the illiterate himself with the collaboration of the teacher" (Freire, 1970, p. 404).

Freire rejected the idea of using primers in literacy training because they are the words of others, not of the learner. "Words should be laden with the meaning of the people's existential experience, not of the teacher's experience" (Freire, 1983, p. 10). The role of the teacher is to enter into dialogue with illiterates about the concrete situations of their lives and to offer them the instruments with which they can teach themselves to read and write.

After leaving Brazil in 1964, Freire worked in West Africa as well as in Nicaragua. He continued to develop his liberatory pedagogy, defending it with an exposition of dialogic pedagogy, which must be characterized by structure, discipline, and rigor. Teachers and students must transform themselves despite their fears and the risks of transformation. He has continued to explore whether "first world" students need liberating, how teachers can overcome language differences with the students, and how to begin practicing liberatory ideas in the classroom (Shor & Freire, 1987).

Organizational Involvement

The U.S. Military

The Armed Forces have conducted the most consistently funded and energetically pursued adult literacy programs in the United States. Since many recruits are insufficiently literate to perform their tasks, the military has been forced to provide job-oriented and functional literacy training. In wartime, the services have had to induct and train large numbers of people deemed illiterate; in peacetime, the process is more selective. Duffy (1985, p. 114) noted:

> Because of the strong technological base of the military systems, the use of printed text is not only more pervasive than in society as a whole, but text is also a more critical component of daily life. It is the primary means of transmitting technical information to millions of personnel distributed worldwide.

Goldberg's (1951) study of literacy training in the Armed Forces yielded a remarkable picture: more than 250,000 men learned to read in 12- to 16-week training sessions. During World War II, Goldberg assisted in the development, coordination, and supervision of the Army's literacy program, and studied the program's effectiveness. He wanted to identify components of the Army's programs that could be applied in civilian education. Goldberg described the Army program as "a necessary and expedient means of preparing hundreds of thousands of marginal [slow learning] soldier personnel for effective Army service" (p. 267). He concluded that the majority of the men taught in the program were "salvaged for useful Army service" (p. 272).

During World War II, the Army took three distinct approaches to induction of illiterates. The first effort followed a 6-month period at the beginning of the war, during which the Army observed adjustment difficulties by illiterate recruits. Then the Army began classifying as "illiterates" men who could not read at the fourth grade level, and deferring them from military service until they could learn to read. Nevertheless, coordinated efforts to increase literacy outside the military before induction were unsuccessful.

When this first effort failed to produce literate recruits, literacy requirements were first liberalized, then tightened, and finally dropped. At first, up to 10 percent of registrants could be illiterate (defined as reading below the fourth grade level). Six months later, the waiver level was reduced to 5 percent. Five months later, all literacy restrictions were removed as long as the recruits met the mental standards as determined by the Army's intelligence test.

Goldberg (1951, p. 1) described the Army's efforts as "a comprehensive and systematic program of literacy training." The training consisted of three components: academic (instruction in reading, language expression, and arithmetic), military (prebasic training), and general (orientation, current events, workplace attitudes). The standard length of training was 12 weeks, although trainees sometimes were retrained for as long as 16 weeks. Trainees were transferred as soon as they were judged ready for regular training.

Goldberg noted that comparisons between the Army's program and adult literacy programs in general needed to be carefully made because of significant differences between civilian and military circumstances. First, the men were specially selected for (or excluded from) the programs, in contrast to the open enrollment of most adult literacy programs. Second, the Army's trainees usually were not "remedial" readers, but rather those who had had no previous access to education. Many were from rural areas.

Goldberg suggested that the Army's effort may have suffered from inefficiency because of the demands of the war, and that "civilian education, unhurried by the pressures of war, will be able to benefit from and improve upon the Army's program" (1951, p. 3). The opposite seems to have been the case; periods of mobilization have proved to be among the best opportunities for literacy campaigns (Arnove & Graff, 1987; Bhola, 1984). The Army's program was speedy and its results extensive and impressive.

Today's literacy programs often suffer from conditions Goldberg noted as having made the civilian preinduction programs difficult and ineffective: lack of requirement to attend, difficulty in scheduling, and insufficient funding. Some welfare programs compel attendance at either skills or job training, and some literacy classes are held at places of employment at any hour of the day or night. However, lack of funds remains a constant in adult literacy work. The Army's program did contain some characteristics that could be incorporated into civilian literacy efforts—for example, the development of appropriate materials, small teaching groups, and diversified methods of instruction.

Appalachian Adult Education Center

From 1967 to 1978 the Appalachian Adult Education Center (AAEC) was the source of a series of studies that informed regional adult literacy practice in schools, libraries, and educational television. In the mid-1970s, due to federal funding cuts, the center was restricted to serving the state of Kentucky only. Learning Center guides are still available, and the center maintains an active presence in the area through VISTA volunteers working with a local TV station. In one year (1987-1988), the center reported 8,500 inquiries, 2,000 enrollments, 1,438 GED-bound students, and 1,169 GED attainments.

George Eyster and his colleagues worked with disadvantaged adults (people over age 16 who are out of school without a high school diploma with a family income below the poverty level), categorizing them into four groups with differing needs. Membership in any category may change as circumstances change.

Group 1: Secure and self-directed, respond to group and individual instruction, can be recruited through the media

Group 2: Less economically and personally secure than Group 1, eager learners, unable to attend classes regularly because of seasonal work schedules

Group 3: Only sporadically employed, require individualized recruitment and one-to-one instruction

Group 4: Most in need but least accessible, the stationary poor, require individualized recruitment and one-to-one instruction (Hunter & Harman, 1979, p. 55).

Eyster has subsequently expanded these four categories considerably.

In the early 1970s the AAEC examined the role of libraries in adult education. Their position was that institutions must understand and accept their service role before they can serve effectively. They characterized libraries and public schools alike as resisting changes that would allow them to better serve disadvantaged adults. They provided models for service as well as lists of materials for people with reading difficulty. In their analysis of educational television, the AAEC recommended that the broadcasts be linked to a network of counselors and teachers who could help and encourage individual learners.

British Broadcasting Corporation

Great Britain and the United States have many characteristics in common: language, diverse populations of natives with their own dialects, newly immigrant groups needing instruction in the national tongue, and a need for increased literacy among all citizens. Hargreaves (1980) wrote about the BBC's contributions to the Adult Literacy Campaign in Britain, during which an estimated 125,000 adult nonreaders received some remedial instruction for the first time since leaving school. The Adult Literacy Campaign exemplified what collaborative efforts can accomplish.

The BBC's involvement in adult literacy began in the early 1970s with concerns that several million people in Great Britain were insufficiently literate to meet the demands of daily life. It was thought that radio and television might effectively reach people with literacy problems. The BBC developed three television shows, *On the Move*, *Your Move*, and *Next Move*. The programs aired during prime time and featured well-known personalities who attracted an audience regardless of their literacy status. *On the Move* contained key environmental or "survival" words and testimony from former non-readers. *Your Move* contained more direct instruction, and *Next Move* featured famous people giving 5-minute readings coordinated with widely distributed texts so that learners could read along.

The focus of the campaign soon broadened to include "multiple and overlapping educational needs," such as numeracy, and two new programs were added: *Make It Count* and *It Figures*. The television and radio broadcasts were only one portion of a plan that relied on bringing learners into contact with people who could help and encouraging them to stay with learning despite their personal and individual difficulties.

Case Studies: Close Encounters with New Readers

CJ: Motivation at Work

Seldom in adult literacy work do we have the luxury of working with a highly motivated student under the nearly ideal conditions with which Newman and her colleagues worked with CJ for 31 months. A felicitous set of circumstances had brought CJ's brother to the Reading Practicum Center at Indiana University, seeking help for CJ at the same time Newman was working on the Literacy Instructor Training films and manual. They struck a bargain. CJ would participate in the production of the films and tapes; Newman and her staff would teach CJ to read.

The history of CJ's progress serves as a model for many of the points illustrated in *Adult Basic Education: Reading* (Newman,

1980). It is important to document CJ's uniqueness, a quality shared by all adult literacy learners. CJ entered the Armed Forces as an avenue to education, but he was discharged after 6 months because of his reading and writing problems. He was reading and writing at about a first grade level when he began his literacy training. His previous educational experience had ground to a halt when he was placed in special education classes in fourth grade: "The teachers didn't know what to do with me, so they put me in special ed, and from then until high school graduation, I didn't learn anything."

After two years of literacy education, CJ was reading at a seventh grade level. Throughout the experience with CJ, which by any standards was a rich one, his teachers kept his needs and interests uppermost. In addition to Newman's tutelage, graduate student instructors worked with CJ, so he received at least 3 hours of instruction per week. When he insisted on enrolling for college classes, he was persuaded to start with swimming and bowling. He later took a class in first aid, then in beginning writing. The most successful class in helping CJ to identify his strengths was a film class in which the instructor observed that CJ had one of the most perceptive visual senses in the class, in spite of his vision impairment and thick corrective lenses.

CJ's instruction included language experience stories, individualized reading, daily writing, and pursuing goals of his choosing—getting a driver's license, locating want ads for used cars and jobs, and reading about people who had made something of themselves. Instruction also was based on such interests as CJ's guppy collection, the Navy manual (early in the instruction he was still looking to the Navy as a career), and his desire for employment. Instruction in skills was given as needed; however, as CJ seemed "hopelessly lost in spelling" (Newman, 1980, p. 153), work on spelling was postponed.

CJ's experience may help to explain why progress is so slow in adult basic education. CJ benefited from careful, highly individualized attention for at least 3 hours a week (attention that is not realistic under usual conditions in ABE instruction). Without this attention, Newman concluded that CJ might have needed months to make the kind of progress he made in weeks (p. 156).

4/19/76

[handwritten] Dune Buggies
The story is about first kind of Dune Buggies
and how they are made and they have different kinds races
they have treasure hunt to

4/20/76

6. if you had been the co. would you have kept jack at cc
why? Becuaa he woys a good man

5/14/76

[handwritten] The first car I had at the age of
fourteen, was a 1962 Galexty 500.
The The sencnd car, I bohot on
my hone was a F85. I pid 90 for it and

The first car I had. At the age of,
was a 1962 Galexty 500. The sencond c
bought on my own was a 1966 F.85. I p

7/76

[handwritten] My destination is South Haven, Indiana,
place that my family lives. I am starting

7/76

[handwritten] The role of women in society in the

First lines of stories written by C.J. during the initial months of his tutoring. Note the progression in handwriting, spelling, and most especially content, over four months of instruction.

Although CJ was not provided with a formal phonics program, he gradually began to use sounds to help figure out new words, receiving on-the-spot reinforcement from the ABE teacher. Three months after he had started the program, his tutor noted:

> He read some more in *Lou Gehrig*. He read much more fluently and is behaving differently where word attack skills are concerned. He appears to be thinking more in terms of phonemes when he attacks words now and is trying to link his knowledge of sounds in his oral language to what he now sees in print (p. 156).

One year later, CJ's writing instructor reported that he was doing "a lot better than last year." Over the months, in his desire to establish independence, CJ had added more outside jobs to his schedule. Soon he was talking about a life of his own, independent of his brother. One year after instruction had begun, CJ wrote a paper on Jimmy Hoffa, which he researched independently at the Indiana University library. Overwhelmed by the enormity of the task, he came to the office in despair. "I'll never be able to finish this," he said. But Newman offered to type it for him, and the result was a documented tribute to his growth and to the strength of his instruction.

The contrast between the pitiful young man who started and the assured, sometimes brash fellow during the second year was striking. "Occasionally CJ will call me on the telephone," Newman wrote. "He always calls me by my first name, and his voice is so assured that I sometimes don't recognize him" (p. 164). This assurance was intimately bound to CJ's new confidence as a literate person.

CJ also was reading more outside of class 2 years after instruction began. About *People* magazine he wrote:

> There was an article about John Travolta and 'Livia Newton John. They were in *Grease*. That was a good picture. I browse. If I like the picture on the cover, I read it. I read one article about Israel and Egypt. If it's of interest, I read it (p. 167).

When interviewed on national television and asked what he was reading, CJ said he kept a book about stocks in his locker and read it whenever he could. "That's the only way I'll ever get ahead." His experience proved that remarkable progress can take place in a relatively short time if the ingredients are right. In CJ's case, these ingredients included sensitivity to the learner's interests and objectives, attention to both strengths and weaknesses, and instruction based on use of the learner's language in reading and writing, without waiting for spelling to be mastered.

In her longitudinal study conducted from 1964 to 1985, Newman began in 1964-1966 by studying the lives of 406 children in the lower third of their first and second grade classes, in what was initially one of 27 "First Grade Studies" (Bond & Dykstra, 1967). From 1974 to 1976, Newman interviewed 20 of the children and their parents again, this time when the children were juniors and seniors in high school. The results of this stage of Newman's study, which were published in *Twenty Lives* (1978), initiated the examination of five variables to be further investigated in subsequent studies: models, motivation, interest, perseverance, and positive pressure.

Expanding the research questions to include the impact of literacy on occupations and schooling, Newman published new results in *Twenty Lives Revisited* (1980). Broadening her questions still further, she examined the five variables identified earlier as they related to the schooling and educational growth of young adults in her final report, *Twenty Lives Nineteen Years Later* (1985). The last set of interviews yielded information far from what might have been predicted, given the less-than-auspicious beginnings of the participants. One participant was in law practice, another was being groomed to take over the family company, and a third was working as a legal secretary. These interviews suggested that less tangible variables, most especially motivation, interest, models, perseverance, and positive pressure, had exerted strong influence on these learners.

By contrast, another student (one of the higher scorers of the low group in first grade) graduated from high school with difficulty, was plagued with continuing illness, was psychologically at odds with his family, remained unemployed, and spent 10 hours a day watching television. After interviewing his mother, Newman summarized some of the problems MK faced after high school:

> He doesn't really like to read....He can't find a job....He has a short attention span....[He] has been under pressure all his life. He has always felt he could not measure up to the accomplishments of his older brother or meet the expectations of others. Mrs. K tried to get him into a special education class when he was younger but was told his IQ was too high.

These two cases, MK and CJ, present a sharp contrast. Although they came from similar socioeconomic backgrounds, their lives took different paths. CJ attended special education classes without attaining much literacy; MK graduated from high school in regular classes. Nonetheless, it was CJ who progressed rapidly from his initial first grade reading level. CJ sought instruction; MK avoided it. CJ recognized the difference education could make in his life; MK appeared not to care. Adult literacy instruction for these two young men would have to be entirely different. We juxtapose these two cases to suggest that unless an illiterate person desires to learn, we cannot teach. America's underclass in need of further literacy is made up of people like CJ and MK. Efficiently meeting needs as diverse as these is a major challenge to the literacy worker.

Laura: Learning to Fall

Forester (1988) wrote about her close look at Laura, a part-time college student who could recognize only about 50 sight-words (words she knew without having to decode). Worse than most college students, Laura could print or write in cursive but had no spelling or composing skills. Her individual tutor used a finger as a place guide while reading text to Laura. Laura copied portions of the text to try to learn the words, and answered comprehension questions, but made little headway.

Then the instructor changed approaches. She asked Laura to begin independent writing with invented spelling. Laura's writing evolved from a few words to pages of letters and descriptions. The conventionality of her spelling increased as her letter-sound correspondence (closeness to conventional uses of letters to represent sounds and morphemes) and her reading improved with the extended practice of spelling. Laura had believed that she must spell accurately at once. Realizing that independent writing for Laura would require invented spelling in the beginning, the instructor helped Laura work through her either/or insistence on correctness or nothing.

Forester contended that the discovery of an enabling metaphor was a key to Laura's progress. As a skating instructor, Laura acknowledged that beginning skaters must fall down as they practice, that this was necessary to their development as skaters. The instructor suggested that Laura would similarly be "falling" as she practiced writing, but that it was necessary. This metaphor helped Laura overcome her insistence on instant correctness in spelling, allowing her to take risks as she wrote. Many adult learners have all-or-nothing expectations of themselves. Forester proposed that finding parallel metaphors in the experiences of any learners might help them accept the risk-taking required in learning to read and write.

Forester (1988) maintained that "learners of all ages have their ways of unfolding their literacy learning." She proposed a literacy continuum of stages for oral language development, spelling and printing, writing and composing, and reading. She asserted that both children and adults move through these stages. Forester theorized that learners who can use their own knowledge of language and their own learning strategies "show themselves to have resources that far exceed expectations" (p. 604). She believed that adult learners must move forward to "personal involvement and active thinking-trying" (p. 605), and that they must use more cognitive processes than just memory and motor skills. They must have a sense of taking charge, decreased dependence on the teacher, and a focus on meaning. Forester made the following recommendations on the basis of her experiences with Laura and other adult learners.

- Help students realize how familiar with print they already are.

- Use discussion to link sight-words with student interests.
- Encourage students to work with partners or in small groups based on shared interests, not on ability level.
- Model fluent reading for students when it seems appropriate.
- In one-to-one sessions, encourage students to read along with you as you read aloud (if they are unable to read with fluency).
- Use books on tape from the library and produce personalized tapes for students.
- Use cloze materials (passages with words replaced by blanks so readers can predict what would make sense with the rest of the passage) to reinforce the use of syntactic, semantic, and experiential aids in making meaning.
- Motivate students by discussing their reasons for wanting to learn to read.
- Invite students to bring their own reading material, and do not reject anything on the grounds that it is too hard or too easy.
- Trust students to find their own level. Encourage them to use everything available to help them read.
- Make learning "safe."
- Place learners in charge of their own learning.

Forester's last two suggestions are more easily recommended than accomplished, but consideration of these factors can make an important difference in the willingness of adults to take chances and to learn. Providing emotional safety is an especially difficult task because adults who have experienced repeated failures as learners often are ready to flee at the first sign that they are in danger of failing again. When students can "own" their learning, direct it, and assess it, they are more likely to feel safe and to be willing to remain in the learning situation.

What We Have Learned from Pioneer Literacy Workers

The harvest of adult literacy we are now reaping was planted by some charismatic leaders with strong visions of the meaning and importance of literacy. Gray talked of the inspiration and transcendence possible in literacy. Laubach believed that people were transformed by becoming literate. Stewart and others held that power within society resides in literacy—that literacy is necessary for democratic citizenship and for action on behalf of one's own needs.

These early literacy workers treated adults as adults. They saw their potential and their need to be lifelong learners. Stewart and Goldberg chronicled rapid acquisition of literacy, while others registered their sense of the barriers to literacy. The pioneer instructors included both professionals and volunteers. Others stressed the importance of peers as teachers, affirming that peers know how to approach learning for members of their own communities. Gray campaigned for professionalism in literacy instruction.

All emphasized the importance of continuous learning by instructors as well as by students. In most of these cases, literacy learning has been embedded in the larger context of multiple literacies and multiple reasons for reading or not reading. Many, including Laubach, have held that there must be a focus on local needs and that those needs may extend beyond the bounds of a narrow definition of literacy curriculum, as Fitzgerald documented. Instruction often has been most effective for small groups and can be either formal, as Goldberg demonstrated, or informal in the style of Wallace. If a common theme runs through the experiences of the pioneers, it is that the literacy learner is a whole person for whom success will most likely come in terms of what is meaningful and what works best in the specifics of that one human life.

The first gardeners who sowed the seeds of adult literacy dug deep and planted strong roots that will grow tall trees when properly tended. Their thoughtful approach to literacy instruction challenges us to keep in mind the needs of the individual learner in the larger context of society and to enact with energy our shared vision. They remind us that we need to keep on planting the garden and tending the trees. People of vision can share this picture of a literate society, and brave leaders can allocate resources. Then each individual learner can be given due attention.

References

Adams, F., & Horton, M. (1975). *Unearthing the seeds of fire: The idea of Highlander.* Winston-Salem, NC: John F. Blair.

Arnove, R.F., & Graff, H.J. (Eds.). (1987). *National literacy campaigns: Historical and comparative perspectives.* New York: Plenum Press.

Bhola, H.S. (1984). *Campaigning for literacy: Eight national experiences of the twentieth century with a memorandum to decision makers.* Paris: UNESCO.

Bhola, H.S. (1988). The politics of adult literacy promotion: An international perspective. *Journal of Reading, 31*(7), 670.

Blodgett, J. (1894). Illiteracy in the United States. *Educational Review, 8,* 227-235.

Bond, G.L., & Dykstra, R. (1967). *Final Report.* Project No. X-001, Contract No. OE-5-10-264. Minneapolis, MN: University of Minnesota.

Brown, D.A., & Newman, A.P. (1968). *A literacy program for adult city-core illiterates: An investigation of experimental factors pertinent to reading instruction.* USOE Project No. 6-1136. Buffalo, NY: State University of New York.

Cook, W.D. (1977). *Adult literacy education in the United States.* Newark, DE: International Reading Association.

Duffy, T.M. (1985). Readability formulas: What's the use? In T.M. Duffy & R. Waller (Eds.), *Designing usable texts.* Orlando, FL: Academic Press.

Fitzpatrick, A. (1919). *Handbook for new Canadians.* Toronto, Ontario: Ryerson Press.

Forester, A.D. (1988). Learning to read and write at 26. *Journal of Reading, 31*(7), 604-613.

Freire, P. (1970). The adult education process as cultural action freedom. In E.R. Kintgen, B.N. Kroll, & M. Rose (Eds.), *Perspectives on literacy* (pp. 398-409). Carbondale, IL: Southern Illinois University Press.

Freire, P. (1983). The importance of the act of reading. *Journal of Education, 165,* 5-11.

Goldberg, S. (1951). *Army training of illiterates in World War II.* New York: Publications, Teachers College, Columbia University.

Gray, W.S. (1956). How well do adults read? In N.B. Henry (Ed.), *Adult reading.* The Fifty-fifth Yearbook of the National Society for the Study of Education. Chicago, IL: University of Chicago Press.

Gray, W.S. (1933). Catching up with literacy. *National Education Association Proceedings, 71,* 280-281.

Gray, W.S. (1925). *Report of the national committee on reading.* The Twenty-fourth Yearbook of the National Society for the Study of Education, part 1.

Gray, W.S., & Monroe, R. (1929). *The reading interests and habits of adults.* New York: Macmillan.

Gray, W.S., & Rodgers, B. (1956). *Maturity in reading: Its nature and appraisal.* Chicago, IL: University of Chicago Press.

Hargreaves, D. (1980). *Adult literacy and broadcasting: The BBC's experience.* London: Frances Pinter.

Hunter, C.S., & Harman, D. (1979). *Adult illiteracy in the United States.* New York: McGraw-Hill.

Kearnery, L. (1988). *Frank C. Laubach, literacy pioneer.* (ED 296 278)

Laubach, F.C., Kirk, E.M., & Laubach, R.F. (1981). *The Laubach way to reading* (3rd ed.). Syracuse, NY: Laubach Literacy.

Meyer, V., & Keefe, D. (1988). The Laubach way to reading: A review. *Lifelong Learning, 12*(1), 8-10.

Mobilizing for action. (1962, October). *The Illiterate American, Overview, 3,* 33-35.

Newman, A.P. (1980). *Adult basic education: Reading.* Boston, MA: Allyn & Bacon.

Newman, A.P. (1978). *Twenty lives: A longitudinal study of the effects of five variables on the lives of 20 students who were low readiness in first grade (1964-1976).* Bloomington, IN: Indiana University.

Ohles, J.F. (Ed.). (1978). *Biographical dictionary of American educators*. Westport, CT: Greenwood Press.

Pearpoint, J.C. (1987). Frontier College: Literacy education since 1899. *Prospects, 17*(2), 279.

Shannon, P. (1985, October). Reading instruction and social class. *Language Arts, 62*, 604-613.

Shor, I., & Freire, P. (1987, November). What is the "dialogical method" of teaching? *Journal of Education, 169*(3).

Stevenson, J.A. (Ed.). (1985). *William S. Gray: Teacher, scholar, leader*. Newark, DE: International Reading Association.

Stewart, C.W. (1917). *Moonlight schools*. Indianapolis, IN: Indiana State Teacher's Association.

Stewart, C.W. (1922). *Moonlight schools: For the emancipation of adult illiterates*. New York: E.P. Dutton.

Swenson, S. (1988). *Welthy Honsinger Fisher: Signals of a century*. Stittsville, Ontario: Swenson.

Van Dyken, J.R. (1984). *What literacy teachers should know about language: An assessment of inservice training needs of reading acquisition teachers in southern Sudan using the Gudschinsky literacy method*. Unpublished doctoral dissertation, Indiana University, Bloomington, IN.

Wallace, M.C. (1965). *Literacy instructor's handbook: An adventure in teaching*. Chicago, IL: Follett.

5

Adult Literacy Research: Surveying a New Field

A dult literacy is a relatively new field of academic study, a field that is changing rapidly. Researchers in a number of cognate disciplines are making substantial contributions to the literature on adult literacy. We do not claim to have read all the relevant work. At this stage of development, we must content ourselves with a discussion of the challenges inherent in research on adult literacy and an overview of the field, including a closer look at social considerations, as well as intergenerational and workplace literacy.

Vexations of Research in Adult Literacy

Decision making depends on the quality of our knowledge, as well as on the political climate and special circumstances surrounding the decision. Decision making takes place at the personal level of the instructor and learner, at the larger level of the program, and the still larger level of the state and national arenas. Ever present in these discussions is the knowledge that we succeed with some students but not with others. Because we want to know why, we look for scientific data to help us make the right decisions. But our demand for answers is often frustrated; we can find many handbooks, materials, and descriptions of single programs, but little research data (Darkenwald, 1986; Fingeret, 1984).

Debates and deficiencies notwithstanding, research in adult literacy is needed to find out what works, to guide funding decisions, and to lead in the eradication of illiteracy. The challenges of the field, however, make research in adult literacy more difficult than equivalent educational research with younger learners.

Intermittent Funding

Research in adult literacy receives inadequate and intermittent funding. Literacy has become a fashionable topic, generating more attention but not much more money. Much of the research work was done with "soft money" from the Right-to-Read Decade, and from Adult Education Act 309-310 grants, which supported only short term projects rather than sustained programs. Section 310 provides for the "use of funds for special experimental demonstration projects and teacher training" and stipulates that not less than 10 percent of the funds allotted to a state be used for innovative adult literacy projects or programs of national significance.

Research in adult literacy often is characterized by interruptions between projects and between research opportunities, a result of the irregular flow of funding. Once disbanded, staff and working teams often are impossible to reassemble when the next injection of money comes. Meanwhile, precious time is consumed searching for the next funding "fix."

Difficult Research Conditions

One problem for the adult literacy researcher is meeting adult learners in their own communities during hours when they are not working. Many among the populations served by the adult literacy movement live transient lives. In this situation, 6 months of study can be labeled "longitudinal." Only in prisons and the military can control be exercised over the duration of, and attendance at, literacy programs. Literacy instructors can be similarly transient, hired for a few months here and a year or two there, often with no sense of continuity or security.

Learners willing to attend literacy programs may be substantially different from those never seen in such programs. For this reason Fingeret (1987) contends that generalization from students to the larger group of illiterate adults is without justification, and that using students in research conceals the fact that "we know very little, actually, about illiterate adults in the United States—only the small minority of whom are literacy students (p. 1).

Facing these conditions, many literacy workers and researchers suffer from a sense of frustration, which is further compounded by the scarcity of research centers for adult literacy. There are only four such centers in the United States: the Center for the Study of Adult Literacy at the University of Pennsylvania, the Institute for the Study of Adult Literacy at Pennsylvania State University, the Center for the Study of Adult Literacy at Georgia State University, and the North Carolina Center for Literacy Development at North Carolina State University. These centers enjoy the use of important tools of substantial research: the help of graduate students, extensive libraries, computers, and database facilities. Nevertheless, because few students specialize in adult literacy, university resources are seldom allocated to literacy work. Few scholars have been attracted to the field because of its low prestige. The field is full of confounding variables and complexities that keep studies from being easily contained and that make solid research difficult, even when people are interested. Fortunately, this situation is about to change somewhat with the proposed Center on Adult Literacy funded under the Office of Educational Research and Improvement (OERI) of the U.S. Department of Education, as well as through prospective adult literacy funding under legislation currently being considered in Congress.

According to Sticht and McDonald (1989) student researchers are not equipped to carry out long term action research—the kind of study that is carried out in real world settings and that draws its power from practice as well as from research. They described cognitive action research, findings of which could be applied and tested even while they were being generated:

> With multidisciplinary scientists and practitioners working on significant educational problems, located in geographical areas where the problems exist, and over long periods of time, scientifically valid knowledge could be developed about the linguistically and culturally diversified populations that make up the U.S. citizenry. Research findings would not lie dormant on library bookshelves before being applied (p. 15).

Newman and Beverstock

Research is further hampered by the relative inability of teachers in adult literacy to take advantage of developments in research conducted by teachers. Interest has been growing in elementary and secondary education with the notion that teachers should view themselves as inquirers (see Fargo & Collins, 1989; Watson, Harste, & Burke, 1989). However, most adult literacy instructors teach part time and feel they do not have the time to engage in inquiry; nor are they part of social or academic structures that foster inquiry.

Many practitioners who work part time do not identify themselves with the profession sufficiently to join professional organizations and to participate in discussions within them (Fingeret, 1985). This is not for the lack of organizations to join. A number of professional organizations exist in which the interests of literacy researchers are addressed. The International Reading Association, the American Association of Adult and Continuing Educators, and the National Council of Teachers of English, are but three of them.

Another difficulty is that researchers naturally have different questions and agendas for their work. The research "consumer" needs to understand these agendas in order to evaluate the products of the research. Some descriptive studies examine who the adult learners are and why they appear in literacy programs. Other so-called studies are merely justifications for continued funding of present programs (Diekhoff, 1988). Then there is always the researcher whose aim is to prove that a favorite theory or approach works.

New Questions

Fingeret (1987) points out that despite the proven potential of ethnographic studies, they continue to be "viewed warily and published infrequently" (p. 9). She states that the domination of traditional research, to the exclusion of ethnographic studies, has impoverished the field of adult literacy research:

> We continue to operate literacy programs on the basis of untested assumptions and the "tradition" of experience that has proven to be of limited success over the past 20-odd years.

We are beginning to recognize that there are some very basic questions yet to be answered, such as "How do nonliterate adults approach the process of learning to read and write?" "What are the functions of literacy in the lives of nonliterate adults living in the U.S.?" and "What is the relationship between cultural background and classroom learning?" Our traditional quantitative approaches to research are not appropriate for responding to these questions. Due to the constraints of the quantitative paradigm, it has not been possible to view adult literacy students more broadly as adults or to investigate issues such as the relationship between program factors, cultural background factors, and learning (p. 1).

In advocating the use of ethnographic research in adult literacy, Fingeret states that the "fundamental strength of ethnography is to provide insight into the perspective of the informants" (p. 3). She suggests that an ethnographic perspective helps researchers understand how informants understand their lives, literacy, and literacy programs. Relationships between the student's culture and classroom behavior can allow or prohibit learning. Characteristics of the classroom culture often are habitual and unexamined—they may seem natural to the instructor, but may in fact be profoundly limiting or even offensive for would-be learners. Ethnography also can illuminate issues of social class, gender, race, and stage of life in relation to reading skill attainment or disability. Community values about reading program participation contain potential insights. Basic skills instruction within industry has its own cultural load, and we need to know how it helps or hinders learning. Finally, the dynamics of change are profound as someone becomes a functional reader. We need to know the supporting or limiting factors in new readers' social networks.

Fingeret concedes that ethnographic inquiry can be "threatening to researchers and professionals who have been taught that they are experts." Researchers need to see themselves as learners under instruction from their respondents.

Michael Kamil (personal communication, March 1989) describes a cycle of research that begins with an ethnographic examination of the context as a whole, case studies to focus carefully on a few individuals, empirical testing of new approaches, and a return to ethnography to see how the new procedures work in an entire context. Sticht has called for action research melding the insights of daily practice and the larger contexts of theory building and testing. Rose (1988), who worked closely with people whose literacy in writing is perceived as substandard, reviewed research in perception, neurophysiology, psychology, and linguistics that is sometimes used to explain students' apparent inability to meet the academic standards of writing. Although Rose's immediate focus is college writers, his observations are applicable to the range of questions across adult literacy.

> Human cognition—even at its most stymied, bungled moments—is rich and varied. It is against this assumption that we should test our theories and research methods and classroom assessments. Do our practices work against classification that encourages single, monolithic explanations of cognitive activity? Do they honor the complexity of interpretive efforts even when those efforts fall short of some desired goal?...Do they urge reflection on the cultural biases that might be shaping them? We must be vigilant that the systems of intellect we develop or adapt do not ground our students' difficulties in sweeping, essentially one-dimensional perceptual, neurophysiological, psychological, or linguistic processes, systems that drive broad cognitive wedges between those who do well in our schools and those who do not (p. 297).

Overviews of U.S. Adult Literacy Programs

Jack Mezirow, Gordon Darkenwald, and Alan Knox
Mezirow, Darkenwald, and Knox reported on an ethnographic study undertaken through the Center for Adult Education at Columbia Teachers College. They studied programs in six cities and employed a national survey to describe programs, classroom interaction, and the viewpoints of the people in the programs. Their book, *Last Gamble on Education* (1975), is a vivid look at the

classes of the 1970s. They found lonely students, severely limited approaches to teaching and learning, and administrative emphasis on attendance rather than on the quality of offerings.

The researchers characterized ABE programs as a "loner's game" with isolated students who might be acquainted with several teachers but with none of their fellow students. They found that classes were made up of people with widely differing levels of literacy; a single class might include learners of basic education, secondary education, and English as a second language (ESL). Whereas evening students tended to be employed and more serious, day students were younger, unemployed, and casual about their classes. Students could be categorized as learners, attenders, or occasional attenders, with varying seriousness implied in these labels. Two thirds of urban ABE students were young to middle-aged women; many had had at least nine years of schooling without becoming sufficiently literate, and 15 to 25 percent were on welfare. The effort to take classes to learners resulted in classes being held in the "often dirty, noisy, uncomfortable, and cramped" facilities of community organizations. Nonetheless, these locations were regarded as preferable to school buildings.

Attendance-taking exerted a tyranny over class life; attendance was recorded meticulously, and teachers alternated between begging students to attend class and threatening them. ABE instruction reminded the researchers of their own school experiences: there was a pervasive "present-recite/test-correct" approach.

> The mode of instruction in many ABE classrooms is that of the elementary school of the 1920s before all those "progressive" educators began their tinkering. Drill, recitation, group chalkboard work, doing assignments in class, using workbooks, and routinization are familiar hallmarks (p. 18).

Student behavior and class atmosphere were informal, friendly, and pleasant. The content of instruction focused largely on achievement test results and preparations for taking the General Educational Development Test (GED). Reading, writing, and arithmetic predominated over the rare instances of instruction in "coping skills." ESL classes had broader contents—to fulfill an Americanization role and to break the dull routine of drill and practice. Teachers practiced an "ideology of minimum failure" by constantly redefining tasks and working to prevent students from confronting difficulty and leaving the class.

Mezirow, Darkenwald, and Knox advocated taking into account learners' goals and the time required to achieve them. They suggested the use of temporary "feeder classes" established in housing projects near students who usually did not attend classes. Once trust was established, people could be moved to permanent classes in central locations. They also identified other pressing needs, including counseling for students, as well as curriculum and staff development.

Carman Hunter and David Harman

At UNESCO's 1972 International Conference on Adult Education in Tokyo, delegates were impressed by the descriptions of successful new approaches to adult learning reported by a Thai official. Subsequently, delegates at the conference urged World Education (an umbrella organization working with governments and secular organizations, known for its many years of pioneering work in nonformal education and functional literacy in developing countries) to apply its international experience to the literacy problems of adult learners in the United States.

Funded by the federal government, World Education mounted a series of experiments in eight states and found that the "self-defined concerns, needs, and objectives of the participants were similar to those they had encountered in the developing countries" (Hunter & Harman, 1979, p. xi). But there were two exceptions: 1) American adult literacy enrollees were largely self-selected and, therefore, not representative of the "functionally illiterate" in the country; and 2) adult illiteracy was difficult to address and assess because schooling was compulsory and available and because the magnitude of the problem was largely unappreciated.

In 1976, when the Ford Foundation asked World Education to undertake another study of adult illiteracy in the United States,

Hunter and Harman became the principal investigators. They interviewed educational agency personnel, examined documents from various government departments, read the literature, and talked to experts. They stated: "Our work on this study has been something like an archaeological expedition—successful digs, each uncovering new layers of materials and insights" (p. 3). The result was the comprehensive *Adult Illiteracy in the United States* (1979).

Hunter and Harman categorized into four groups attitudes on adult illiteracy. First, some regarded adult illiteracy as a failure of the schools and recommended school reform. Others believed that adult and special education must be improved for those with literacy difficulties. Still others advocated changes in the entire educational system to foster lifelong learning for all people. The fourth view—and the one taken by Hunter and Harman—was that each of the three previous views was too limited to "address the root causes of adult illiteracy" and that "only a radical rethinking of the purposes and patterns of education as a function of the larger social system can achieve long range changes" (p. 8).

They also categorized literacy programs into three types: the volunteer organizations and ABE programs that focused on "conventional skills," competency-based programs that emphasized the "skills and competencies needed by the learner for life—either personal or job-related," and broadcast media. The programs of the ABE and volunteer organizations made basic education generally available, but served only an estimated 2 to 4 percent of the target population.

Hunter and Harman believed that the literacy efforts involving broadcast media used the media for one of three purposes: as a motivator, as a tool for discussion and assessment of the learning needs of adults, or as a means of presenting subject matter such as GED preparation. They concluded that funding was better for producing broadcast programs than for using them effectively with learners, that the target audience did not watch public television, that a lack of coordination existed between public broadcasting and adult education, and that there was a gap between "the delivery capability of the media and community/regional planning for utilization" (p. 97).

The programs they labeled as competency based had been influenced by the American Performance Level Study and subsequent conferences. They included in this group such diverse organizations as the Armed Forces, labor unions, cultural and ethnic organizations, and museums and galleries. A strength of competency-based programs was that they had the potential to overcome tension between institutional and individual goals. The unstructured programs served as models to inform alternative approaches to learning. The advantages included the involvement of community agencies, resources, people, and institutions outside the strictly educational world; a focus on individual assessment of interest and need, and on appreciation of participants' backgrounds; pressure (from students and the situation itself) to invent broader methods, materials, approaches, and linkages than already existed; and an emphasis on outcome criteria that allowed learners to start wherever they were and move at their own pace toward meaningful objectives.

Hunter and Harman arrived at the following conclusions about the literacy systems they had investigated: (1) the most impoverished and least educated adults seldom participate in traditional adult education programs, (2) the cost of adult education services is higher for the less advantaged, and (3) the greater needs of the disadvantaged are ignored in many current assumptions about educational services. Hunter and Harman called for a major shift in national educational policy and for the "establishment of new, pluralistic, community-based initiatives whose specific objective will be to serve the most disadvantaged hard-core poor" (p. 105).

Hunter and Harman's study is one of the most quoted studies of adult literacy in the United States, and their inclusive analysis of the contexts of literacy issues has had a pervasive influence. In the preface to the 1985 paperback edition, the authors reaffirm their belief that community-based programs have the potential to clarify research agendas, to link with larger political movements, and, if supported by national policy and funding, to enable "democratic educational renewal."

Janet McGrail

McGrail's (1984) survey, part of the National Adult Literacy Project, brought together the available statistics on the insufficiently literate and on literacy programs. McGrail drew data from a variety of sources, including the Census Bureau, the Adult Performance Level Study, and two studies by Harris (1970, 1971). She focused on groups that evidenced high rates of illiteracy: the elderly, the poor, and the unemployed. She reported on literacy programs provided by ABE funds, and on volunteer-based organizations, correctional institutions, the armed forces, business and industry, and universities. The analysis was complicated by the overlap among groups. For example, literacy learners in an ABE program may be simultaneously enrolled in a library-based volunteer program, and in tallying participants, some people are counted twice, causing an overestimate of numbers served. Although McGrail's review was extensive, she concluded:

> At present, it is not possible to provide a complete and accurate picture of adult illiterates and literacy programs in the 1980s using existing data. Most of the needed information is not available. Information that is available is often out of date, incomplete, or inaccurate. In some cases, existing data suggest additional questions to a greater extent than they answer questions previously posed (p. 21).

Finally, McGrail recommended that new counts not be instituted, suggesting instead that more useful and accurate data would be generated if programs gathered and reported such information routinely, allowing the data to be a natural part of the ongoing programs.

Donald McCune and Judith Alamprese

In *Turning Illiteracy Around: An Agenda for National Action* (1985), McCune and Alamprese describe the activities and resource needs of 50 representative local literacy programs and the national organizations that supplied them with leadership, coordination, and technical assistance. The researchers make suggestions for expanding the literacy system; give guidelines for new organizations and agencies; and recommend increased involvement by state and federal governments, as well as business and industry.

McCune and Alamprese conclude that:

- local programs and national literacy organizations need more resources;
- the combined efforts of state and federal government and the private sector are required to make substantial gains where currently we are making only minimal progress;
- doubling or tripling the present literacy system will not meet the literacy needs of the country's 27 million functionally illiterate adults;
- increasing the literacy system will cost billions of dollars and will require alternative services and programs using computers and mass media; and
- greater attention must be given to quality instruction, professional instructors, and staff management.

The researchers recommend expansion of local literacy providers and national organizations. They call for new funding for ABE at the federal level, use of ABE funds for a wider range of literacy providers, expansion of the technical assistance capacity of the Office of Adult Education, funding of volunteer organizations, and the establishment of an independent institute on adult literacy. At the state level, they suggest increased funding, establishment of statewide councils, the funding of ongoing technical assistance, and the use of "310 monies" to fund the pilot phase of programs. For business and industry, they recommend grants for operating costs in local and national organizations, donation of in-kind services, encouragement of employees to become literacy volunteers, and provision of grants for research and development. They also call for more funding from professional organizations.

Renee Lerche

Lerche (1985) and associates carried out a major study for the National Adult Literacy Project to identify "promising practices" in literacy training efforts. Of 335 exemplary programs nominated for inclusion in the study, 38 were visited by the research team. Lerche realized that it would be neither possible nor appropriate to complete the study with a single design for all literacy programs because the philosophy, "sector," goals, and nature of the student population all would influence the planning of the individual programs. The study was a report on eight components of literacy programs: recruitment and public relations, orientation, counseling, diagnostic testing, assessment, instructional methods and materials, follow up, and program evaluation.

Each section ends with recommendations for good planning in that program component. Lerche recommends that recruitment and public relations planners "begin with the needs of the community, select appropriate recruitment and public relations strategies, tailor the message, and make recruitment a dialogue between you and the community and other constituencies" (p. 53). Four recommendations for orientation were to "be sensitive to the affective needs of students, organize your information needs, tailor sessions to the program's role in the community, and be alert to changing needs and goals of students" (p. 66). For counseling, Lerche recommends that planners "develop a system for identifying counseling needs of individual students, develop a system for responding to the counseling needs of individual students, explore methods of using peer support, and provide inservice training in counseling techniques for all program staff" (p. 81).

Lerche and her associates recognized that the area of diagnostic testing was "hotly debated," but affirmed that methods of placement were necessary, that assessment should be ongoing, that criterion-referenced tests (tests that measure specific skill attainment rather than the relative test performance of norm-referenced achievement tests) may be best for planning instruction (though not so useful in supplying evidence to funding agencies), and that tests must be appropriate for adults. Lerche recommended that planners "clearly define the instructional mission and goals of the program, develop expertise in educational psychology and measurement, translate the students' and programs' goals into sets of clear and measurable objectives, and build a regular and frequent schedule for assessment" (pp. 97-98).

Lerche acknowledged that there are many ways to teach adults reading, writing, arithmetic, and applications skills; hence, a single recommended method would not be appropriate. Instead, the research team suggested that designers of instructional programs should "recognize that the student population is made up of adults, supply opportunities to apply skills in adult functional contexts, involve students in making decisions about their educational program, anticipate the multiplicity of learning goals and learning styles with a variety of program options, build a true instructional management program based on clearly stated behavioral objectives, and build a system of documenting student progress and achievement" (pp. 154-155).

Programs in which no follow up is done yield no solid understanding of why learners leave programs or whether the program has been effective in changing students' literacy. Thus, Lerche recommended that literacy workers "maintain up-to-date files on all students, establish a policy under which teachers identify possible dropouts for follow-up contact, and establish target dates on which the program will conduct a study of the long term effects of the program on the lives of its students" (p. 170).

Program evaluation was seen to be an area of weakness in the programs. Lerche asserted that the evaluation procedures were generally "not very sophisticated." She found substantial disagreements among practitioners on what "evaluation is, how one goes about it, and even how useful it is" (p. 171). Evaluation often was limited to either required reporting or occasional efforts. Lerche and her team felt that program goals and objectives should be more clearly defined and suggested that teachers become more knowledgeable about evaluation, both for decisions about the success of a program following its initial adjustment period, and for the planning stages and first portion of a program to find information to use in making program adjustments. They further recommended that new evaluation instruments be designed and used, and that a unified system of collecting, analyzing, and using data be established for making changes in program components. Lerche's published report, *Effective Literacy Programs*, is a comprehensive discussion of program decisions, models for collecting information within programs, and sources for more information on the approaches described.

Association for Community Based Education

The Association for Community Based Education surveyed literacy providers throughout the United States to prepare the *National Directory of Community Based Adult Literacy Programs* (1989). They borrowed mailing lists from many organizations and made substantial efforts to contact all programs; they received 796 responses. The people served in these programs are the "hardest to reach and the most in need section of the U.S. population" (p. 69). The report contains specific figures on the educational attainment, income, ethnicity, and gender of the learners in these programs:

> Fifty-seven percent of the students enter the programs with reading skills at less than the fifth grade level, and another 27 percent come with skills at the fifth or sixth grade level. Seventy percent have family incomes of less than $10,000; another 26 percent have family incomes between $10,000 and $20,000. Thirty percent are Hispanic, 26 percent are black, 13 percent are Asian, 3 percent are native Americans, and 4 percent are of other racial and ethnic groups. Seventy percent of the programs serve at least some nonnative English speakers. Fifty-six percent of the students are female and 44 percent are male (National Directory, 1989, p. 69).

Teaching approaches are described as nontraditional and include one-on-one tutoring (83 percent), individualized instruction (58 percent), interactive groups (52 percent), traditional classroom lecturing (32 percent), combinations of two or more approaches (71 percent), and using all four approaches (21 percent). Nonnative speakers comprise 70 percent of the learners, so some programs offer general ESL instruction (66 percent) and some offer Spanish literacy instruction (12 percent) or literacy instruction in other languages (9 percent). The programs do not focus on literacy instruction alone. They also are involved in the "broad empowerment" of participants. Wider projects reported included job training and placement (40 percent), cultural activities (25 percent), community organization (24 percent), housing activities (22 percent), parenting programs (20 percent), and economic development (18 percent).

The report concludes that, taken together, nonliteracy activities made up an average of 44 percent of the programs' activities.

About two-thirds of the funds come from state, federal, and local governments; and one-third comes from foundations, corporations, the United Way, religious organizations, and tuition fees. They estimate a per-pupil expenditure of $331.

Case Study Close-Ups

Individual case studies allow close examination of the differences and similarities between people and programs. They allow us to focus on learning strategies, people's beliefs, and the exploration of what these mean in the new reader's life.

Public policy is set and implementation takes place on the basis of nationally representative samples of the broad population. Nevertheless, a change in literacy is an intensely personal matter. We must balance national generalizations about the extent of functional illiteracy with insights from "close readings" of individual lives and the wisdom spawned from thoughtful instructors. While each student is unique, we can learn lessons from each experience that can be applied to encounters with other students.

Peter Johnston

Johnston (1985) worked with Jack, Bill, and Charlie—45, 26, and 43 years of age, respectively. His study was based on tape recordings of individual instruction sessions ranging from 45 minutes to 2 hours with each man. Johnston categorized his findings into five areas: conceptual problems, strategies, anxiety, attributions, and goals and motivation. His purpose was to present a "multifaceted yet integrated picture of adult reading failure" (p. 174).

Conceptual problems have to do with readers' understanding of what reading is, and their consequent "allocation of attention." Johnston found that all three men maintained incorrect sound-symbol generalizations and viewed reading as an act of remembering, and that both of these mistakes interfered with their reading. He concluded that less proficient readers may be attending to less useful characteristics of print (paying attention only to the first letter of words or counting the letters instead of using them as reading cues) and missing more useful ones. As adults, they have experienced years of not knowing what to attend to; they are afraid that others will succeed while they fail. Johnston suggested that Clay's (1979) work in early intervention to prevent the development of erroneous or restricted concepts might be helpful to avoid these predicaments.

Strategies pose another point at which readers can wander off track. Johnston categorized the men's strategies as either for general coping ("passing" as literate) or for specifically coping with not reading. They avoided reading by listening carefully and by using family and friends as readers. Their strategies left them with little practice in reading, no opportunity to develop fluent reading, and little flexibility in reading strategies. Johnston found that these men were using whole-message strategies (getting the gist, guessing from the context) to the exclusion of more print-based strategies (sounding out words). (This is consistent with Carrell's 1984 finding that second-language readers either pay attention to constructing the larger message of the print or read word by word, but do not manage both at the same time.) The men's strategies, although dysfunctional, were strongly ingrained in their practice; both close attention and self-understanding would be required to enable the men to exchange them for more useful strategies.

With reference to *anxiety*, Johnston maintained that "the effect of anxiety in reading difficulty cannot be overestimated, although its circular causal properties are difficult to demonstrate" (p. 167). In many situations, the men were unable to perform tasks they had performed earlier or would perform again later without difficulty. The severity of their tension warranted the label of neurosis. They displayed the following symptoms: resistance to entering the learning situation, fear responses (trembling, hiding, attempting to escape from the learning situation), inability to resist making incorrect responses, compulsive responding, regressive behavior, loss of the ability to delay a response, and changes in social behavior (p. 168). Any instructor of people with reading difficulties has encountered learners with these characteristics. Adding to the anxiety load, many adults who are insufficiently literate feel utterly alone and unable to talk about their difficulties.

Attributions are another source of literacy difficulty. When people decide they cannot read because they are stupid, they are attributing their difficulty to a factor beyond their control. Stupidity, they reason, is not something they can change. This attitude induces helpless passivity. One strand of research has examined the differing treatment of students by teachers on the basis of how able the teacher believes the students to be. Teachers sent "less able" students different messages about what they can do, as well as different strategy instructions for reading (Shannon, 1985).

Finally, Johnston considered *goals and motivation*. For illiterates, maintaining secrecy or believing they are stupid are forces so strong that even stringent requirements to increase literacy may have little effect. Learners often leave even good programs quickly. Johnston suggested that disabled learners vacillate between involvement in the task at hand, which produces progress, and shielding their fragile egos, which blocks progress.

Johnston suggested that the familiar learning plateau where learners "rest" after spectacular (or at least steady) gains also may be explained by switches in attention from learning to feeling inadequate. For example, Jack reached a plateau at a sixth to seventh grade level after his initial reading progress, and he was stuck there for nearly two semesters. He was reluctant to part with "regular contact with a concerned female tutor." He also seemed to be struggling with his sense of what was possible. For years, Jack had believed that he could not read; now he had evidence that he could have become literate earlier. To admit that would force him to contemplate what might have been—a question he found dismaying. Literacy providers must work to make learners feel "safe" with literacy.

Johnston concluded that explanations of reading disability as neurological and processing deficits are not useful. He recommended that we focus on "educationally modifiable components" through early intervention to prevent reading difficulty. For instructors of adults who have not learned literacy, he suggested concentrating on the five factors he found in his study.

Mussaret Sheikh

Sheikh (1986) examined the responses of adults ranging from absolute nonreaders to mid-level readers. Sheikh developed and tested a Computer Assisted Instruction/Adult Basic Education (CAI/ABE) model for the prediction of success of illiterate adults in learning to read by using computers. Including a broad array of cultural, physiological, psychological, and educational characteristics of learners, Sheikh tested the application of her model to ascertain its explanatory/predictive ability. She then verified the outcomes of the model with a computer diagnostic program, Outcome Advisor (Fattu & Patrick, 1983).

A major finding was that adult learners coming from diversified backgrounds have vastly different personalities and needs; they do not fall into neat categories. Learners were examined for how well they fit into the Eyster categories: Group 1, secure and self-directed; Group 2, time problems; Group 3, sporadically employed; and Group 4, stationary poor (Hunter & Harman, 1979). None of the five learners clearly fit in one group, and three of the five exhibited characteristics from all five categories. Sheikh noted:

> It does not seem appropriate to label them into the different groups simply from their background. Instead, the diversified information provides us with a useful framework for organizing the learning situations, by understanding, interpreting the first-hand information people give us about their lives and aspirations....Many illiterate adults are downgraded by the larger society. Many of such illiterates possess the common sense and the ability to abstract and analyze necessary for learning if they are provided the appropriate attention and instruction (pp. 227-228).

Further, Sheikh cautioned against using categorizations to plan instruction. In our haste to categorize people, we tend to label (often mislabel) in the process. At one time in their lives, students may be sporadically employed (Group 3); at another time they may have scheduling problems (Group 2). As handy as it is to say, "She's a Group 2 type person, and therefore we can expect so-and-so," we are talking about people, and we must remember that statistics come after, not before, the individual. Many crucial learner characteristics are overlooked or ignored because they cannot be measured with a standardized test. The Sheikh study demonstrated the importance of considering a broad array of emotional, attitudinal, and other learner characteristics.

A second major finding of the study was the speed with which even the most academically disabled learners could achieve their goals, given appropriate instructional support. When HH, a 62-year-old man, started the program he could not write one letter of the alphabet. Nevertheless, in 12 1-hour sessions, using computer assisted instruction and the language experience approach, HH achieved his goal of "writing a letter before I die." In fact, he wrote several letters. His experience demonstrates that the CAI/ABE model contributed to his overall success.

Another of the study's findings had to do with the diagnostic and predictive power of the computer program Outcome Advisor(R) compared with two commonly used standardized tests in identifying learner characteristics most likely to predict success. Sheikh's work focused on the learner, taking into consideration the cultural, physiological, psychological, and educational characteristics to decide on instruction. More recent work in this area brings up to date the application of the Consult-I(R) program, developed by Fattu and Patrick (1983) and now being applied to the learning needs of adults in the workplace. The Reading Practicum Center staff at Indiana University has worked since 1983 to apply Outcome Advisor and Consult-I to the needs of children and adults to diagnose and recommend treatments that focus on learner needs. Work with the Indianapolis Network for Employment and Training suggests that Consult-I applications in education are as effective as they have been in medicine, business, agriculture, and earth science.

The Sheikh study contributed much to our knowledge about the instruction of the adult learner. It emphasized the obligations of both instructor and learner; it showed that building on crucial, detailed background information could lead to more effective instruction; it proposed that the power of sophisticated technology might assist in literacy instruction; and it underlined the importance of knowing the learner's wishes.

Social Perspectives on Literacy

Although much concern about illiteracy concentrates on individuals, inquiry in literacy also must consider the larger social contexts of literate communication. Literacy research needs to address the distribution of literacy in a community in terms of age, sex, and socioeconomic class; the settings of "literacy acts"; the accepted means for distributing information (oral, written); dependence or independence of social status on literacy; and how and why literacy is acquired in a particular "communicative community" (Szwed, 1981, p. 310).

Social perspectives on the literacy of native speakers are complemented by current findings and questions in ESL research on U.S. communities not based in English. Migrant workers and illegal aliens are among the most isolated and least known residents of the United States. Hiding from deportation, they keep to themselves and do not seek learning situations. Many who have not had opportunities for education, are not literate in their first language, let alone English.

Since the passage of amnesty legislation that requires applicants for legal status to demonstrate English skills, aliens have emerged and, in some areas, deluged ABE programs. Their teachers report that their English is rudimentary and their skills in speaking English have "fossilized." These people have been able to get their message across without accurate vocabulary and syntax. What the teachers perceive as bad habits have been working for these language learners; therefore, they are reluctant to learn the more conventional patterns offered by ESL teachers. They complain the conventional language is "high fallutin' " and not necessary for them to learn.

The question posed by these learners' reluctance to change their ways of speaking raises an important question for instruction in any language: Is a focus on accuracy the key to proper fluency in the language being learned? (Higgs & Clifford, 1982). A related and also unanswered question is: Should instruction in literacy skills be delayed until "oral competence" is established, using an instructional progression of listening, speaking, and only then introducing literacy in the language? If learners are literate in their first (or second or fifth) language, should they be limited to only the oral learning of a new language? And for those who are not literate in any language, should literacy learning begin in their first language to allow them to build literacy concepts in their strongest language for later transfer to any written language, even if it is not English?

Two other issues have emerged in ESL work that are relevant to a discussion of social and cultural impact on literacy instruction. As we read, we use what we know to predict the meaning of the text. Our predictions and guesses arise from our cultural backgrounds, experiences, and value systems. When the readers' value systems are at odds with the text, readers are challenged additionally in an already challenging enterprise. Language teaching must include instruction in culture so the new reader can make sense of the printed text by reference to its cultural framework (Carrell, 1979).

Nyikos (1989) theorized that language learning proceeds on the basis of associations between what the learners already know and the new material; therefore, more associations mean easier retrieving. She suggested that the way people memorize is a function of socialization, which is different for men and women. In a study of vocabulary learning, Nyikos found men and women to be significantly different in their memorization. The women did best with just a color clue; the men did best with picture and color clues. Rote learning and picture associations were less helpful for both men and women.

Nyikos' findings continue the discussion of gender differences in learning begun in the work of Gilligan (1982) and Belenky et al. (1986). We can relate Freire's (1970) ideas of a "culture of silence" among the marginal people in a society to the metaphors of silence and voice in their work, which examined women's ability to speak for themselves. A similar silence may describe the conditions for many marginalized people.

Persons who operate in culturally induced silence have little opportunity or motivation to further their own literacy. In fact, traumas of past abuse may make any effort to communicate prohibitively dangerous to psychic comfort. Literacy requires a belief that communication, spoken and written, will make a difference. In the absence of this confidence, lack of literacy skills is understandable.

Kazemek (1988) discussed the need to examine gender implications in literacy learning and attainment, and notes that programs organized as "individually oriented" may be antithetical to the connectedness required by women's ways of knowing. It was noted that in individualized instruction, the learner is isolated, as literacy learning is isolated from the rest of the learners' concerns in daily life. Kazemek argued that we need to explore learning circles to help establish an "ethic of caring" among the members with shared responsibility taking the "tremendous onus off the individual." We can use the "collaborative models of teaching which are sensitive to women's ways of knowing and, at the same time, are not antagonistic or detrimental to men" (1988, p. 24). Kazemek noted Fingeret and Heath's observation:

> We need to carefully examine Belenky's contention that teachers should be "midwives." And we need ethnographic/ case studies which compare specific approaches to literacy education (one-on-one vs. collaborative) and their effectiveness for women.

We also need to ask about men, youths, and dropouts who may not be served well by present programs.

The work of Heath and Fingeret furnishes insights into the literacies of these special social segments that many literacy workers do not know well. While descriptions of illiterates on first glance may seem quite similar, these descriptions offer different meanings for different interpreters. Fingeret (1984, p. 13) suggested that literacy educators were "influenced deeply" by the "war on poverty" perspective of the 1960s that portrayed individuals as embedded in a culture of poverty. If being poor is equated with being culturally impoverished, the result is a deficit perspective that "establishes middle class culture as the norm and judges others by it." Norman and Malicky (1986, pp. 13-14) described people at "lower levels of literacy development" as "print deprived and literally not part of the literate culture around them." They also noted a paradox: when these people come to learn to read, they often think of reading as decoding, or letter-by-letter recognition of words, a view that is "often counterproductive because there is no match between this means to literacy and the major goals for literacy development, which are primarily social in nature." Gardner's (1983, p. 391) theories of multiple intelligences may provide metaphoric as well as practical insights into the lack of development of literacy in some people. He suggests that for "individuals who have initial difficulty learning to read text, it may make sense to begin with an introduction to some other symbolic system." Knowledge differences as well as cultural differences can be used to expand learners' sense of language use, power, and variations.

From another sociocultural point of view about sources of illiteracy, we may contend that illiteracy has been induced by social inequalities in schooling. These inequalities take the form of no school at all, unequally funded schooling (there is a vast difference in per-pupil expenditures between wealthy and poor school districts), and schools that are unresponsive to children who are culturally different from the middle class (Erickson, 1984; McDermott & Gospodinoff, 1979; Ogbu, 1982; Shannon, 1985).

We conclude that no single explanation is adequate for differences in literacy in the print-rich society of the United States. The examination of social contexts and culture allows us to consider a variety of meanings, expressions, and values of literacy. We need to consider the similarities and differences between literacy learning among those who have never had an opportunity to become literate and those who are surrounded by a print-based culture but still fail to become sufficiently literate. One factor in this analysis may be the relative importance of subculture membership in groups that do not value or use literacy in the same ways dominant cultures in the United States do.

Shirley Brice Heath

Heath (1983) focused her work on the social base of literacy. She believed "the place of language in the cultural life of each social group is interdependent with the habits and values of behaving shared among members of that group" (p. 11).

Heath's work furthered understanding of differences in communicative traditions and the impact those traditions made on the varying uses of literacy. From 1969 to 1978, she investigated three communities in North Carolina to discover what becoming literate and orally competent meant in those societies, how oral and literate traditions interrelated, and whether ways of thinking about literacy were distinct among the three communities. She designated the three communities as Maintown, the middle-class section of the town; Tracton, the nearby working-class black community; and Roadville, the nearby working-class white community.

Heath found that each community had its own ways of "taking" meaning from print and oral language, and each also interacted differently from the others with oral language and print. The ways of taking meaning from books were learned from the people with whom the learner associated, and were not based on texts or the reading process.

Heath told stories of the confusion that arises between people of differing traditions:

> To the chagrin of the townspeople...[Roadville] mill people were scornful of school. One young man, apprehended out of school, indicated his father was the source of his low estimation of schooling: 'Pa says tain't nothin' ter it. He says he got 'long 'thout it' (1983, p. 23).
>
> [The Roadville adults] used literacy in ways that differed from those of academically motivated parents. Among these adults, reading was a social activity, involving more than the individual reader. Solitary reading, in fact, was often interpreted as an indication that one had not succeeded socially; women who read "romance" magazines or men who read "girlie" magazines were charged with having to read to meet social needs they could not handle in real life. Written materials were often used in connection with oral explanation, narratives, and jokes about what the written materials meant or did not mean. The authority of the materials was established through social negotiation by the readers (1980, p. 128).

In contrast to the view that literacy is a solitary enterprise, Heath defined a literacy event as an occasion when "the talk revolves around a piece of writing." She considered the time talking about the text to be an integral part of the reading of the text and noted that these "literacy events" have social interactional rules that regulate the type and amount of talk about the text.

Heath's findings explain the congruence, or lack of it, that children and adult learners find between their experience and use of print at home, and how print is viewed and used in schools. In Tracton, for example:

> Individuals have relatively few occasions to focus on specific decoding skills such as letter-sound relationships. Weak readers can always find someone else to read aloud, so that the negotiation of text meaning can take place in the group....Since reading is a social activity of the group, there are few opportunities when individuals practice extracting meaning and achieving the final synthesis or re-integration of meaning on the basis of only their own experiences (1983, pp. 386-387).

When Tracton students were asked to read and respond individually in school, the request denied the essential process of group literacy that people from Tracton valued and used. For people from Maintown, whose reading and writing behaviors at home were like those valued in schools, there was little tension or dissonance. Tracton residents thus did not recognize the connections or see the value of the skills promoted at school.

Heath maintained that "a strict dichotomization between oral and literate tradition is a construct of researchers, not an accurate portrayal of reality across cultures" (1982, p. 73). Because the customs of literacy vary, the behavior of certain groups may not seem to be literate to outside observers. Both oral and written language uses must be considered in drawing a portrait of the literacy event in a community.

Arlene Hanna Fingeret

As literacy workers, we have declared our allegiance to the importance of literacy. However, there are people whose views of literacy differ from those of their literacy teachers. Many who might be classified as functionally illiterate do not see themselves as needing literacy because the social payoff is not visible to them. When an adult comes for help, the literacy skills to be taught should be scrutinized by the program staff in terms of what kinds of reading and writing the learner needs and wants: Is there a match between the program and the prospective learner?

Fingeret's studies allow us to examine why some people fail to value literacy. Those who do not respond to literacy invitations already have a social group in which they operate successfully. In a medium-sized Northeastern urban setting, Fingeret interviewed 43 illiterate adults about education, their jobs, goals, and accomplishments. She disputed the deficit perspective often attached to illiterate adults and offered the alternative portrait of an "oral subculture." Fingeret documented an interpretive community made up of family and close friends who negotiated meaning face-to-face through verbal behaviors such as ritual speech. One of her informants described his understanding of such speech:

> When somebody is just throwing hard words at you, you have to answer back....If you don't say nothing, it's a weakness....I enjoy the word games on the streets. I'm a Leo and Leo is fire...the most powerful sign. I love the power of words. Words and fire....You got to know how to conversate [sic], how to use your words, like how to use your mind (1983, p. 156).

Performance speech preserves social distances and controls information and social status. Life in an oral subculture includes a greater emphasis on face-to-face interaction, reliance on personal experience as the "primary source of legitimate knowledge," and common sense derived from the collective experience of the elders and tested day to day in the social world. "In the oral subculture, events structure time, rather than the reverse. The material conditions of poverty, a reality for many illiterate adults, further encourage a culture of 'getting by.' " Fingeret added to the literate/illiterate contrast by asserting that when members of the oral subculture contrast their ways with those of the literate culture, they view "efforts to 'think about' rather than to 'do' as energy which is misdirected and dubiously productive" (p. 158).

A deficit model of illiteracy predicts that adult illiterates would be unable to handle the demands of daily living in a print-saturated society. However, Fingeret characterized her respondents not as dependent but as interdependent in inner (frequently familial) and extended networks that can include consistent relationships with people such as employers or representatives of caretaker agencies. The latter are less likely than the former to be called upon for help. Illiterates share their own skills with the literacy helpers through an informal barter system in which one person may read and write letters, while another may take care of the children.

Fingeret also examined the social contexts of ABE. Ten years after Mezirow, Darkenwald, and Knox studied ABE programs, Fingeret completed her study in North Carolina (1985). Many of the difficulties found earlier were still evident. Teachers (mostly elementary) were isolated, having little or no opportunity to consider their teaching assumptions and beliefs. They were not involved in ongoing training and professional organization, or in contact with other ABE people. While students, instructors, and administrators were positive about their programs, Fingeret found both a lack of assessment and the possibility of comparison from instructor to instructor or program to program. Among other problems, Fingeret listed low instructor salaries, lack of payment for preparation time, lack of supervisor training, dependence on part-time instructors, and use of materials in group settings that were designed for one-to-one instruction.

Intergenerational and Family Literacy

Programs in family and intergenerational literacy aim to prevent further generations of children from growing up in environments that do not support the development of literacy. Intergenerational literacy gleams with the attractive quality of a Norman Rockwell painting of a family (like the image of the father and child reading together that was used during the National Coalition's campaign). It is attractive to imagine the prevention of illiteracy; doing the hard work of ameliorating adult literacy seems to some to be too little, too late.

Sticht was one of the earliest advocates of intergenerational literacy, first presenting a paper on the topic in 1979. Both Sticht and Kozol testified before Congress on the link between parent and child education (Sticht, 1989). Sticht and McDonald (1989) also argued in favor of teaching literacy intergenerationally; their 1989 conference report on the intergenerational transfer of cognitive ability was intriguingly titled "Making the Nation Smarter." They argued that children acquire their cognitive ability within the family, and that the social environment "provides the basic tools of thought, language, concepts, and the means and motivation for intellectual activities" (p. 1). According to cognitive development theory, intergenerational literacy efforts "are about human and social capital."

The rationale for intergenerational literacy is the need to strengthen the child-adult connection in order to break "the intergenerational cycle of undereducation by improving parents' childcare skills and uniting parents and children in a positive educational experience" (Darling, 1989). Since literate parents read to their children, help them learn to write, and surround them with sources of literacy, their children are more likely to become literate. Evidence suggests that school achievement and scores on national tests (such as the NAEP) are higher for children whose parents have more education and who have books in their home (Applebee, Langer, & Mullis, 1988). Conversely, parents who are less literate are less supportive of their children's literacy learning and less able to pass on positive feelings about schooling and the importance of literacy.

Ruth Nickse

Nickse, for many years the director of Collaborations for Literacy in Boston, is one of the pioneers of intergenerational literacy. Her program focused on providing positive one-to-one learning experiences for low-literate adults who then would be able to pass the experiences on to their children. The tutors were paid with college work-study monies and trained by the Literacy Volunteers of Massachusetts. The content materials were books from the *Reading Rainbow* television series, books covering occupational and career awareness, functional materials required in the parents' lives, and children's books.

Nickse was commissioned by the U.S. Office of Education, Research, and Improvement to write an overview of intergenera-

Newman and Beverstock

tional and family literacy programs (1989). In her comprehensive report, she covered the research base, motivation, administration, designs, variations, effectiveness, issues, and concerns. As complex as the challenges are in assembling program information and research on general adult literacy, Nickse said the search was even more complicated in intergenerational literacy because the range of funding and sponsoring agencies was wider, no single national outlet for information had been established, and the concept of intergenerational literacy was relatively new.

Nickse categorized intergenerational programs into four types:

Type 1	Direct service to adults and children
Type 2	Indirect service to adults and children
Type 3	Direct service to adults with indirect service to children
Type 4	Indirect service to adults with direct service to children

Nickse's classification makes obvious the variety of programs and the multiplicities of approaches possible under this classification system. Her own program was an example of Type 3. Although some efforts were already under way—notably the Kenan Trust Family Literacy Project in Kentucky (Type 1)—others had been funded for too brief a time to have made a substantial difference in the literacy of parents and children.

Other issues identified by Nickse included the need for multidisciplinary staffing "with representation from adult basic education, child development, reading, and family systems theory" (p. 3); collaboration across many agencies; appropriate sites (especially for programs that include both parents and children); culturally sensitive and appropriate curricula; assessment; dissemination of program models; successful practices; and technical assistance (particularly difficult because there is no central information source). Nickse emphasized that sensitivity is required in telling parents how to act. People who are threatened by the criticism of their way of life implied by the demand that they become more literate sometimes regard intergenerational literacy programs as a form of "cultural imperialism" (Auerbach, 1989). Nickse cautioned that since we don't yet know what works best, we need to try many variations.

Sharon Darling

Darling (1989) reported on the programs of the Kenan Family Trust operating in Kentucky and North Carolina. In these programs, parents and preschool-age children attended school together and worked with a staff that included an adult education teacher, a preschool teacher, and an assistant preschool teacher. These programs fit into Nickse's Type 1 category, since direct services are provided to both parents and children. The instructional components of the program for the parents included individualized literacy training (about 3 hours a day), parenting practice (directed parent/child activities), parent education (sessions devoted to the parents' needs and concerns), and preemployment education. The children enjoyed 3 hours of preschool while their parents were in class.

Darling reported a variety of indicators of the success of the programs. Parent accomplishments included acceptance of responsibility in getting jobs and participating in their own and their children's schooling. Their parenting skills increased, as did their awareness of themselves as worthwhile adults. Darling categorized child accomplishments into indications of maturity (desire to attend school, arrive on time, take turns), cognitive growth (think better, make choices and decisions, follow through on activities with less direction), and affective growth (develop distinct personalities, talk about personal feelings). Darling's approach to family literacy captured national and international attention. Within a relatively short period of time, more than 1,000 requests for information were filled, 10 states appropriated funds to set up similar programs, and 100 locations applied for Even Start monies to fund programs. She serves as consultant to the Barbara Bush Foundation for Public Literacy.

Ruth Handel and Ellen Goldsmith

Handel and Goldsmith (1989, 1990) worked in New York community colleges and directed voluntary workshops for students.

Their workshops are another example of a Type 3 program, one that focuses primarily on the adult but expects changes in the children as well. The workshops included a discussion of home read-aloud strategies, an instructor read-aloud, presentation of a children's literature selection and modeling of the accompanying reading strategy, practice of the strategy through role playing and discussion, presentation of an adult reading selection and review of the reading strategy, and the lending of books to read to the children at home.

Handel and Goldsmith discussed the difficulties in evaluating this kind of program which, for the most part, must depend on self-reports of the participants and can be confirmed only with informal observation. The authors reported that the most dramatic testimony to the motivational value of the program was the participants' transformation from apathetic students in the remedial classroom to eager, competent adults in the workshop. This transformation was supported by the increased reading test scores of the participants.

Handel and Goldsmith undertook case study interviews to examine the results of the program. They found that the parents developed home literacy environments to foster the development of their children, involved their children in reading activities, and often became active in their children's schools. For parent readers in the program, the results included personal "validation, a timely reminder [to read to their children while they were young], a chance to reexperience childhood, new learning, confidence, a social context of peer support, and lack of pressure." They concluded that "the affective components of the project—experiential curriculum, peer interaction, building on parent motivation, the enjoyable nature of children's literature—are instrumental in developing the students' cognitive competencies related to literacy and in promoting abilities to transfer them to their children" (p. 16).

Eunice Askov, Connie Maclay, and Brett Bixler

In a program focused primarily on parents, Askov and her colleagues reported on the use of computer courseware with parents of children in Chapter 1 programs (federally funded reading improvement programs for disadvantaged children). In a survey of informational materials routinely sent to parents of Chapter 1 children, Askov, Maclay, and Bixler found that the materials inadvertently perpetuated illiteracy because they "were of a high read-ability level, too difficult for the low-literate parents of children being served in compensatory reading programs" (1988, p. 2).

In order to provide a whole family approach, the authors initiated the Penn State Adult Literacy Courseware project. The courseware involved a whole word approach along with some word-building activities to expand the word recognition of adult nonreaders. In 46 sites in Pennsylvania, parents of "Chapter 1 identified" children were invited to visit schools, libraries, or churches and use the courseware. In some cases, individual parents were oriented to the program without their children and then were able to come and use the computer during class time. Sometimes both parents attended, and the teacher worked with one parent while the other used the computer. Other times, the children attended with their parent or parents. In many cases the presence of the children was positive for both parent and child, but in other cases the parents were embarrassed to display their rudimentary reading skills to their children. When the children did not attend, child care was important. Scheduling was both important and difficult to arrange, and seemed easiest when the computer was located in either the teacher's or the student's home.

The authors had to overcome several difficulties in order to start the project. The teachers in the program had little or no experience in working with adults. In some cases, they were unfamiliar with and apprehensive about the use of computers. Recruiting parents was a hurdle that seemed to disappear when word got around; adult learners saved face by saying they were learning to use computers.

The researchers documented a gain of 1.5 years in reading grade levels (tested with the Slosson Oral Reading Test, two parts of the Baltimore County Design, and the Bader Reading and Language Inventory in just 20 hours of instruction. Askov and her team noted that comparable gains "usually take a minimum of 50-80 hours" (1988, p. 9). The children's achievement also improved (although not significantly more than other Chapter 1 children), and their attendance increased.

Workplace Literacy

The workplace is the arena where public and economic needs most directly collide with personal illiteracies. What we do not know makes our pictures of workplace literacy partial, our basis for action questionable, and our need for further information urgent.

The key word in workplace literacy is *technology*. Technology is the most frequently cited culprit in causing longtime workers to become unemployed and unemployable when their jobs are automated beyond their schooling and skills. But technology also is regarded as a potential savior because it is a rapid and efficient means for teaching workers basic and new skills.

Some studies suggest that rapid initial learning is possible (Askov, Maclay, & Bixler, 1988; Taggart, 1986), but in the longer term, it is debatable whether such rapid progress can be sustained (Sticht, 1982). In computer-aided literacy programs, the least literate have been the most enthusiastic about computers; their optimistic attitude is that they can finally control something (Askov & Brown, 1988). But we do not know if this new control transfers to any other aspects of their lives. In addition to questions about feeling in control, questions remain about the transfer of what is learned using the various forms of teaching technology (computer-aided instruction, interactive video) to print tasks in the real world.

The basis of the U.S. economy is changing from manufacturing to service. When there is a mismatch between workers' literacy and the task at hand, employers have three choices: increase the workers' literacy, modify the task and materials to suit their skills, or lay them off (Bormuth, 1973). But people disagree about the trend in skills requirements on the job. Various views include: skills requirements are being upgraded; skills requirements are being downgraded; skills requirements are being polarized with no middle level; some new jobs require more skills and some require fewer skills than previously. Some fear that a permanent class of unskilled workers is being established. In the future, workers will make as many as 10 job changes in their lifetimes. These changes will require both specific new job skills and the ability to learn rapidly. A disturbing change concerns the decrease in internal promotions that has come about because employers are finding there is a big difference between entry-level skills and those of the higher rungs on the ladder (Collino, Aderman, & Askov, 1988). These trends are of great concern to literacy providers for future planning.

The question of skills requirements is intertwined with the minimum levels of education employers seek in filling positions. The real requirements of a job are elusive, unlike the indicators of attainment officially cited in the ad. For example, high school diplomas or college degrees may be regarded as direct certification of the applicants' skills, or they may be valued as an indirect indication of such attitudes and habits as timeliness and amenability to taking directions from others. The use of general standardized reading tests as screening devices in employment was judicially struck down (Mikulecky & Coy, 1989); only measures that are directly related to the actual skills required on the job are legal.

Money comes up in any discussion of business and industry, and the cost of workplace literacy is no exception. Collino, Aderman, and Askov (1988) quoted the American Association for Training and Development (ASTD) as stating that combined formal and informal training on the job costs $210 billion a year. ASTD estimated the cost of remedial training and the lost productivity of underskilled workers at about $25 billion annually. Xerox estimated that 1 percent of industry's training costs — roughly $2 billion a year — goes toward teaching basic skills. These dollar amounts make adult literacy educators gasp at the disparity between what workplace illiteracy is costing America and the amount of money allocated to correcting the problem.

From 1980 to 1985, state administered adult literacy programs received about $100 million a year. Since then, the funds dedicated to adult literacy have steadily risen. Most recently the amounts have doubled, and it is expected that they will continue to rise dramatically. In the language of business and industry, educating for literacy is more cost effective than paying the price of illiteracy. Sticht, who has done much of the pioneer research on literacy in work contexts, suggests:

> Business and industry are going to have to pick up a greater portion of education. It would probably cost between $5 bil-

lion and $10 billion over the next few years to establish literacy programs and retool current ones. But the returns of that are going to be tenfold (U.S. Department of Education, 1988, p. 40).

Partnerships are needed among government, literacy providers, and business and industry, so that each can inform the others and work toward creating programs that benefit everyone.

Thomas Sticht

Sticht began his study of adult literacy in the 1960s. The study of workplace literacy stands on the foundations he has laid. Much of his research was conducted in the context of military literacy. His research has covered most of the field. He has examined the reading and basic skills demands in the military and other work environments, appropriate text and manual design, high school environments, assessments, the learning potential of the "marginally literate," readability formulas for technical material, and the intergenerational transfer of cognitive skills.

Sticht et al.'s (1972) study, "Project Realistic" was contemporaneous with the first of the national studies of functional literacy in the United States (Harris, 1970, 1971). Project Realistic was an indepth examination of the functional literacy demands of three occupations in the military (each of which had civilian counterparts) — cooks, vehicle repair technicians, and supply clerks. The researchers based their assessment of the literacy demands of each occupation on what they called job knowledge and job performance data. Their assessment included reading, listening, and arithmetic, tested both with multiple-choice exams covering job knowledge and with 4-5 hours of individual simulations of job performance. The readability levels of the materials used on each job also were estimated, although the researchers noted that the application of readability formulas designed for estimating the grade level of children's materials yielded "ridiculous conclusions," such as a "grade level requirement for cooks at 9.0, for repair technicians at 14.5, and supply clerks at 16+" (p. 460).

These high estimates of reading difficulty did not match the educational attainment of the people in these jobs. Sticht et al. found that reading materials in the repair technician and supply clerk categories exceeded the average reading abilities of the high aptitude personnel by four to six grade levels and of low aptitude personnel by six to eight grade levels (1972, p. 460). They theorized that people who use these materials "develop specialized bodies of knowledge that help them comprehend the relatively narrow domain of job literacy materials." Applying these insights in *Forecast*, his special readability formula for technical materials, Sticht (1988) put less emphasis on the difficulty of long words than do more traditional readability formulas. He reasoned that the long words are apt to be familiar terms used frequently on the job, and they do not present the challenge that long, unfamiliar words do. *Forecast* allowed the reduction of estimates of required reading skills by as much as five grade levels.

Sticht found that people's degree of literacy depends in part on their knowledge of the content as well as on their language and reading skills. He also found that more proficient readers read more on the job, while less proficient readers (grade levels 4-6.9) were more likely to ask others for help instead of reading to find answers to their questions. Standardized reading tests were reliable predictors of ability to perform adult-level reading tasks. Sticht et al. concluded that eighth grade level was a "reasonable general purpose target for functional adult basic education," and that sixth or seventh grade levels were reasonable targets for arithmetic skills (1972, p. 463).

An error in test scoring has added interesting information concerning appropriate literacy levels for job performance. Sticht et al. (1987) examined the results of a miscalibrated aptitude test, and found that more than 300,000 "lower aptitude" people, who ordinarily would have been rejected, had entered military service between 1976 and 1980. Examination of their records showed that 80 percent had achieved satisfactory job training and job ratings. Sticht calculated that this group "performed 80-95 percent as well as average-aptitude personnel," and concluded that "great caution ought to be exercised in declaring people functionally incompetent because of their performance on literacy or other types of aptitude tests" (Sticht, 1988, p. 70).

Job performance also depends on the understanding of, and fluency in, reading learned in school. While school reading theoretically prepares students for the reading they will do for the rest of their lives, the reading demands common to school tend to be quite different from those expected in job and other adult settings (Sticht et al., 1977). School reading can be characterized as "reading to learn," or reading toward a goal of remembering what has been read. In contrast, occupational reading is "reading to do," or reading toward a goal of locating information for immediate use that need not be recalled later. In examining the reading uses of high school students, technical school students (civilian and military), technical school instructors (military), and job incumbents (civilian and military), Sticht found a "complete reversal in the frequency with which these two classes of tasks are performed" between "traditional academically oriented high schools" and the workplace (1985, p. 317).

Even taking into account the mismatch between school and job literacies, illiterate adults who seemingly have had opportunities to become sufficiently literate pose questions for literacy workers. Because literacy is language-based, some have wondered about the oral language capacity of the inadequately literate, and whether oral language can be the basis for reading improvement. Sticht (1982) investigated the reading potential of marginally literate adults and the assumption that adults are able to learn to read more quickly than children because they have a larger base of language and experience. Contrary to expectations, Sticht found that they are not. Sticht also compared literacy gains for the marginally literate between those who participated in brief, general literacy programs and those who received job-related instruction. Marginally literate adults made twice as much progress in job-related instruction as they did in the general literacy program. Sticht concluded that reading instruction should center on job-related literacies.

If adults are underliterate and make slow progress in literacy instruction, the question arises whether it might be better simply to teach those people using means other than reading. Sticht, Hooke, & Caylor (1982) tested both reading levels and listening levels. They concluded that the substitution of oral instruction would not be very productive.

Since the research was carried out with academic materials, Sticht warned that the same people might have performed differently with real world tasks, which he termed more "ecologically representative reading and listening tasks" (1985, p. 328). Kirsch and Jungeblut (1986) later confirmed Sticht's conclusions, using tasks that were more typical of daily life.

Sticht and Mikulecky (1984) examined job-related basic skills in three cases, including the Functional Literacy Project (FLIT) of the U.S. Department of Defense. They advanced a psycholinguistic model of literacy, according to which language, cognition, and perception are critical to using literacy. The worker must know about the job (background knowledge) and must have higher level cognitive skills (reasoning) to read job-related materials successfully. Sticht and Mikulecky recommended that literacy programs include the objectives of the business, have a functional context, require active learning, and use competency-based mastery learning.

Workplace Literacy Questions

Workplace literacy remains an inadequately researched area of concern. Mikulecky, a foremost analyst of workplace literacy, stated that "no coherent body of research exists on the cost effectiveness of technology-driven basic skills education and of workplace basic skills education" (1989). Industry sponsorship of literacy and basic-skills instruction challenges literacy providers to keep at least two sets of agendas in mind. The employers need job-literate workers to improve their skills as rapidly as possible; workers need to fulfill both their employer's specific skill requirements and their own objectives. Displaced workers have special needs, but they may not always be motivated to embark on a course of technical training for a new job. They may be more inclined to participate in training if technical and more general literacy are offered in an integrated program (Park, Storlie, & Dawis, 1987). Stein (1989) contended that the most effective workplace literacy programs allow these agendas to coexist. Thus, while workers meet job requirements, they also gain a sense of improving for themselves. Employers report better teamwork, higher morale, and greater productivity.

Mikulecky (1989) suggested that levels of skills required by the workplace can be classified into three problem areas: (1) extremely low-level literates (those unable to function independently with even simple print); (2) new and experienced workers who can read at a moderate level (the sports page), consider themselves to be literate, but derive little benefit from expensive training because of insufficient reading, computing, and study abilities; and (3) workers at any ability level who make some job-related literacy mistakes that influence safety, productivity,and promotability (p. 20). These skill levels require different approaches; Mikulecky suggested a "multistrand approach" to address the literacy learning needs of people at each of these levels.

While there is evidence that basic skills are learned in the context of job-specific training, questions remain about the appropriate balance of technical training and basic skills instruction (Phillipi, 1988). In a study of language use in 10 occupations, Rush, Moe, and Storlie (1986) emphasized the importance of organizing information meaningfully and relating it to the learner's knowledge and interests.

Askov suggests there may be a learning cycle that begins with instruction in *reading to do* in specific job training and later broadens into *reading to learn.* That broadening of purpose and content could be termed *education* as opposed to the more limited scope of *training.* This cycle was instituted in Philadelphia in a nursing home that offered basic instruction to improve employees' skills in filling out myriad forms. At first, instruction was focused on the forms; but when the instructor learned that the employees were motivated to earn their GEDs and to move beyond their present employment, the classes were broadened in scope. The employers, at first dismayed by the change of focus, came to believe that it was their social obligation to continue the class, even if it qualified workers to move on to different employment (Askov, personal communication, October 1989).

Instructional approaches to the teaching of basic skills also raise questions about whether discrete teaching of basic skills in a workbook approach can be sufficient, or whether the skills should be contextualized into larger frames of metacognitive awareness and problem-solving models (Mikulecky, Ehlinger, & Meenan, 1987).

Solid Indicators and Remaining Questions

We have learned many lessons from research on adult literacy. We need better basic information; we must see literacy learners as more than deficient individuals; we need to know more about the function of social networks as they affect literacy and learning; we must remain leery of categorizing people; we must look beyond the unexamined application of conclusions about children's literacy to adults; and we need to know more about workplace literacies and how to efficiently provide workers with what they need to know.

Alamprese's (1988) general research agenda suggested the development of "an underlying base of knowledge and expertise that can move the current state of operations forward." The four areas she identified were research on learning, research on instruction, development of assessment and accountability systems, and research on the organization and delivery of services. We concur that adult literacy stands in need of additional understanding and development in each of these areas.

Because counting procedures vary greatly, even the simple question of how many people are being served in literacy programs is difficult to answer. Alamprese called for the establishment of a national database including learner and program characteristics, program impact, and fiscal support.

> The lack of a reliable national database...presents a major barrier to the establishment of a cohesive system for adult basic skills education. Better information about the status of our current literacy efforts is needed by individuals at all levels of government, as well as by those responsible for designing and operating basic education programs (p. 6).

The social perspectives on literacy expounded by Heath and by Fingeret give us help in perceiving literacy learners as more than deficient individuals. Their results demand that we examine literacy as a part of the entire social fabric, rather than as isolated skills and attainments. We cannot expect to see changes in literacy if we do not take into account its meanings and uses for a variety of literacy learners and nonlearners. And we need to know more about the social networks and connections for learners that promote rapid literacy development. We join Sheikh in her mistrust of overly tidy labeling of learners, and expect that as we have better descriptions of learners, there will be less temptation to label. In this socially centered work, as well as with intergenerational and family literacy programs, we are challenged to respect learners' cultures before suggesting additional or alternative literacies.

We join other reviewers of research in being wary of applying to adults data from studies of children (Fingeret, 1984; Sticht, 1988). However, Sticht calls for unified theories, practices, and policies that bring together child and adult literacy development. He suggests that we need a unified theory for both old and young, and a simultaneous awareness that the "functional contexts of childhood and adulthood are not the same" (p. 85). Perhaps some of the unified theory Sticht calls for will emerge from intergenerational and family literacy efforts. These diverse programs have a common function in their dual goals of encouraging a wide range of family literacies and preventing the development of further generations of cognitively deficient, illiterate adults.

Developments in the workplace require us to look beyond the traditional educational infrastructure to business and industry. Literacy providers find themselves with at least two clients—workers and employers—and literacy workers need to know more in order to fill the orders they are receiving. Sticht concludes that more research is needed to determine whether demands in the workplace are actually increasing, whether workers' skills are indeed insufficient for their jobs, and whether "approaches to literacy education can be developed that are attractive to both industry and the work force" (1988, p. 84). Alamprese calls for the assessment of the utility of approaching literacy education through functional literacy education (programs that integrate literacy with job development) for "developing both the specific and general literacy skills and content knowledge adults need to operate successfully in society" (1988, p. 23).

Mikulecky (1986) suggests the need for the following lines of research: 1) examine the literacy process in workplace settings and describe "how one reads most effectively in the workplace"; 2) examine and test the Sticht model of developmental information processing in the workplace; 3) determine the costs of workplace literacy deficiencies and then calculate "who is worth training" and when it is cost-effective to seek alternatives to further training; 4) learn more about the degree of transfer of training; 5) address the direct teaching of metacognitive strategies for workplace training and application; and 6) develop and test the use of various expert systems for the teaching of job literacy tasks.

Close examination of adult literacy leads us to further questions. The challenges are substantial, the foci as diverse as literacies are various, and the demands pressing. As Sticht suggests, we need problem solvers—thoughtful people working in the field to build and test understanding and theories while implementing them experimentally.

References

Alamprese, J.A. (1988). *Adult literacy research and development: An agenda for action.* Paper prepared for Project on Adult Literacy, Washington, DC. (ED 302 676)

Applebee, A.N., Langer, J., & Mullis, I. (1988). *Who reads best? Factors related to reading achievement in grades 3, 7, and 11.* Princeton, NJ: Educational Testing Service.

Askov, E.N., & Brown, E.J. (1988). Attitudes of adult literacy students and their teachers toward computers for instruction: Before and after use. In D. Lumpkin, M. Harshbarger, P. Ransom, & J. Williams (Eds.), *The dilemmas of teaching reading.* Muncie, IN: Ball State University.

Askov, E.N., Maclay, C.M., & Bixler, B. (1988). *An intergenerational study of the impact of computer-assisted reading instruction with low-literate parents.* University Park, PA: Institute for the Study of Adult Literacy, Pennsylvania State University.

Auerbach, E.R. (1989). Toward a social-contextual approach to family literacy. *Harvard Educational Review, 592,* 165-181.

Belenky, M.F., Clincy, B.M., Goldberger, N.R., & Tarule, J.M. (1986). *Women's ways of knowing: The development of self, voice, and mind.* New York: Basic Books.

Bormuth, J.R. (1973). Reading literacy: Its definition and assessment. *Reading Research Quarterly, 9* (1), 7-66.

Carrell, P. (1979). The components of background in reading comprehension. *Language Learning, 33,* 183-207.

Clay, M. (1979). *The early detection of reading difficulties: A diagnostic survey with recovery procedures* (2nd ed.). Portsmouth, NH: Heinemann.

Collino, G.E., Aderman, E.M., & Askov, E.N. (1988). *Literacy and job performance: A perspective.* University Park, PA: Pennsylvania State University.

Darkenwald, G. (1986). *Effective approaches to teaching basic skills to adults: A research synthesis* (Contract No. OERI-P-86-3015). Paper prepared for the Office of Educational Research and Improvement of the U.S. Department of Education, Washington, DC.

Darling, S. (1989). *The Kenan Trust Family Literacy Project: Preliminary final report.* Unpublished report, Louisville, KY.

Diekhoff, G.M. (1988). An appraisal of adult literacy programs: Reading between the lines. *Journal of Reading, 31*(7), 624-630.

Drew, R., & Mikulecky, L. (1988). *How to gather and develop job specific literacy materials for basic skills instruction.* Bloomington, IN: Office of Education and Training Resources, Indiana University.

Erickson, F. (1984). School literacy, reasoning, and civility: An anthropologist's perspective. *Review of Educational Research, 54*(4), 525-546.

Fargo, J.E., & Collins, M. (1989). Learning from researching: Literacy practitioners and assessment of adults' reading progress. *Journal of Reading, 33*(2), 120-127.

Fattu, J.M., & Patrick, E.A. (1983). *Outcome Advisor: A computer diagnostic program.* Englewood Cliffs, NJ: Prentice Hall.

Fingeret, A. (1984). *Adult literacy education: Current and future directions.* Columbus, OH: ERIC Clearinghouse, Ohio State University.

Fingeret, A. (1987). *Directions in ethnographic adult literacy research.* Paper presented at the Thirty-Second Annual Convention of the International Reading Association, Anaheim, CA.

Fingeret, A. (1985). *North Carolina adult basic education instructional program evaluation.* North Carolina ABE Evaluation Project. Raleigh, NC: North Carolina State University.

Fingeret, A. (1983, February). Oral subculture membership: A nondeficit approach to illiterate adults. *Lifelong Learning Conference Proceedings.* College Park, MD: University of Maryland. (ED 226 228)

Freire, P. (1970). The adult education process as cultural action freedom. In E.R. Kintgen, B.N. Kroll, & M. Rose (Eds.), *Perspectives on literacy* (pp. 398-409). Carbondale, IL: Southern Illinois University Press.

Gardner, H. (1983). *Frames of mind: The theory of multiple intelligences.* New York: Basic Books.

Gilligan, C. (1982). *In a different voice: Psychological theory and women's development.* Cambridge, MA: Harvard University Press.

Goldsmith, E., & Handel, R.D. (1990). *Family reading: An intergenerational approach to literacy.* Syracuse, NY: New Readers Press.

Handel, R.D., & Goldsmith, E. (1989). *Intergenerational reading: Affecting the literacy environment of the home.* Paper presented at the annual meeting of the American Educational Research Association, San Francisco, CA.

Harris, L., & Associates. (1970). *Survival Literacy Study.* Washington, DC: U.S. Government Printing Office.

Harris, L., & Associates. (1971). *The 1971 national reading difficulty index: A study of functional reading ability in the United States.* Washington, DC: National Reading Center.

Heath, S.B. (1980). The functions and uses of literacy. *Journal of Communications, 30*(1), 123-133.

Heath, S.B. (1982). What no bedtime story means: Narrative skills at home and school. *Language in Society, 11*(2), 49-76.

Heath, S.B. (1983). *Ways with words.* New York: Cambridge University Press.

Higgs, T., & Clifford, R. (1982). The push toward communication. In T. Higgs (Ed.), *Curriculum competence and the foreign language speaker.* Skokie, IL: National Textbook.

Hunter, C.S., & Harman, D. (1979). *Adult illiteracy in the United States.* New York: McGraw-Hill.

Hunter, C.S., & Harman, D. (1985). *Adult illiteracy in the United States* (paperback edition). New York: McGraw-Hill.

Johnston, P. (1985, May). Understanding reading disability: A case study approach. *Harvard Educational Review, 55*(2), 153-177.

Kazemek, F.E. (1988). Women and adult literacy: Considering the other half of the house. *Lifelong Learning, 11*(4), 23-24.

Kirsch, I.S., & Jungeblut, A. (1986). *Literacy: Profiles of America's young adults.* NAEP Report No. 16-PL-02. Princeton, NJ: National Assessment of Educational Progress.

Labov, W. (1972). *Language in the inner city.* Philadelphia, PA: University of Pennsylvania Press.

Lerche, R.S. (1985). *Effective adult literacy programs: A practitioner's guide.* New York: Cambridge.

McCune, D., & Alamprese, J. (1985). *Turning illiteracy around: An agenda for national action.* Working paper No. 1. New York: Business Council for Effective Literacy.

Adult Literacy Research 165

McDermott, R.P., & Gospodinoff, K. (1979). Social contexts for ethnic borders and school failure. In A. Wolfgang (Ed.), *Nonverbal behavior*. New York: Academic Press.

McGrail, J. (1984). *Adult illiterates and adult literacy programs: A summary of descriptive data*. San Francisco, CA: Far West Laboratory for Educational Research and the Network. (ED 254 756)

Mezirow, J., Darkenwald, G.C., & Knox, A.B. (1975). *Last gamble on education: Dynamics of adult basic education*. Washington, DC: Adult Education Association of the United States.

Mikulecky, L.G. (1986). *Job literacy research: Past results and new directions*. Paper presented at the Thirty-Second Annual Convention of the International Reading Association, Anaheim, CA.

Mikulecky, L.G. (1989). *Second chance: Basic skills education*. Paper No. 999 45700904 commissioned by the U.S. Department of Labor, Commission on Workforce Quality and Labor Market Efficiency. Washington, DC: U.S. Department of Labor.

Mikulecky, L.G., & Coy, J. (1989, June). *Legal aspects of testing in the banking industry*. Paper presented at the American Bankers' Association Conference, Chicago, IL.

Mikulecky, L.G., Ehlinger, J., & Meanan, A.L. (1987). *Training for job literacy demands: What research applies to practice*. University Park, PA: Pennsylvania State University, Institute for the Study of Adult Literacy.

National directory of community based adult literacy programs. (1989). Washington DC: Association for Community Based Education.

Newman, A.P. (1980). *Adult basic education: Reading*. Boston, MA: Allyn & Bacon.

Nickse, R. (1989). *The noises of literacy: An overview of intergenerational and family literacy programs*. Paper No. 403J47900343, commissioned by the Office of Education, Research, and Improvement. Washington, DC: U.S. Department of Education.

Norman, C., & Malicky, G. (1986, May). Literacy as a social phenomenon: Implications for instruction. *Lifelong Learning*, 9(7), 12-15.

Nyikos, M. (1989). *Sex-related differences in adult language learning: Socialization and memory factors*. Paper presented at Research Perspectives in Adult Language Learning and Acquisition, Ohio State University.

Ogbu, J.U. (1982). Cultural discontinuities and schooling. *Anthropology and Education Quarterly*, 13(4), 291-307.

Park, R.J., Storlie, R., & Dawis, R.V. (1987). *The educational needs of dislocated workers in Minnesota*. Minneapolis, MN: University of Minnesota, Center for Urban and Regional Affairs.

Phillipi, J.W. (1988). Matching literacy to job training: Some applications from military programs. *Journal of Reading*, 31(7), 658-666.

Rose, M. (1988). Narrowing the mind and page: Remedial writers and cognitive reductionism. *College Composition and Communication*, 39 (3), 267-302.

Rush, R.T., Moe, A.J., & Storlie, R.L. (1986). *Occupational literacy education*. Newark, DE: International Reading Association.

Shannon, P. (1985). Reading instruction and social class. *Language Arts*, 62, 604-613.

Sheikh, M. (1986). *Computer assisted instruction in adult basic education: A model to predict success of illiterate adults in learning to read*. Doctoral dissertation, Indiana University, Bloomington, IN.

Stein, S.G. (1989). *What we have learned and are still learning*. Paper presented at the American Association for Adult and Continuing Education Conference, Atlanta, GA.

Sticht, T.G. (1982). *Evaluation of the reading potential concept for marginally literate adults*. Alexandria, VA: Human Resources Research Organization.

Sticht, T.G. (1983). *Literacy and human resources at work: Investing in the education of adults to improve the educability of children*. Professional paper 2-83. Alexandria, VA: Human Resources Research Organization.

Sticht, T.G. (1985). *Problems of illiteracy in the United States and literacy issues affecting the military*. Testimony before the House Subcomittee on Elementary, Secondary, and Vocational Education, and the Senate Subcommittee on Education, Arts, and Humanities, Washington, DC.

Sticht, T.G. (1988). Adult literacy education. In E. Rothkopf (Ed.), *Review of research in education* (vol. 15). Washington, DC: American Educational Research Association.

Sticht, T.G., Armstrong, W.B., Hickey, D.T., & Caylor, J.S. (1987). *Cast-off youth: Policy and training methods from the military experience*. New York: Praeger.

Sticht, T.G., Caylor, J.S., Kern, R.P., & Fox, L.C. (1972). Project REALISTIC: Determination of adult functional literacy skill levels. *Reading Research Quarterly, 7*(3), 424-465.

Sticht, T.G., Fox, L.C., Hauke, R., & Welty-Zapt, D. (1977). *The role of reading in the Navy* (NPRDC TR77-40). San Diego, CA: Navy Personnel Research and Development Center.

Sticht, T.G., Hooke, L.R., & Caylor, J.S. (1982). *Literacy, oracy, and vocational aptitude as predictors of attrition and promotion in the armed services*. Alexandria, VA: Human Resources Research Organization.

Sticht, T.G., & McDonald, B.A. (1989). *Making the nation smarter: The intergenerational transfer of cognitive ability*. San Diego, CA: Applied Behavioral and Cognitive Sciences.

Sticht, T.G., & Mikulecky, L. (1984). *Job-related basic skills: Cases and conclusions*. Columbus, OH: ERIC Clearinghouse on Adult, Career, and Vocational Education.

Szwed, J. (1981). The ethnography of literacy. In E. Kintgen, B. Kroll, & M. Rose (Eds.), *Perspectives on literacy*. Carbondale, IL: Southern Illinois University Press.

Taggart, R. (1986). *The comprehensive competencies program: A summary*. Alexandria, Va: Remediation and Training Institute. (ED 275 869)

U.S. Department of Education/U.S. Department of Labor (1988). *The bottom line*. Washington, DC: U.S. Department of Labor.

Watson, D.J., Harste, J.C., & Burke, E. (1989). *Whole language: Inquiring voices*. New York: Scholastic.

6

The National Coalition for Literacy

T he adult literacy movement has been a huge puzzle. Puzzle pieces prior to 1980 were scattered but significant. Newman first encountered the needs of nonreading adults in 1960 at the University of Iowa when a young man who could not read came to the Reading Clinic for help. Newman wrote to the U.S. Office of Education for help. The response was two small pamphlets—an indication of the low level of interest in adult literacy in 1960. The work of the Armed Forces in increasing the literacy of recruits during World War II had not been extended effectively to the civilian population.

The landmark Adult Education Act of 1966 changed this situation. Part of plans for the "great society," the Adult Education Act was the first piece of legislation for adult literacy. It provided for acquisition of eighth grade functional basic skills. The 1970 amendments to the act authorized instruction through the high school level. The fundamental purpose of the act continued to be the provision of adult education for those most in need of assistance. As a result of this legislation, Brown and Newman conducted one of the first pieces of civilian research on adult illiteracy, from 1966 to 1968. At the time, the study was heralded as a breakthrough. The research questions were:

1. What common characteristics do adult city-core illiterates exhibit when measured by the Wechsler Adult Intelligence Scale, the Leiter Adult Intelligence Scale, the Davis-Eells Games, and the Experience Inventory?

2. Do adult city-core illiterates make significantly faster gains in beginning reading achievement when the program uses the Initial Teaching Alphabet (i.t.a.), presents materials prepared specifically for adult interests and paced to their learning rate, and provides consultant and training services for the teachers in the program?

3. Are there significant correlations between gains in reading achievement and factors in the measuring devices mentioned above, and is there a cluster of measurements that will predict gains in reading achievement for adult city-core illiterates? (1968, p. 4).

These questions are still under consideration by the research community, even though the specifics of the measures are different.

At about this same time—during the Civil Rights era—the Right-to-Read Campaign presented literacy as a right and the lack of literacy as a national shame. In the 1970s, along with innovations in community-based education programs, the establishment of reading academies, and the search for model programs, came a reduction in the naive belief that some quick fix could completely eradicate illiteracy from the United States within a few years. The American public perceived a lowering of educational standards in the schools, which raised concerns about education at all levels. This increasing awareness was moving adult literacy to the forefront of the nation's consciousness.

Communication, Cooperation, Collaboration

In 1981 several literacy groups in the United States became members of a coalition working toward increasing literacy. As enthusiastic as we were, we little realized we were on the brink of the explosive "decade of adult literacy" and the discovery of learning as a lifelong pursuit. We represented 11 charter organizations, which together became the National Coalition for Literacy (Table 1).

At each meeting of the coalition a major new literacy development arises—a new group joins, a new event is planned, or a new political move is launched. These are heady times for literacy workers. Prepare! Consolidate! Don't lose momentum! These are the im-

Table 1

Charter Members, Coalition for Literacy

American Association for Adult and Continuing Education (AAACE)
American Association of Advertising Agencies (AAAA)
American Library Association (ALA)
B. Dalton Bookseller
Contact Literacy Center
International Reading Association (IRA)
Laubach Literacy Action (LLA)
Literacy Volunteers of America (LVA)
National Advisory Council on Adult Education (NACAE)
National Commission on Libraries and Information Science (NCLIS)
National Council of State Directors of Adult Education (NCSDAE)

perative thoughts of the "old timers" in the coalition. A decade ago we could not imagine what the 1980s would bring; at the beginning of the 1990s, we have to run to keep up.

The 1980s saw the birth of America's awareness of the needs of adult new readers. Millions wanted a new start, and in 1990, they have many places to turn. The national hotline directs calls for help to a listed local agency or literacy support group, television programs and radio announcements give encouragement and directions for finding help with learning, and media events are staged to raise funds. Legislators are introducing bills at the state and federal level to supply more financial backing, to promote better teaching, and to build a national literacy center. Business and industry are reorganizing their energies toward work-related literacy training, and unions and management alike are seeking to help workers who are inadequately literate overcome their vulnerability. The most visible champion of adult literacy is First Lady Barbara Bush, who is continuing her own long-time involvement as a literacy worker.

The new readers themselves are now emerging at the national level. People who dared not speak out before are speaking now. Their words are being heard at historic meetings: in Philadelphia at the First Adult Literacy Student Congress in 1987, and in Washington, DC, at the Second Student Congress in 1989. Their messages are disseminated among the coalition's member groups, and they are being heard over the phone at the Indiana University Reading Practicum Center: "Rhonda at the detox center told me to call you. She said you could help."

I talk with Rhonda's friend. His life is falling apart. He's separated from his wife. He stays away from home to avoid his 12-year-old son, who needs help with his homework—help he knows he can't give. He is a Vietnam vet who has trouble being with people. But here he is—on my phone—searching for a new start at age 41. "My life is a mess," he says. "I've got to do something. Can you help?" We start the wheels rolling. We find a tutor, work out tutoring times, and search for meaningful materials for this literacy beginner.

Every group is working toward the same end: new readers who suddenly are doing what they had been afraid to try before. These organizations form the coalition, which fosters ongoing communication, cooperation, and collaboration on the national literacy scene. Communication within the coalition and the literacy field has been greatly enhanced by *The Written Word*, the bimonthly newsletter published by the Contact Literacy Center in Lincoln, Nebraska.

In 1985, when the coalition reexamined its purpose, the members recognized that one of the greatest advantages of the regular meetings was increased communication among members. The meetings kept members informed, allowed cooperative planning among groups, and prompted new ideas to be tried. In 1988, when the group again reassessed its reason for being, the highest priority was placed on communication. The first of the newly developed objectives was to "provide for ongoing communication among national groups whose primary and continuing interest is literacy." Cooperation among the member groups has included working together on campaigns, sharing limited funds, and sharing staff.

Campaigns and the Coalition

Forerunner of the many literacy activities spawned during the 1980s, the Coalition for Literacy, along with the American Advertising Council, sponsored a nationwide advertising campaign in 1985. The media contributed over $24 million worth of free advertising during the campaign, and millions of people got involved.

There is a difference between campaigns and coalitions. Campaigns tend to be run by a few leaders, burn hot for awhile, and accomplish an important but sometimes limited result. Coalitions, on the other hand, need to be broadly representative and long lasting, and must serve the needs of diverse interests and individuals.

The National Coalition for Literacy started out as a campaign, achieved early success, and then metamorphosed into a coalition for a longer run and long term productivity. The coalition was the broadly democratic outcome of initiatives from many sectors— public, private, corporate, and professional. Early contributors to the coalition included the U.S. Department of Education, B. Dalton Bookseller, the Business Council for Effective Literacy, General Electric, and Time, Inc.

The people and the organizations that produced the initial campaign each had their own special interest in literacy. The American Library Association (ALA), for example, took an interest because a literate populace gives libraries their reason for being. But it could not mount a literacy awareness campaign alone—its interest was too narrow and its resources too few. In the ALA's realization that it must involve others, the idea was born of a literacy coalition representative of the varied literacy interests in the United States. The coalition met the American Advertising Council's criteria for a national campaign: it was of broad benefit, and it had many groups behind the effort. The Ad Council took on the project.

Effects of the Volunteer Against Illiteracy Campaign

Except for a brief National Literacy Crusade in 1924 (Cook, 1977), the Coalition for Literacy/Ad Council Volunteer Against Illiteracy campaign was the first national effort exclusively for the benefit of adult literacy to be attempted in the United States. The initial purposes, processes, and outcomes are documented in the evaluation study completed by Newman in 1986. This was a first for the Advertising Council, as it had not had resources to evaluate any of its earlier campaigns. Evaluation also enabled the coalition both to assess the impact of the Ad Council's campaign against illiteracy and to document achievement of the two major goals of the campaign: raising awareness of the problem and increasing resources for tackling it.

Awareness of the problems faced by functionally illiterate adults and out-of-school youths increased markedly during 1985. Calls to the Contact Literacy Center increased from 962 in January to a high of 3,587 in September 1985. The Ad Council's Benchmark Study showed that awareness of advertising about illiteracy had increased from 21.4 to 30.0 percent, that people recalled specific advertising elements, and that the general public had become more familiar with the issue by the end of the year. The ad campaign spurred concern and encouraged volunteerism.

The Survey Research Center surveyed a random sample of literacy-related programs to determine the changes in resources devoted to literacy efforts between Fall 1984 and Fall 1985. Some results are summarized in Table 2 (Newman, 1986, p. 53). The study found that enrollments and budgets in literacy programs had increased slightly; that growth in enrollment was more evident among volunteer programs than among Adult Basic Education (ABE) affiliated programs; that the number of volunteer teachers had increased by almost 29 percent during the year; and that 8,000 new teachers and 10,000 new students had come to literacy programs via the Contact Literacy Center telephone referral service. The center had referred at least one volunteer to each center polled.

Table 2
Changes in Students, Teachers, and Budgets
of Literacy Programs, Fall 1984 to Fall 1985

	Fall 1984	Fall 1985	Percent Change
Number of Programs Surveyed	567	567	
Estimated Number of Students	395,000	400,000	+ 1.3%
Estimated Number of Volunteer Teachers	75,000	96,000	+ 28.7%
Estimated Total Literacy Program Budgets	$100 million	$109 million	+ 9.0%

Budgets for literacy programs during the survey period grew for all types of programs. Funding for the Literacy Volunteers of America (LVA), libraries, and unaffiliated programs had the greatest percentage increases. Because these were the smallest of the programs, their increases seemed more spectacular. More disappointingly, total funding increased only 9 percent—not much above the inflation rate and not a tremendous gain, particularly for the large ABE programs serving larger numbers of people.

Other findings were more encouraging. Two volunteer tutor groups, Laubach Literacy Action (LLA) and LVA, reported that requests for help rose 100 percent. The U.S. Department of Education reported a whopping increase of 243 percent in its National Adult Education Volunteer Network between 1983 and 1985. The surge in literacy workers helped meet this new demand. In addition to the increase in the number of volunteers, the number of paid workers in volunteer organizations rose substantially. In addition, the number of LVA sites increased 137 percent in 1985, while Laubach sites increased 24 percent, and ABE sites 37 percent.

One of the most dramatic increases in resources came from grants. The dollar amount contributed by foundations, businesses, and industries rose from under $1 million in 1980 to over $85 million in 1985. Increased media time, materials contributions, volunteer contributions (other than tutoring), and in-kind contributions from coalition member groups (printing, mailings, travel) all attest to the phenomenal increase in giving for literacy (Newman, 1986).

Each group within the coalition continued its individual activities; therefore each continued to need its own financial support. Raising funds was one of the most serious difficulties to threaten the coalition. Through lean years, each group continued to raise funds for itself instead of for the Coalition as a whole; nonetheless, representatives of the 11 charter member organizations recognized that they could achieve more through united efforts than they could alone.

Inside the Media Blitz

When the American Library Association applied to the Advertising Council with the hope of mounting a national advertising

Newman and Beverstock

campaign against illiteracy, it was with the knowledge that campaigns such as "Smokey the Bear" and "Crime Prevention" were among the most effective means of communicating with the greatest number of people. The Ad Council's campaign requirements included that such campaigns be noncommercial, nondenominational, nonpartisan, national in scope, and of sufficient seriousness and public importance to warrant donations of space or time by national and local media. (For complete coverage of the initiation, progress, and detailed outcomes of the early phases of the Volunteer Against Illiteracy campaign, see Newman, 1986.)

The Ad Council calculated that its distribution system to the top 75 markets and networks reached 80 percent of all TV households in the United States. Radio and newspaper ads also reached large audiences.

In addition, Benton and Bowles, the advertising agency that volunteered to develop the ad campaign for the coalition, developed and distributed consumer magazine ads, hosted a special meeting of leading publishers to promote the campaign, and sent a special mailing to selected top publications. Ads were also developed and distributed in a special kit to the business press. The Ad Council promoted the campaign at the national meetings of the American Business Press, resulting in still more advertising. Finally, in an innovative move, book ads were developed and distributed. In all, an estimated $40.5 million of free ads ran.

All of the advertising featured the toll free number of the Contact Literacy Center. The center handled calls generated by the ad campaign. Brochures written and distributed free (in the thousands) by coalition members included *Basics of Public Relations, Help Your Child Succeed in Reading, How to Form a Community Volunteer Literacy Program, How to Form a State or Local Literacy Coalition, One-to-One Tutoring,* and *27 Million Americans Cannot Read and Guess Who Pays the Price.*

Advertising is regarded by some as a high art. When coalition members started meeting with the representatives of Benton and Bowles to discuss the development of an ad campaign, we were cautioned that we must choose a single message; more than one message would confuse the public. Many meetings were dedicated to defining what we hoped to communicate. We came to the conclusion that our initial efforts must be devoted to recruiting volunteers for tutoring; if we targeted learners first, the field would be swamped with requests that could not be met. We assumed that the process of requesting volunteer help would stimulate an awareness and a willingness to contribute resources.

The ads that focused on volunteers provoked resistance among some of the coalition's executive board members. One ad stated: "All you need is a degree of caring." This appeal for nonprofessional or professional volunteers grated on some professionals who had invested thousands of dollars and years of effort in becoming certified teachers.

Some literacy workers were concerned about adult learners' possible negative feelings about the advertising. Many illiterate adults who were friends of instructors and were productive, hardworking people, heard the term "ill-literate" as demeaning. "We're not ill. We just don't know how to read. Give us a chance!" Prior to the campaign, the underliterate had been better able to mask their difficulties (protected by friends and family) and retain a fragile measure of self-respect. Now they were unmasked by the push to raise literacy levels. We needed to develop means of acknowledging and upholding literacy learners' sense of self-respect while they were upgrading their skills. Some literacy workers questioned whether the campaign might have been better focused on the theme of citizens' worth: "You are valued, needed, wanted." Still, the campaign was effective, touching millions of Americans.

ABE Workers and Literacy Volunteers

Meanwhile, the largest providers of adult literacy instruction (outside of business and industry) had been the federally funded and state administered ABE programs. The coalition member representing state ABE programs brought to early meetings the viewpoint of those who had been doing literacy work in official programs since the mid-1960s.

In the flush of our enthusiasm and gratitude for the efforts of volunteer programs, we must not forget that most of the teaching of adult new readers has been and continues to be done by nonvolunteer, professional programs under the provisions of the Adult Education Act (1966, amended 1978). The statistics tell the tale of hard work accomplished: the U.S. Department of Education reported 3 million students enrolled in adult basic education classes for the school year 1988-1989.

The contents of ABE programs vary from state to state, and even within states. But the basic purpose of the programs remains the same: to serve the needs of the undereducated adult. State ABE teachers must be certified. Their certification is usually in elementary or secondary education, since no certification programs have been established in adult literacy. ABE group classes meet in local elementary, secondary, or vocational schools or junior colleges; church basements; or other community centers.

In the late 1960s, communication between state-supported and volunteer programs was poor. The use of volunteer tutors in conjunction with certified classroom teachers was rejected in one large city in New York State. Cooperation and collaboration were nonexistent. At this time, many of the ABE teachers were moonlighting from daytime jobs to pick up extra income. They were not necessarily well qualified for, or enthusiastic about, a nighttime job that required no special training and had minimal supervision, unimaginative curriculum and materials, and low pay. Efforts to introduce volunteers into the programs met stiff opposition from ABE administrators. "The volunteers won't know what they're doing and will be in the way," complained the professionals. This blanket rejection of offers by volunteers to collaborate was eventually withdrawn, however.

Part of the reason for this capitulation was the need to resolve a persistent dilemma with which state ABE programs had struggled for years. Ten percent of the funding of these programs is allocated to innovation in teacher training, computer training, and staff development. The other 90 percent goes for books, facilities, and staff. As states worked out formulas for spending the money, it was natural for them to concentrate funds on the learners who were easiest to reach—those heading for a high school diploma or the GED. As time went by, the federal government and state adult education officials worked harder to enforce the requirement to concentrate more of the funding on the least served. This hardest to reach segment of adult new readers, with the lowest potential for success, takes the most time to bring to literacy and therefore costs the most. The tax-funded programs were never able to accomplish this task cost-effectively. Volunteer programs were a partial answer to this need.

The two major volunteer literacy programs in the United States, LLA and LVA, have made a tremendous contribution to the success of adult literacy instruction. These groups, together with the Association of Community Based Organizations (CBOS), are now the backbone of basic volunteer literacy provision.

The contributions of the volunteer groups and the CBOS differ in several ways from the professional approach. The volunteers have the freedom to do what they think needs to be done to meet the needs of the individual learners. They can produce their own materials, prescribe their own methodology, and train their own tutors. On short notice, they can draw on a volunteer labor pool that is not accessible to the state ABE programs, confined as they are to the use of certified teachers. The volunteer tutors meet one-to-one with their learners at times and places of mutual convenience. Learner identity is strictly protected, if the learner so desires. Perhaps most important, volunteer groups work out of generous commitment to ideals that give their groups a hard-to-match esprit de corps. Knowing that their "pay" comes from the satisfaction of learners who become readers, they often contribute time and resources far beyond what certified teachers can afford.

The flip side of the volunteer movement, of course, is that nonprofessional tutors, sometimes with as little as 12 to 20 hours of training, are dealing with one of the most difficult populations to teach. By contrast, the certified teacher may have had upwards of 2,400 hours of professional education. The two major volunteer groups see themselves as "feeder" groups to the ABE programs; they take the nonreaders and low-level readers, work them up to a fourth grade level, and send them along to the local ABE program. Difficulties sometimes arise when minimally trained tutors deal with the learning disabled, the psychologically damaged, and the people with entrenched nonproductive approaches to reading and writing. Both tutors and learners suffer the consequences.

Newman and Beverstock

Due to the nature of the volunteer programs, record keeping is difficult to maintain, and experimental research is almost impossible to conduct. The volunteer leaders are aware of these limits, and respond that their main purpose is to teach people to read, not to conduct research. They note, however, that as they have grown in numbers and sophistication, they have moved into a better position to cooperate or even collaborate with researchers.

Volunteerism: The American Way

From barn raisings in the settling of the West to the fleamarket capitalism that prompts the Internal Revenue Service to ask, "Have you engaged in barter this past year?" Americans love the sociability of working together informally. American social know-how means finding a way around aggravating circumstances in spontaneous and inventive ways and sometimes in spite of, rather than with the help of, government efforts. This is not to say that we eschew government leadership, coordination, and support. It does suggest that the best ideas come from the people, later to be picked up by the government for routinization, elaboration, and application on a larger scale. Likewise, in the many sectors of the literacy community, we have learned some important lessons about the strength of partnership, networking (Richardson, 1988), and mutual involvement.

If we expect to continue to make progress in adult literacy, we must continue to look to the goodwill and dedicated efforts of combined private and public sector initiatives. When private groups pool their own best interests to produce an outcome that meets the best interests of the most people, we all win.

The successes of the adult literacy decade were the results of the cooperative efforts of many groups and individuals. Their ability to cooperate was slow and delicate, and now, in a new decade, let us not attempt to strong-arm the growth process. The gradual unfolding of communication, cooperation, and collaboration could not be pushed at the beginning of the process, no matter how hard some of the coalition members tried. The payoff will come in its own good time. The first small step was communication, which continued for years before evolving into collaboration. Still more years of press conferences, media involvement, and the uneasy cooperation of rival organizations had to take place before we reached our current status.

Networks of communication kept members apprised of one another's efforts; organizational representatives served on one another's steering committees and boards; new groups coalesced (the State Literacy Initiatives Network, the Working Group, the National Governors' Association, and the Literacy Network). The machinery moved and clanked, and the newly literate were served. The National Coalition for Literacy was born out of the belief that the problem of adult functional illiteracy was too big to be handled by any one group alone, and that the cost was too big for federal, state, or local governments to assume by themselves. The more realistic, if slower moving, solution was a strong partnership among education, government, business, volunteer, and professional organizations all working toward a common goal. Communication is still one of the coalition's primary objectives (Table 3).

Table 3
National Coalition for Literacy 1989 Objectives

1. *Communication.* To provide for ongoing communication among national groups whose primary and continuing interest is literacy.
2. *Information and Referral Policy.* To establish policies and actively support the operation of a literacy telephone information and referral service.
3. *State Initiative Ties.* To develop and maintain ties with state-level initiatives.
4. *Public Awareness Campaigns.* To stimulate, review, and guide public awareness campaigns targeted to particular populations or purposes.
5. *Public Policy.* To influence public policy at the federal, state, and local levels in support of adult basic education.
6. *Research and Development Forum.* To provide a forum for the examination of relevant research and development projects in adult literacy.
7. *National Initiatives Forum.* To provide a forum for the discussion of new national literacy initiatives.
8. *Needs Assessment/Service Development.* To assess national needs, identify gaps in services, and promote the development of services to meet needs.

A decade after its founding, the coalition's quarterly meetings are marked by the camaraderie of people accustomed to communicating with one another—people who have cooperated and collaborated over the years to produce brochures, sponsor conferences, and meet the press. Other organizations have been added to the coalition's steering committee to broaden and strengthen its base. A new spirit of unity and trust is enabling coalition members to promote one another's causes and reach larger, mutually beneficial goals. The coalition's early efforts are now paying off in an explosion of new initiatives on behalf of the emerging adult reader.

References

Brown, D.A., & Newman, A.P. (1968). *A literacy program for adult city-core illiterates: An investigation of experimental factors pertinent to reading instruction.* USOE Project No. 6-1136. Buffalo, NY: State University of New York.

Cook, W.D (1977). *Adult literacy education in the United States.* Newark, DE: International Reading Association.

Newman, A.P. (1986). *An evaluation of the impact of the Advertising Council's "Volunteer Against Illiteracy" campaign on public awareness of the resources devoted to adult literacy for 1985.* Bloomington, IN: Indiana University.

Richardson, J.W. (1988). Networking for adult literacy: A position statement. *Adult Literacy and Basic Education, 12*(1), 27-32.

7

Literacy Initiatives

The National Coalition for Literacy was not the only literacy program begun in the 1980s. The decade saw an unprecedented explosion of literacy initiatives at the federal, state, and local levels. Some of the new organizations formed were related to the National Coalition; others were not. Some were direct providers of literacy services; others were bodies of public representatives who recognized that their own best interests were served by addressing the issue of literacy.

Direct Literacy Providers

The Adult Literacy Initiative

The roll call of new initiatives starts with the Adult Literacy Initiative (ALI) launched in 1983 by President Ronald Reagan. In line with the Reagan Administration's reduction of the federal government's role in the social sector, the government sought solutions to literacy needs by appealing to private volunteer groups. Little new funding was provided for the ALI ; nevertheless, according to Delker (1984), the ALI was the federal government's first endorsement of a minimal education level for adults. Delker does not specify what that minimal level was, but he notes that promoting literacy was a bipartisan concern in Congress.

In 1982, the Subcommittee on Postsecondary Education of the House Committee on Education and Labor had initiated hearings on adult literacy. Hence the ALI was to some degree a response to the Congressional investigation of adult illiteracy. Some critics saw the ALI as merely recapitulating efforts that had gone before.

Kazemek and Rigg (1985) were skeptical about what they saw as the redundant declaration of a "crisis." They questioned whether any literacy campaign, making lofty promises to solve complex social, political, economic, and moral problems, can succeed when its progenitors have a brush fire interest that burns briefly and then is extinguished.

In 1986, the ALI reported on the initiative's progress. The National Adult Literacy Project (NALP) had commissioned an 18-month study of adult literacy programs and had produced 10 papers, 1 of which evolved into *Effective Adult Literacy Programs: A Practitioner's Guide* (Lerche, 1985). In addition, the ALI staff had worked on the development of the National Assessment of Educational Progress Young Adult Literacy Study; numerous literacy councils at local and state levels had been established or planned; the Federal Interagency Committee on Education (FICE) had commissioned a governmentwide survey of literacy and literacy-related programs; and in the College Work-Study Student Program, 68 institutions had received a total of $1.8 million of "unexpended work-study monies" for literacy projects. The ALI had also urged colleges and universities to grant credit for literacy activities and to become otherwise involved. Finally, the ALI had developed the Federal Employee Literacy Training (FELT) program, which recruited tutors from the ranks of federal employees and trained them to teach individuals to read. The program placed about 500 literacy instructors.

Many of these spinoff initiatives of the ALI have continued, and some have expanded. For example, nearly $5 million was made available in 1989-1990 for the development of the Student Literacy Corps, a program designed to train student tutors through university coursework.

American Association for Adult and Continuing Education

Also a charter member of the National Coalition for Literacy, the American Association for Adult and Continuing Education (AAACE) was created to provide leadership in advancing the education of adults in the lifelong learning process. The association provides many services, including unification of the profession, development of human resources, encouragement and use of research, communication with members and the public, and other efforts to further adult education. The AAACE also serves as the voice of adult and continuing education.

Association for Community Based Education

The Association for Community Based Education (ACBE) was founded in 1976 as a national organizing body for institutions involved in the education and development of communities. It provides educational programs linked to the needs, cultures, and traditions of their communities, which are often made up of low-income residents and ethnic minorities. The ACBE's activities include the development of a database of literacy organizations and resources, information and referral services, minigrants for program improvements and innovations, community based literacy programs, a professional development program, and several publications dealing with literacy issues.

International Reading Association

The International Reading Association (IRA) was founded in 1956 to improve reading and develop literacy around the world. Specifically, IRA strives to improve the quality of reading instruction at all levels, to develop an awareness of the impact of reading among all peoples, and to promote the development of a level of reading proficiency commensurate with each individual's capacity. In the area of adult literacy, IRA publishes books, runs a regular newspaper column devoted to adult literacy issues, holds conferences, works with UNESCO, and supports local adult literacy efforts around the world. IRA is also a charter member of the National Coalition for Literacy.

Laubach Literacy Action

Laubach Literacy Action (LLA), the U.S. program of Laubach Literacy International, is another charter member of the National Coalition for Literacy. Its primary purpose is to enable illiterate adults and older youths to acquire needed listening, speaking, reading, writing, and mathematics skills. LLA focuses on literacy training that helps people solve the problems they encounter in everyday life and that allows them to take advantage of opportunities in their environment and participate fully in the transformation of their society.

Literacy Network, Inc.

Literacy Network, Inc., is an expansion of the Urban Literacy Network, which was a spinoff project of the B. Dalton Bookseller National Literacy Initiative. The group's emphasis is on supporting literacy collaboration. It sponsors national meetings and publishes regular communication pieces on urban programs and resource development. The network also provides demonstration grants, training, and direct assistance to 11 urban literacy initiatives. In addition, it works in collaboration with other national organizations to develop and influence federal and state policy.

Literacy Volunteers of America

Literacy Volunteers of America (LVA), also a charter member of the National Coalition for Literacy, was organized in 1962, with the purpose of guaranteeing the right of every citizen to read. LVA tutors focus on learner needs and interests as well as on student problems and motivation. The organization also publishes tutor training materials and provides technical assistance as time and budget allow.

National Council of State Directors of Adult Education

The National Council of State Directors of Adult Education (NCSDAE), founded in 1980, is a charter member of the National Coalition for Literacy. The group's goal is to make maximum use of literacy resources to provide a comprehensive literacy program for each state. NCSDAE establishes coordination and cooperation between state literacy associations, local literacy councils, local school districts, libraries, state agencies, and businesses.

Sponsors with a Vested Interest

Several organizations that are not direct providers of literacy instruction, but that do have a vested interest in literacy, have become leaders in the literacy movement. These organizations, which come from a variety of sectors, have a great impact on the field.

Book Publishers and Booksellers

"What's good for literacy is good for the industry." This conclusion was taken seriously by newspaper, magazine, and book publishers in the 1980s. It has been estimated that booksellers contributed $20 million worth of free literacy-related advertising in 1985 alone. Contributions of this kind boost awareness of literacy needs tremendously.

America's booksellers began to take an active interest in the literacy campaign in the 1980s, especially during a massive fundraising effort begun late in the decade. In theory, every bookstore in America was to have an attractive canister by its cash register with the slogan "Give the Gift of Literacy." The money was to be collected from the stores by a volunteer group of retired AT&T workers and distributed according to a predetermined formula to literacy groups all over the country. In practice, because the AT&T retirees were unevenly located across the country, money collection became a nightmare. The effort was disbanded, and what money was collected went either to the Contact Literacy Center (to maintain the 800 number) or to the Reading Is Fundamental effort.

Education Writers

The Education Writers Association performs a useful service by producing a series of papers containing solid information about literacy myths: *There's an Epidemic of Illiteracy in American Society*, *Illiteracy Can Be "Cured" in One Generation*, *Literacy Programs Are Fail-Safe*, and *The "Feds" Are Readying a Campaign on Literacy*. (Copies of the papers are available from the Education Writers Association, 1001 Connecticut Avenue, NW, Suite 310, Washington, DC 20036.)

Libraries

In 1981 the American Library Association (ALA) brought together various national organizations to form the National Coalition for Literacy. Through its Office for Library Outreach Services, the ALA plays a major role in developing library literacy programs at the local level. The U.S. National Commission on Libraries and Information Science (NCLIS) is also a charter member of the National Coalition for Literacy. In addition, local libraries around the country make great contributions to the advancement of literacy.

Newspapers

The American Newspaper Publishers Association (ANPA) and the ANPA Foundation continued their literacy efforts after the 1985 campaign and made significant contributions with their "Press to Read" campaign and Showcase of Newspaper Adult Literacy Projects (*Press to Read*, 1989). They sampled newspaper literacy efforts nationally, describing 160 activities from Medford, Oregon, to Bangor, Maine. The *Medford Mail Tribune* sponsored a literacy walk in targeted neighborhoods. The *Bangor Daily News* installed a toll-free number for information regarding literacy in Maine.

In 1989 ANPA published *Newspapers and Literacy,* a statement of why newspaper people care and how they are helping. The publication included a four-page listing of resources, including newspaper, support, and instructional organizations, as well as literacy resource materials.

Project Literacy U.S.

One of the most successful partnerships to grow out of the literacy activities of the 1980s was the Project Literacy U.S. (PLUS) campaign. PLUS, a joint effort by the Public Broadcasting System (PBS) and the American Broadcasting Company (ABC), marked an unprecedented joining of national television forces on a long term basis.

PLUS started as a two-phase project, encompassing outreach for mobilizing community resources and awareness-raising through on-the-air programming. With the avowed goal of supporting or establishing a central literacy task force in all PBS/ABC communities, PLUS announced that "those who need and want help and those who are able to help will know where to turn in every sizable community in the U.S."

The list of PLUS backers includes more than 100 names, ranging from ACTION to ZONTA. There are many local coalitions. An impressive campaign of television and radio programming supports the local efforts. Following the PBS documentary, *First Things First,* the Contact Literacy Center received 2,500 calls.

On November 15, 1988, PLUS and the National Coalition for Literacy hosted the National Literacy Honors dinner in Washington, DC, to raise funds for the literacy movement. "The world we live in runs on words," announced Peter Jennings, ABC anchor and host for the evening. During the ceremonies, Jennings presented awards to First Lady Barbara Bush, as the outstanding leader of literacy in the United States, and to the 20 PLUS Learners of the Month who had won trips to Washington to receive the personal congratulations of the First Lady.

PLUS is now looking to the next generation. Youth PLUS is focusing on solutions to the major problems of the young: illiteracy, drug and alcohol abuse, unemployment, teenage pregnancy, dropout rates, and delinquency. The group's emphasis on intergenerational literacy undoubtedly will characterize the 1990s.

Universities

In 1985 the Institute for the Study of Adult Literacy and Technology was founded at Pennsylvania State University. The Institute's research on adult literacy and its development of literacy-oriented materials are prodigious. The Institute newsletter opened a new avenue of communication, and its publications on intergenerational literacy, staff development and training, workplace literacy, special needs populations, and the use of technology fill a void in the field.

Other universities also are involved. The Literacy Research Center of the University of Pennsylvania conducts important work on assessment in adult literacy. At Georgia State University, the Center for the Study of Adult Literacy is examining standards for evaluating programs in adult literacy. At Indiana University, a broad array of literacy activities are under way. The North Carolina Center for Literacy Development at North Carolina State University also has made important contributions.

Support from Other Sources

Commitment to adult literacy instruction is spreading to non-literacy related organizations. Some of the groups volunteering to support the cause of literacy are Altrusa, the Rotary Club, the American Legion, the American Association of University Women, the American Bar Association (ABA), and United Way of America. The ABA and United Way have elected to become sustaining members of the National Coalition for Literacy. The ABA's Task Force on Literacy publishes *Lawyers for Literacy* and conducts national conferences and institutes. ABA members support literacy work in their communities by donating legal services, advocating literacy, and tutoring. For example, 150 young lawyers meet weekly in Washington, DC, for literacy tutoring and sharing box dinners with a group of homeless youngsters.

The American Legion is taking a different tack. At its national convention in September 1989, it promoted a series of literacy videotapes that Legion posts might purchase to place in their local libraries.

Altrusa, a national service organization for professional women, began promoting literacy in the mid-1970s, and its chapters continue to sponsor literacy projects nationwide in the 1990s.

Business and Industry

Until recently, few educators knew that business, not the Department of Education, is the big spender on education. B. Dalton Bookseller gave more than $3 million to the cause in the early 1980s. Time, Inc., Prudential Insurance, Nabisco, and many others have contributed cash or in-kind contributions for literacy work during the past decade. A discussion of all the literacy activities of business and industry would fill volumes. We tip our hats, however, to Harold McGraw, Jr., a prime mover in involving business in literacy. In 1985, with a $1 million gift, he established the Business Council for Effective Literacy. The BCEL newsletter is a source of literacy information for thousands of people in the business community.

Private Foundations

Another remarkable change that took place during the 1980s was the involvement of private foundations in the literacy movement. In 1980, 15 foundations were listed as contributors to literacy; in 1985, 36 were listed — a 240 percent increase. During the

5-year period from 1980 to 1985, 112 foundations made specific contributions to literacy. The Gannett Foundation alone contributed $6 million for adult literacy in the latter half of the 1980s.

Another private foundation, the Kenan Trust Family Literacy Project, reflects the growing understanding that the illiteracy cycle can best be broken by going beyond the confines of the traditional classroom. The project intervenes early in the cycle of illiteracy by combining efforts to provide high quality, early-childhood education with efforts to improve the literacy and parenting skills of under-educated adults. The stated goal of the Kenan Project is to "break the intergenerational cycle of undereducation by improving parents' child care skills and uniting parents and children in a positive educational experience" (Darling, 1989). The vision manifested in the Kenan Project is being multiplied across the country. "Thousands of requests for information about the Project have been received. Well over 1,000 orders for materials developed by the Project have been honored....Forty-five states and three foreign countries have requested information" (p. 4).

First Lady Barbara Bush

First Ladies develop different roles as their husbands carry out their presidential duties. But no First Lady has ever stepped into the White House and espoused a cause with more alacrity, sincerity, and willingness to serve than Barbara Bush has done for literacy. Her championing of the cause was welcomed by the literacy community during the eight years her husband was vice president. Since her husband has been president, her leadership has put literacy at the center of national attention.

Barbara Bush's contribution to literacy is personal as well as national. Reel and Lewis (in press) tell the story of the 1988 July 4 celebration in St. Louis, at which J.T. Pace—a 63-year-old newly literate man—was to read the Preamble to the Constitution while America watched on television. When Pace arrived at the Gateway Arch, where the celebration was to be held, he met Barbara Bush, who was to appear on the platform with him. He explained to her that he couldn't read the Preamble after all, because he couldn't pronounce the word *tranquility*.

J.T. and Barbara sat down on the couch to talk things over. She agreed that he must do only what was comfortable for him. Then she took his hands in hers and asked him gravely: "What if you and I read the Preamble together?"

A moment of silence followed, and then J.T. smiled and said: "I'd like that."

So, the First-Lady-to-be and the retired construction worker read the Preamble together sitting on the couch; and when they had finished, they gave one another a big hug. Under the Arch, J.T. had no trouble with *tranquility* at all. (*Tranquility*, incidentally, was Barbara's Secret Service code name.)

We herald especially the First Lady's establishment of the Barbara Bush Family Literacy Foundation. The foundation is contributing to a major breakthrough in our approach to literacy development. Literacy begins, and is nurtured, in the home; literacy's progress is enhanced at home as well as in school; literacy thrives when all generations — children, parents, and grandparents — abetted by teachers, neighbors, and friends share in the work and blessings of literacy for all. Literacy is an intergenerational event.

The State Literacy Initiative

Our story about the growing momentum of the adult literacy movement would be incomplete without at least mentioning the developments among official state literacy organizations. As with the volunteer groups, with determination, vision, and inventiveness people in state organizations are taking the initiative to form partnerships and networks, recognizing that turf battles will not win this fight, but teamwork will. The State Literacy Initiative (SLIN) is one such network. SLIN was designed to serve as an informal source of support and communication for literacy services at the state level. A set of guidelines that grew out of the SLIN meetings has been distributed nationally. In 1990, more than 40 states are participating in SLIN, following the literacy guidelines.

Many other individuals and groups, whom we have not mentioned, are demonstrating initiative in small and grand ways on behalf of adult literacy. Years from now, the explosive quality of this decade of adult literacy—with its astonishing mass of personal commitment and organizational energy—will be easier to describe. Our documentation of adult literacy initiatives provides only a sample of this unprecedented movement in intellectual history. The message is a simple one: There is room for all. New initiatives are welcome and encouraged because the challenges are numerous and great.

References

Darling, S. (1989). *The Kenan Trust Family Literacy Project: Preliminary final report.* Unpublished report, Louisville, KY.

Delker, P.V. (1984). *Ensuring effective adult literacy policies and procedures at the federal and state level.* Washington, DC: Office of Vocational and Adult Education. (ED 260-281)

Lerche, R.S. (1985). *Effective adult literacy programs: A practitioner's guide.* New York: Cambridge.

Newman, A.P. (1986). *An evaluation of the impact of the Advertising Council's "Volunteer Against Illiteracy" campaign on public awareness of the resources devoted to adult literacy for 1985.* Bloomington, IN: Indiana University.

Press to read. (1989). Washington, DC: American Newspaper Publishers Association Foundation.

Reel, J., & Lewis, W. (in press). *First lady: Life stories of the women behind America's most powerful nonelective office.*

8

The Challenges of Adult Illiteracy

I lliteracy alarms were ringing as early as the 1950s. In *The Uneducated* (Ginsberg & Bray, 1953), the authors analyzed the problems of illiteracy during World War II as well as the literacy demands of work in the mills and factories in the South. Popularizations of *The Uneducated* in national magazines such as *Newsweek* drew attention to literacy as an American issue.

The enhanced public awareness of adult literacy during the Right to Read years of the 1960s and 1970s brought illiteracy in the United States shockingly to the attention of the people. Most had assumed that this country of power, wealth, and a long history of public education could claim the highest literacy rate among the major industrialized nations. Margaret Heckler, representative from Massachusetts, included the results of the Survival Literacy Study (Harris, 1970) in the Congressional Record. She lamented the embarrassing revelations about "a nation which prides itself on making quality education available to the greatest possible number of its citizens" (1970, p. 38036).

Ruth Holloway, then director of Right to Read, dismayed Americans further when she declared:

> One would assume a nation as wealthy and prosperous as ours would have no illiteracy. In spite of the excellent educational system, the fact is that the United States is plagued with enormous reading problems (Holloway, 1973, p. 27).

Holloway linked literacy levels to the ability to earn a decent living and emphasized a correlation between functional illiteracy and other social problems.

> Our nation finally realized, officially, that it must pay for problems one way or another, and it decided that eliminating illiteracy would be far cheaper than continuing to support the bitter harvest of social ills that illiteracy has reaped (p. 33).

The publicity surrounding studies of functional illiteracy in the 1970s fueled these worries. As the results of each study became known, concern grew. The crisis of illiteracy had stepped onto center stage. By the 1980s, people were moved to take new kinds of action.

Articles on illiteracy were written by both private and government writers (Copperman, 1980; Darling, 1984; Smith, 1983). In *Adults in Crisis: Illiteracy in America,* Johnson (1985) stated, "A major social problem in our country is rapidly assuming crisis proportions....The problem is nationwide, cutting across geographic boundaries and social distinctions in every city and every neighborhood in the country" (p. 1). The English Language Proficiency Survey (ELPS) pointed to a bottom line: 13 percent of all Americans were illiterate.

Kozol's books *Illiterate America* (1985) and *Where Stands the Republic?* (1986) fanned the fire. People were flabbergasted to read Kozol's statistics extrapolated from the American Performance Level study: 25 million functionally illiterate Americans were reading below fifth grade level, and 35 million more were functioning at lower than a ninth grade reading level. According to Kozol, one third of America's adults in 1984 were illiterates.

> The cost to our economy...is very great. The cost to our presumptions and our credibility as a democracy is greater still. The cost in needless human pain may be the greatest price of all (1985, p. 12).

In Kozol's opinion, neither government nor private organizations had been able to address the problem effectively. In 1984 only about 2 million people were enrolled in literacy programs, and Kozol questioned the efficacy of those programs. The cycle of illiteracy was continuing as children were raised in households empty of books. Kozol stated that the literate may fear loss of status should the illiterate learn to read and write; hence the ruling class had not made war on illiteracy because they wanted to protect their advantages and privileges.

Like Flesch's *Why Johnny Can't Read* (1955) and Hunter and Harman's *Adult Illiteracy in the United States* (1979), Kozol's *Illiterate America* (1985) was the most widely read book on adult literacy of its decade. Kozol made vivid the personal struggles of the insufficiently literate; his book is a call to arms against illiteracy. Kozol told stories of individuals who lived in fear, frustration, and shame at not being able to read adequately in a highly literate society. He cited statistics about the costs of illiteracy, not only to individuals but also to businesses and society at large.

Kozol's declaration of war on illiteracy drew a large response from both professional education journals and the public press. One reviewer characterized the work as "another angry book" that discounted the efforts of innercity teachers, and asked: "How many problems of race, poverty, social class structure—and, in addition, reading—ought to be solved by public schools?" (Leary, 1986).

Part of the strength of Kozol's book, and the ferocity of the reactions to it, stemmed from his essentially political analysis of illiteracy. He proposed a grassroots national literacy movement to replace ineffective programs and to break the illiteracy cycle. He argued that neighborhood problem-solving groups ought to get people involved in public housing, schools, and health care. He proposed that centers be established away from traditional school sites and that volunteers (including college students and the elderly) be used as well as professionals. Both methodologically and ideologically, Kozol leaned on the work of Freire, especially on the idea of "generative" words, personal narrations, and oral history. He suggested that new primers be written and that the many books publishers destroy each year be given to new readers. (Because publishers must pay taxes on unsold books in their warehouses, they often destroy them.)

> Illiteracy...may represent the one important social, class, and pedagogic issue of our times on which the liberal, the radical, and the informed conservative can stand on common ground and toil, no matter with what caution and trepidation, in a common cause that offers benefits to all (1985, p. 199).

Is There a Literacy Crisis?

In 1985, Hunter and Harman's *Adult Illiteracy in the United States* was issued in paperback. In the new preface, they offered the following assessment of the dangers of declaring a "crisis":

> We must finally disabuse ourselves—especially those responsible for public policy and funding—of the idea that we face a crisis that can be overcome by a one-shot effort. Neither optimistic rhetoric nor armies of volunteers will reduce the numbers of young people with educational deficiencies who graduate from or drop out of our high schools each year. We can seek to understand the context within which both schooling and adult programs take place—the influence of subtle systemic racism, the exclusion of poor minorities, and the persistence of structures of domination. We can address the problem of the schools and the problem of the educationally disadvantaged adults as one problem demanding a unified solution (pp. xix-xx).

In his review of the literature on adult literacy, Sticht (1988) stated that while the country had been responding to the social crises identified with adult literacy, efforts had been so misplaced in quick-fix programs that research in adult literacy actually had been hindered. He asserted:

The crisis mentality has retarded not only the development of a knowledge base for adult literacy education, but also the preparation of a cadre of professionals competent to design, develop, implement, and teach in adult literacy programs that take into account the little professional and research-based knowledge available (p. 62).

The Public Debate

For the general public, the meaning of the statistics from the functional literacy studies was elusive. Moats (1986) was scornful of what seemed to her to be feeble attempts by the federal government to ascertain the true level of literacy in the United States. She included in her article some of the test items from the 1982 ELPS. Incredulous at what seemed to be ridiculously easy questions on the survey, Moats quoted Robert E. Barnes, Acting Director of the U.S. Department of Education's Planning and Technical Analysis Division: "I could imagine giving people a three-page text and asking them to write a one-paragraph summary and having a result of 85 percent adult illiteracy including college graduates. So, I don't think we found the right number. I think we found a floor." Then Moats quipped, "Barnes, honey, I think you found the basement" (Moats, 1986, p. 11-A). Moats' attitude exemplifies the reaction of capably literate people who take their own literacy for granted, and who grasp neither the nature nor the extent of illiteracy problems.

The crisis mentality became acute with the growing sense that American industry was falling behind that of other industrialized countries, that this was the fault of the workers, and that all we needed to do was shore up the literacy levels in the workplace for all to be well. As important as literacy is, a single-issue solution to America's battered pride was not sufficient. Nevertheless, for a while literacy became a convenient whipping boy for the problems of the workplace.

The literacy crisis burst upon the national consciousness at about the same time that a series of educational malpractice suits rattled through the courts and made scandalous reading in the newspapers. In each of these cases, parents were charging that the schools had failed their children. In *Peter W. Doe v. the San Francisco Unified School District* (1972, 1976) and *Donahue v. Copiague School District* (1977, 1978, 1979), the plaintiffs alleged that they were functionally illiterate despite their high school diplomas. The courts decided against the malpractice charges in the Doe and Donahue cases, ruling that even if negligence had been involved, a decision in favor of the plaintiffs would open such a Pandora's box of litigation that a misuse of taxpayers' money would result.

In *Hoffman v. the Board of Education* (1978, 1979), the case was more complicated because of a traumatic experience in Hoffman's childhood that had limited his ability to speak. Misdiagnosed as mentally retarded by a school psychologist who used a verbal-based intelligence test, Hoffman was placed in classes for the mentally retarded and remained there without retesting through 12 years of school. In the suit, Hoffman's mother claimed that she should have been consulted about her son's placement and that he should not have been placed or kept in a classroom for the mentally retarded because his intelligence was normal or above normal. After 12 years of education with the mentally retarded, Hoffman was not prepared to make a living, and had been rendered incapable of believing that he could learn. The Hoffman story further shook public confidence in the schools and school personnel.

In addition to the concerns over educational malpractice, a host of other issues contributed to the public perception of a state of crisis in American literacy. These issues included new demands by women and minorities, the changing requirements of technology, publication of scores on standardized tests (however little these may be understood by the general public), and the "sharp shift over time in expectations concerning literacy" from simple to complex literacies (Resnick & Resnick, 1989, p. 190).

Although the National Assessment of Educational Progress study (Kirsch & Jungeblut, 1986) showed that absolute illiteracy was low among young adults, it also revealed that many could not adequately carry out mid-level and advanced literacy tasks, such as interpreting an employment benefits chart. Resnick and Resnick concluded that the populace had trouble gaining new information from printed texts, and that people are poor at drawing inferences and even worse when it comes to literary allusions, metaphoric expressions, text interpretation, and comparing the meaning of one text with that of another.

Venezky, Kaestle, and Sum (1987) examined the results of the National Assessment Study and saw danger, but not crisis:

> The message from the Young Adult Literacy Assessment is neither of impending doom nor of catastrophe. Contrary to the Cassandra-like warnings issued in recent years of a land populated by hordes of illiterates, America is not steering itself toward such imminent self-destruction. Few cannot read at all, and many of these appear to have multiple problems, of which illiteracy may not be the most severe (p. 52).

They interpreted the results of the Young Adult Literacy Assessment as a warning of persistent problems that must be addressed to keep America from becoming a weak nation in terms of human capital and to avoid wasting the potential, skills, and abilities of Americans. They concluded that there is no crisis, but the need to act is no less than if there were.

What Demographic Shifts Tell Us

Adult education is asked to meet the needs of people who seek instruction in English as a second language as well as those of native speakers of English who need greater literacy. The 1980 census included the estimate that about 2 percent of the population 5 years of age and older speak little or no English. Since that census, the amnesty program has brought forward thousands of people who speak minimal English. The 1990 census certainly will reflect higher numbers in this category.

The demographic literature points to at least two other major population shifts relevant to literacy: the changing workforce and the increasing numbers of the poor. These shifts will continue through the end of the century and will add to the sense of national crisis. How these demographic shifts are interpreted will have a significant impact on our understanding of the needs and goals of adult literacy.

The nature of work in America is changing, and so is the nature of the workforce. Johnston and Packer's (1987) study lends a sense of the magnitude of this shift. According to these authors, while native-born white males made up approximately 47 percent of the U.S. labor force in 1990, by the year 2000, this population will compose only 15 percent of the labor force. The remainder will be nonwhites, women, and immigrants. In addition, they say, the average age of the workforce will rise. At the same time, the pool of young workers entering the labor market will drop by 8 percent.

If we set goals for adult literacy using the demographic statistics on sex, race, and age alone, we will need greater emphasis on special population concerns and reading content appropriate to the cultural as well as the employment needs of the new labor pool. For the immigrant populations, we will need to know the languages represented and the levels of educational attainment in those native languages if we hope to set goals for moving people into functional English.

Since many future jobs will require more education and higher levels of information processing, reasoning, reading, and math, it is obvious that workplace literacy is becoming much more than basic skills training or high school equivalency work. The goals for adult literacy need to include skill with the information and reasoning processes involving the use of English, math, and problem solving. Furthermore, workplace literacy goals need to envelop the concept of lifelong learning. Quick-fix training will be no help to a workforce that is aging and not being replaced by younger or more highly skilled employees.

The second major demographic shift is that of the increasing number of people below the poverty line. This shift is tied closely both to the need for more highly skilled workers and to the growth in numbers of minority employees. The increasing underclass will have the greatest difficulty preparing for the high skill demands of the workplace. This growing underclass will have intergenerational and family literacy needs. The growing body of demographic data describes an underclass of millions of people who are isolated from the mainstream of power, wealth, and education, even though their numbers are projected to make them the majority in America. A

Vision for America's Future (1989), published by the U.S. Government Printing Office, lists these troubling figures:

- If we continue on our present course, by the year 2000 one in four American children will be living in poverty. Today, one in five is classified as poor.

- One in four American families is now a single-parent family, and single-parent families now make up two out of three homeless families.

- One in every 5 girls will have a child by the age of 20, and most of these mothers will not be married. Only 6 of 10 will have high school diplomas, compared with 9 of 10 among their peers who are not parents.

- One out of 3 of the homeless—estimated at between 350,000 and 3 million—is a parent with homeless children.

- High numbers of minority populations are present among the homeless.

- Minority teenagers are likely to live in poverty.

- Poor teens are four times more likely than their nonpoor peers to have below-average basic academic skills.

- A significant number of poor children have parents who do not have a high school education. No matter how motivated these parents may be to help their children learn, they often lack the personal and financial resources to do so.

The consequences for families with low levels of education are far more serious now than in earlier decades. Literacy demands in the workplace and in society in general alienate the illiterate and the uneducated from the more knowledgeable mainstream and contribute to endemic poverty. Regardless of race or ethnic origin, earnings are closely tied to the number of years of schooling completed. The more years of formal education a person has, the greater his or her annual earnings tend to be. In 1985, of the full-time, year-round male workers who were 25 years old and over, those who had not completed high school earned a median income of $18,881; high school graduates earned $23,853; college graduates earned $32,822; and those with professional training requiring five or more years of college earned $39,335. Earnings for women workers at these same levels of educational attainment were around 40 percent lower, at $11,836; $15,481; $21,389; and $25,928, respectively (*The Forgotten Half*, 1988, p. 26).

From 1973 to 1986, the median annual earnings of family heads younger than 30 who were high school dropouts fell 53 percent. Even young family heads who were high school graduates (but did not attend college) saw their earnings drop 31 percent. In contrast, the earnings of those young family heads who were college graduates fell only 3 percent (*Vision*, p. 71). These figures are bleak indeed for the undereducated.

Sticht (1988) pointed out that parents' education levels, particularly the mother's level, affect the child's learning. "One correlation analysis has suggested that a one-year gain in the mother's basic skills may lead to better than half a grade gain in the skills of offspring" (p. 82). Hence, the increasing numbers of single-parent and homeless families, teenage mothers, and population segments with limited education levels suggest an ongoing cycle of greater numbers living below the poverty line. A major consideration for setting literacy goals must be how to raise general adult literacy levels and, thereby, raise family literacy levels for those living in poverty.

A Challenge, Not a Crisis

As Newman (1980) stated, "Whatever we may call it, adult literacy presents us with a problem to be solved." We believe that illiteracy is not a crisis but a challenge. America will lose its position as a world literacy leader if we do not make every effort to solve the multiple problems of adult illiteracy. The loss of that leadership would not be a moral failure only; it also would lead to tremendous economic and social losses. Nevertheless, we resist defining the situation as a crisis because the outcry such terminology causes sets the adrenalin flowing, prompting the animal reaction of flight or fight. What is needed instead is something distinctly human: sturdy reasonableness, visionary clarity, and faith in practicality and progress.

Newman and Beverstock

In denying that illiteracy is a crisis, we do not want to be interpreted as saying that illiteracy is not a critical factor in America's future. Rather, our point is that the problem is not insurmountable; America is facing another of those challenges that, when met, historically have bred new opportunities and optimism for the nation. Once we abolished the slavery of chains; now we need to abolish the servitude of illiteracy.

Our attention should remain focused on abolishing illiteracy. Although illiteracy is tied to many other problems in our society— endemic poverty, homelessness, racial and ethnic prejudice, absent fathers—we must remind ourselves that literacy workers cannot untangle all those intertwining problems. But we can meet the challenges of illiteracy if we keep them before the American mind. Our dynamic, growing society will plow through its inevitable changes to garner a harvest of literacy from this field of crises.

In a characteristically romantic mood, the poet Goethe once said, "Whatever you can do, or dream you can do, begin it." If we dream with Goethe, we can foresee major changes taking place in our country—changes that already have taken place in other, smaller, more controlled situations. We are a nation of people willing to help, wanting to know how we can do better everything that we do—and that includes literacy instruction. We foresee the reflective practitioner combining daily practice with lessons of the past, questions of the present, and possibilites of the future. We foresee leaders who can help us redirect our energies. We foresee thoughtful literacy workers confronting the hard questions posed by illiteracy and coming up with their own new answers.

We are not talking about a one-shot crisis campaign. We are talking about ongoing communication, cooperation, and collaboration. We have to end the isolation of adult literacy. We can do much to achieve a more literate America by working together and drawing strength from the exhilaration of making a difference.

We offer the following concrete proposals toward achieving a literate America. We draw especially on the recommendations made in three earlier reports: Hunter and Harman (1979), the Business Council for Effective Literacy (1988), and Hammink (1989).

Recommendations from Hunter and Harman

Hunter and Harman (1979) offered 11 recommendations for the field of adult literacy. Here we summarize their original recommendations, add brief assessments of progress made on each, and state our own recommendations for the new decade.

Principal overall recommendation. "We recommend the establishment of new, pluralistic, community-based initiatives whose specific objective will be to serve the most disadvantaged hard-core poor, the bulk of whom never enroll in any existing program" (p. 133).

Some community-based initiatives have sprung up in response to the Project Literacy U.S. (PLUS) campaign. But although the discussion of literacy policy has increased overall, the adult literacy movement has not undergone a needed major shift in emphasis. Most people still think largely in terms of national or state initiatives rather than programs focused on the local community's needs. As a result, we are not serving the most disadvantaged, hard-core poor. These individuals are hard to enroll and retain in literacy programs, partly because they take longer to bring to functional literacy, and partly because we as a society have not been willing to pay the high price of this kind of literacy.

The incentive to promote community-based programs has been lacking because money tends to go to programs in response to their success and not to their needs: Adult Basic Education programs need to report success in terms of numbers served. The Job Training Partnership Act ties payment to success at "positive placements" of the newly trained by the organizations that undertook to educate them with the promise of federal subsidy. Nobody knows yet how long it takes to teach the illiterate and the very low literate to read and write at levels required in today's technologically demanding marketplace.

Recommendation 1. "The principal overall recommendation for community-based approaches to the most educationally disadvantaged adult should be given wide dissemination through the distribution of this study to legislators and policymakers, government officials, corporations and foundations, adult education professionals and practitioners, and those in other disciplines who are concerned with community development" (p. 133).

We know of no concerted effort to distribute the overall recommendation for educating the most disadvantaged poor other than the work of the Association for Community Based Education (ACBE), which completed a statistical overview of community-based programs (*National Directory of Community Based Adult Education Programs*, 1989). ACBE has several other information service activities planned.

Recommendation 2. "A series of well publicized regional conferences should be planned and held to gather data and to create a climate for understanding and implementing the central proposal for new community-based approaches" (p. 133).

Some conferences were held in 1989: ACBE, SLIN, the National Forum on Literacy Collaboration and Policy Issues, and the Second Student Adult Literacy Congress all met. However, support is needed for the data gathering to facilitate implementation of new community-based approaches.

Recommendation 3. Develop appropriate means to increase public awareness, involve educators and service professionals in direct contact with community people, prepare concept papers, and compile an inventory of successful community-based programs (pp. 133-134).

Many groups have worked to increase the public's awareness of adult literacy; however, the efforts and accomplishments vary in different regions. Few involve educators and service professionals in direct contact with community people. Several papers have been written on the social contexts of literacy. The PLUS community coalitions are probably succeeding better than any other effort to compile inventories of successful community-based programs. A 1989 Department of Education Request for Proposals to develop a Student Literacy Corps was a move toward national involvement at the community level.

Recommendation 4. A systematic and accurate database about the groups, communities, and general population with which we are concerned should be developed and made available.

Both the 1982 English Language Proficiency Study (ELPS) and the 1986 National Assessment of Educational Progress (NAEP) study are foundations on which a more systematic and complete database can be built. New York City has initiated a comprehensive database for all adult learners (Ragin & Denny, 1989; Schneider & Cook, 1989). Establishing a truly national database will require the combined efforts of the federal government, the computer whizzes of the business world, and representatives of all types of programs to envision, provision, and develop it.

Recommendation 5. A research exchange and planning conference should be held.

Several research-sharing conferences have been held, such as the Adolescent and Adult Literacy Conference staged in January 1990 by the International Reading Association. At the state level, the Indiana Adult Literacy Coalition sponsors an annual research conference and keeps abreast of the state's research needs and developments through its research subcommittee.

Recommendation 6. Case studies should be undertaken to generate information about a range of subjects: integration of community development and adult education goals, models for financing adult literacy programs, flexible approaches for reaching goals, mechanisms for integrated local planning and management of projects that cut across traditional lines of functional responsibility, competencies necessary for participating in community life, and strategies for maintaining programs free of political control by self-selected managers.

The case study written by Johnston (1985) is a comprehensive and insightful description of the emergence into literacy. We reaffirm the value of the case study approach as a viable and significant route to understanding how adults learn literacy. Continuing the collection of case studies on the topics recommended by Hunter and Harman should be part of a comprehensive, cohesive program of research.

Recommendation 7. "Educational agencies and organizations should be...enabled by appropriate funding to establish a number of pilot projects to test the hypotheses of the studies emanating from work carrying out the earlier recommendations" (p. 135).

Laubach Literacy Action is sponsoring pilot community-based programs in California. The group is bringing to the effort the accumulated Laubach International experience in community organizing and a Freirean approach to the local identification of themes and issues for literacy learning.

Recommendation 8. A national commission on community-based initiatives should be established.

Two pieces of legislation, the Sawyer Bill (HR3123) and the Simon Bill (s1310), propose the establishment of a national center for adult literacy, but neither specifies community-based education. We propose that a community-based commission operate as an integral part of the national adult literacy center.

Recommendation 9. "Background studies should be undertaken and alternative proposals tested to determine the most effective ways to obtain legislation and funding necessary if the new approaches are to be implemented nationally on a scale commensurate with the need" (p. 135).

The pursuit of both legislation and funding is under way. But no one has determined how we are going to pay for adult literacy, or even how to test which ways of legislation and funding might be most effective. The work of Brizius and Foster (1987) is a big step in this direction, although it is primarily aimed at providing recommendations for state governors. But it does discuss the role of state governments and gives many useful suggestions that touch on costs.

Recommendation 10. "Citizen groups should be encouraged and enabled to address questions of social purpose and direction through the provision of concrete issue-oriented resource materials and agenda items about specific problem areas and illustrations. At the same time, these materials should be oriented toward the construction of new options for the future" (p. 135).

Laubach Literacy Action was the primary sponsor of two Adult Literacy Congresses (1987, 1989) that tackled some of the tough social issues, and has a third congress scheduled for 1991. Another promising citizens' group activity is the National Issues Forum. Sponsored by the Kettering Foundation, the local forums discuss issues of major concern to the country in town hall fashion. One of their programs includes the newly literate in the discussions by producing easier to read versions of the issues guide. For the emerging literate, this means an opportunity to think about the concerns of the times. Finding their public voice is an important step for new learners in becoming fully literate members of society.

Recommendation 11. Provide instruments for social planning at the national level comparable to those that exist for economic planning.

We are not aware of any instruments for social planning at the national level. We hope that some of the policy recommendations in the *Jump Start* report (Chisman, 1989) will be useful.

In the preface to the paperback reprint of *Adult Illiteracy in America*, Hunter and Harman (1985) added several major recommendations. They recommended that community-based organizations make proposals for research and action in the schools and adult education, that the organizations seek linkages between local initiatives and the larger political arena, and that policymakers and legislators enact legislation to affirm the legitimacy of the literacy movement and to provide fiscal support for making educational renewal a national priority. Their goal is a "learning society."

We believe that people working in community-based organizations have insights about making education viable and possible, empowering people of all ages whom our present educational system is failing to serve. We believe that these neighborly insights can be used to ask better research questions about the people who are hardest to reach. Community-based education, however, is inadequately funded with local, state, federal, and private monies. Community-based programs are democracy at work and are deserving of our vote of confidence, more expert oversight, and a greater and continuous share of the funding. Goals set locally should be supported nationally.

Recommendations from BCEL

The Business Council for Effective Literacy (1988) identified eight major adult literacy issues and problems:

1. Program management and accountability
2. State level policy development
3. Professionalism
4. Professional stature in the field
5. Teacher training
6. Development of supervisory and management personnel
7. Assessment and diagnostic tools
8. Creation of a central source to collect data on programs, enrollments, and funding

Only one of the recommendations (4.) made by Hunter and Harman (1979) is echoed in the BCEL issues list (8.)—the concern for development of a nationwide database. BCEL was right to place emphasis on a central database: business now runs on computers and has developed databases for every conceivable need. Why not engage those splendid resources and the expertise of business and industry to develop a systematic record of programs and populations served? This tax-deductible contribution to the adult literacy movement is one that any number of computer manufacturers could afford to make.

The Hunter and Harman recommendations focus on grass-roots help to the hard-core illiterate, most of whom never enroll in existing programs. The BCEL recommendations, by contrast, focus more on the professional management of the adult literacy field. These differing perspectives are appropriate, considering that Hunter and Harman wrote as academic researchers, whereas BCEL represents the interests of the business community. These differences, each bespeaking valid concerns, suggest the importance of reflecting on everyone's interests before making major decisions and setting policies for the field. As conflict resolution experts Carpenter and Kennedy (1988) advised, one had better ensure that all interests are effectively represented if one hopes to avoid pleasing one end of the spectrum while infuriating the other.

Recommendations from the National Forum

The issues that emerged from the National Forum on Literacy Collaboration and Policy Issues in 1989 focused on yet a different set of perspectives. More than a decade had passed since Hunter and Harman offered their recommendations in 1979, and a year since BCEL offered theirs in 1988. In 1989, a new and different constituency was represented. This time, 200 literacy learners, practitioners, leaders, and policymakers came together—a diverse group of stakeholders in the adult literacy movement. They understood their task to be to confront issues critical to the development of literacy in the future. Specifically they agreed to examine the problems and opportunities accompanying each issue, to consider various collaborative strategies and outcomes, and to develop a consensus on recommendations for action. The National Forum identified the following seven issues as central to the progress of literacy in America:

1. Literacy delivery system capacity (keeping up with the growing literacy needs of the adult population)
2. Quality and standards for literacy programs
3. Literacy and the family
4. Roles of adult literacy learners
5. Basic literacy skills and the workforce
6. Public and private resources
7. Welfare reform

How different this list is from either of the two preceding lists. Here we see concerns stated for adult illiterates. The importance of family literacy is acknowledged; the role of the adult literacy learner as captain of his or her own intellectual ship is affirmed. Literacy is linked with workplace needs. It is acknowledged that resources must be increased if we are to design solutions rather than merely describe problems. Finally, we have faced the question of welfare—the interrelatedness of literacy and deep-rooted poverty.

Coordinated and comprehensive programs to enable people to leave the cycle of welfare and dependency and become employable (and employed) are expensive, but they are possible. Pennsylvania established Single Point of Contact (SPOC), a literacy program to care for the whole person. SPOC addresses an individual in terms of the many stages of life skills development, including basic skills and vocational training. The group also supplies ongoing support and counseling once newly literate clients are placed in jobs. SPOC feeder programs are especially innovative. One of them engages professional actors to train the clients in acting, voice, projection, carriage, and self-confidence: Making-believe makes it so.

Other Emerging Issues

The challenges identified in the preceding sections will engage the adult literacy community for years to come. Beyond these, we face the major challenges of setting appropriate long and short term goals, and the challenge to literacy researchers, to America's business people, and to all of us to hold it all together.

Setting Goals

Goal setting is a multifaceted enterprise that requires us to pay attention to what we already know and to what we still need to learn through research. The shifting character of the U.S population, and thus of the target populations of literacy programs, forces us to face sobering questions about the possibility of eradicating illiteracy.

Langer (1979) stated, "What we know depends on the questions we ask." We might paraphrase that to say, "What we achieve depends on the goals we set." We are in a period of increased awareness of the needs of the adult new reader. Yet sometimes, in our haste to get on with the solutions, we may forget that we do not have enough information about the underliterate. We need to know more about the shifting character of underliterate populations and their needs in order to be able to eradicate adult illiteracy. In this scientifically dominated age, we depend on technical information. We want to make the best decisions possible; thus we turn to the hard data generated by research to guide us in program planning and design.

Unfortunately, a number of obstacles block our use of research. The present knowledge base is by no means adequate. Literacy research is still raising primary questions. Research reports on the ERIC database frequently end with comments by the abstractors that the scholarly articles and speeches that describe how to set up literacy programs and train volunteers frequently contain very little of what might be considered the hard data of research (Darkenwald, 1986; Fingeret, 1984). We are in a period of reassessment of the beliefs that underlie scientific inquiry. This latest paradigm shift is not limited to research in adult literacy, but it does affect it.

As discussed in Chapter 5, literacy researchers in the past 100 years have moved from a primary concern with numbers (How many? How much?) to considering other important questions (Who? Under what conditions?). Whatever research paradigm one employs, the essential question for the literacy worker is "What knowledge do we have that will help us determine the best approach to teaching adults to read, write, and cipher?" Sometimes we rely on empirical research: "How many Vietnamese in the San Francisco area use English instruction?" Other times, ethnographic research tells us what we need to know: "What changes are needed in order to make literacy a reality for the hard-core illiterate?" Still other times it prompts critical analysis: "What are the political meanings of literacy and illiteracy in this community?"

Building on the recommendations of Hunter and Harman, BCEL, and the National Forum on Literacy, we say further:

1. Keep a focus on community-based action. Literacy instruction takes place at the point of human contact between instructor and learner, not in national meetings and academic conferences. Meetings and conferences give focus and direction to local activities, but the work of literacy instruction happens in the field of the local community.

2. Set standards for the field, but resist the demand for state certification. We are not equipped to handle the complications of certifying the experienced but uncredentialed, nor have we achieved sufficient unity of opinion on what certification might entail.

3. Work on identifying which programs are accomplishing what ends and by what measures. The volunteer groups have had difficulty telling others what they do, but so have the ABE programs. We must all improve in describing to one another what we do, and we must learn to communicate in terms understood by our learner communities.

4. Provide money and means to train teachers, counselors, and supervisors as literacy teachers for adults. Foster meetings among literacy workers and continue town hall gatherings of learners and practitioners.

5. Develop a central data bank at the national level that can keep us up to date on important information. We need to know how to redistribute funds to the areas of greatest need.

6. Fund a national diagnostic and treatment center that would be on call through referral by the Contact Literacy Center. This center would be a central place for research and publication of studies and materials, and would

make recommendations for teaching strategies based on learners' individual characteristics. The Reading Practicum Center at Indiana University is working toward being able to provide these services.

7. Explore instruction with larger units. New readers often learn best in groups. In some cases, this means a family; in others, it is four or five people working together in a shelter for the homeless or among welfare mothers. Now is the time for intergenerational and family literacy. Bring more literate friends and relatives of literacy learners into the process so the people who already help learners cope can help them learn as well.

8. Strive to make workforce literacy a cooperative effort of employers and workers, government agencies and the private sector, and ABE and community-based projects, with the support of the universities and the research community—all holding as their common value the well being of the whole learner.

9. Combine public and private resources to meet the funding needs for the national classroom. No one source of funds can cover the cost of adult literacy. No one organization can sustain the movement; all must play their cooperative part. The Job Training Partnership Act (JTPA) Advisory Committee of the U.S. Department of Labor concluded: "In this era of budget stringency, particularly, we should no longer accept a fragmented, uncoordinated approach to the delivery of human services. It is inefficient and wasteful, and it frustrates the consumers of these services: both those who seek training and their potential employers" (*Working Capital*, 1989, p. 3).

10. Collaborate. Collaboration is one of the powerful ideas with which our movement can enter the twenty-first century. It is the "one way" that can embrace all the "many ways" to adult literacy.

11. Define literacy broadly. There are many literacies. We must learn to respond to individual needs, regardless of the expense. All of us must have a broader understanding

of the varieties of literacies and what they open up for all who possess them.

12. Shift the emphasis in measuring literacy status and gain. Such measurement must become broader, more responsive to learners' purposes, and more reflective of the actual activities and goals of the workplace, the classroom, and the literacy support organizations.

13. Suit the effort to the problem. Fighting over how to define illiteracy must yield to working together to overcome it through means appropriate to the situation. Our best literacy workers of the past solved many of the major problems of their times. We must do the same, using today's new tools.

In sum, to meet the literacy challenge, we all must understand that increasing literacy is critical in elementary, secondary, and adult schools, as well as in colleges and universities. Each level of literacy instruction must remain a part of the national discussion. Consequently, there must be adequate monetary, legislative, and moral support for all stages of education. Students, professionals, and volunteers must work together to improve what they are doing and to envision the future of literacy. Literacy efforts must be coordinated as solutions to a variety of needs, not focused exclusively on literacy while ignoring other pressing social problems—poverty, homelessness, and the plight of the children. In the 1970s, America turned some of its attention to literacy; in the 1980s, America expanded its literacy awareness to include adult literacy. The main challenges of the 1990s are to keep broad literacy in the forefront of the nation's mind and for literacy workers to keep advancing on all these fronts.

A Challenge to Labor and Management

The challenge to business in the global era is to explore new frontiers. The successful mind in the corporate world examines alternatives, sifts the evidence, and charts a course that will maximize gain. Counting the high price of illiteracy in the marketplace, the challenging alternative is to explore the cost-effectiveness of investment in the whole worker. The short term gain of teaching workers single functions and then unstopping the technical bottleneck that ensues when the skill runs out by firing them and hiring new workers, cannot compare with the long term gains to be realized through more intelligent investment in human capital. Productivity climbs in an incentive atmosphere, whether the incentive is purely monetary or recognition of worth.

An employer is interested primarily in what works best for the company. Making a long term investment in teaching workers how to solve problems and adapt to new tasks does work. Some of today's most successful businesses and industries are recognizing that their best interests are served when they count their progress in terms of society's progress as a whole. In our view, the resilience of business and industry lies in this investment in human capital. That makes it a win-win situation for all.

The challenge to the worker is finding the solutions most appropriate to his or her immediate need. People who may have to change jobs with some frequency must learn to make changes quickly, to enjoy the challenge of newness, and to accept the adventure of expanding their horizons. Gilder (1989) captured the promise of our next frontier when he wrote:

> Overthrowing the superstitions of materialism—of classical physics, of national and tribal bigotry—modern man is injecting the universe with the germ of his intelligence....The computer will ultimately collapse to a pinhead that can respond to the human voice. In this form, human intelligence can be transmitted to any tool or appliance, to any part of our environment. Thus the triumph of the computer does not dehumanize the world; it makes our environment more subject to human will (p. 120).

We believe that dealing with literacy as a long term investment is the most productive route. A progressive, collaborative approach to meeting the challenges will turn the illiteracy crisis into a literacy bonanza not only for business and industry but also for the rest of society. Long term investment in working to eliminate the causes of adult illiteracy will pay higher dividends than a panicky short term treatment of the symptoms.

A Challenge to Literacy Workers

The United States is now facing the challenge of adult literacy. How can we think as productively, creatively, and humanely as possible about the development and delivery of adult literacy instruction? We are a sleepy Rip Van Winkle, awakening after a long slumber in a shrinking world to behold changes that seem to have taken place overnight.

Culturally, the complexion and character of our neighbors have changed. Cosmopolitan people eat Vietnamese, Ethiopian, Lebanese, and Korean food, as exotic restaurants vie for expendable income. But as we eat our kimchee and couscous, how many of us think of the wives, daughters, sons, or grandparents toiling in the kitchen, who may not read or write in English?

We know that human civilization is interconnected and interdependent. The global dreamers of the 1940s and 1950s are the realists of today as we approach the unification of Europe. The world's major problems—poverty, overpopulation, hunger, environmental pollution, homelessness, discrimination, and illiteracy—probably will best be met through united world action. Each of these problems is too big for one neighborhood or one nation to tackle alone. As the problems of humankind are interconnected, so also is humanity's future; it is better to work on our problems and our future as a whole package than to process bits and pieces as separate items. To cherish, nurture, and develop the intelligence of adult new readers in this era of interconnectedness is to ensure the future.

One of the issues identified by Hunter and Harman (1985) boils down to "How and by whom are the learning needs of adults best defined?" Just as we must arrive at a definition of learning needs collaboratively, so also we must determine the actual instructional content of literacy programs collaboratively. Some adult learners begin as virtual nonreaders and expect to achieve a high school diploma equivalent (GED) overnight. In that moment of high expectation, the sensitive instructor has a delicate opportunity to direct this optimism into more achievable short term objectives. If you make it seem too hard, you lose the learner; if you make it seem too simple, when the going gets tough, you lose the learner anyway. The instructor must deliver kindness, uphold optimism, and develop a keen sense of the possible, while keeping long term goals in focus and working closely with the learner to identify the concrete interests that will lead to the most productive instruction.

One of the misunderstandings most aggravating to adult non-readers is the literate person's suspicion that they are dumb. Adults who have been tough enough to survive for years without reading or writing should not be treated as children. None of us is perfectly literate. The challenge for literacy supporters is to mine the native intelligence of the aspiring adult learner, polish it, and let it shine. Students progress much more quickly when they think of themselves as intelligent.

The road to adult literacy goes on, and sometimes it is rough; but is there another way to go? Literacy work requires a reflective thoughtfulness and human understanding that prompts us to continually question, discuss, and change our approaches if we are to meet the needs of those adults who want to become more literate.

References

Brizius, C., & Foster, S. (1987). *Enhancing adult literacy: A policy guide*. Washington, DC: Council of State Policy and Planning Agencies.

Business Council for Effective Literacy. (1988, January). *BCEL Newsletter, 14*, 6.

Carpenter, S.L., & Kennedy, W.J.D. (1988) *Managing public disputes: A practical guide to handling conflict and reading agreements*. San Francisco, CA: Jossey-Bass.

Chisman, F.P. (1989, January). *Jump start: The federal role in adult literacy*. Southport, CT: Southport Institute for Policy Analysis.

Copperman, P. (1980). The decline of literacy. *Journal of Communication, 30*, 113-122.

Darkenwald, G. (1986). *Effective approaches to teaching basic skills to adults: A research synthesis*. Paper prepared for the Office of Educational Research and Improvement of the U.S. Department of Education, Washington, DC (OERI-P-86-3015).

Darling, S. (1984). Illiteracy: An everyday problem for millions. *Appalachia, 18*(1-2), 21-28.

Fingeret, A. (1984). *Adult literacy education: Current and future directions* (series #284). Columbus, OH: National Center for Research in Vocational Education. (ED 246 308)

Flesch, R. (1955). *Why Johnny can't read*. New York: Harper & Row.

The forgotten half: Pathways to success for America's youth and young families. (1988). Washington, DC: The William T. Grant Commission on Work, Family, and Citizenship.

Gilder, G. (1989, August). The world's next source of wealth. *Fortune*, 116-120.

Ginsberg, E., & Bray, D.W. (1953). *The uneducated*. NY: Columbia University Press.

Hammink, J. (1989). *Report on the National Forum on Literacy*. Minneapolis, MN: Literacy Network.

Harris, L., & Associates. (1970). *Survival literacy study*. Washington, DC: U.S. Government Printing Office.

Holloway, R. (1973). *The worldwide right to read*. In R. Karlin (Ed.), *Reading for all*. Newark, DE: International Reading Association.

Hunter, C.S., & Harman, D. (1979). *Adult illiteracy in the United States*. New York: McGraw Hill.

Hunter, C.S., & Harman, D. (1985). *Adult illiteracy in the United States* (paperback edition). New York: McGraw Hill.

Johnson, J.N. (1985). *Adults in crisis: Illiteracy in America*. San Francisco, CA: Far West Laboratory for Educational Research and Development. (ED 243 755)

Johnston, P.H. (1985, May). Understanding reading disability: A case study approach. *Harvard Educational Review*, 55(2).

Johnston, W.B., & Packer, A.E. (1987). *Workforce 2000: Work and workers for the twenty-first century*. Indianapolis, IN: Hudson Institute, 154-177.

Kirsch, I.S., & Jungeblut, A. (1986). *Literacy: Profiles of America's young adults* (Report No. 16-PL-02). Princeton, NJ: National Assessment of Educational Progress, Educational Testing Service.

Kozol, J. (1985). *Illiterate America*. New York: Anchor Press/Doubleday.

Kozol, J. (1986). *Where stands the republic? Illiteracy: A warning and a challenge to the nation's press*. Atlanta, GA: Cox Enterprises. (ED 281 029)

Langer, S. (1979). *Philosophy in a new key: A study in the symbolism of reason, rite, and art* (3rd ed.). Cambridge, MA: Harvard University Press.

Leary, W. (1986). Review of *Illiterate America*. *Educational Leadership*, 43(8), 86.

Moats, A.L. (1986, May 20). The only way is up for literacy tests. *The Philadelphia Inquirer*, 11-A.

National directory of community based adult literacy programs. (1989). Washington DC: Association for Community Based Education.

Newman, A.P. (1980). *Adult basic education: Reading*. Boston, MA: Allyn & Bacon.

Ragin, D.F., & Denny, V.H. (1989, March). *The relationship between students' goals and patterns of participation*. Paper presented at the annual meeting of the American Educational Research Association, San Francisco, CA.

Resnick, D.P., & Resnick, L.B. (1989). The nature of literacy: A historical exploration. In E.R. Kintgen, B.M. Kroll, & M. Rose (Eds.), *Perspectives on literacy*. Carbondale, IL: Southern Illinois University Press.

Schneider, S.L., & Cook, J.L. (1989). *A longitudinal analysis of adult literacy students in New York City: A two year study*. Paper presented at the annual meeting of the American Educational Research Association, San Francisco, CA.

Smith, E.T. (1983) Adult functional illiteracy: A pervasive problem. *Catholic Library World*, 55(3), 117-121.

Sticht, T.G. (1988). Adult literacy education. In E. Rothkopf (Ed.), *Review of research in education*. Washington, DC: American Educational Research Association.

Venezky, R.L., Kaestle, C.F., & Sum, A.M. (1987). *The subtle danger*. Princeton, NJ: Educational Testing Service.

A vision for America's future. An agenda for the 1990s: A children's defense budget. (1989). Washington, DC: U.S. Government Printing Office.

Working capital: Coordinated human investment directions for the 1990s. (1989). Final report of the Job Training Partnership Act Advisory Committee. Washington, DC: U.S. Department of Labor.

Newman and Beverstock